Design Beyond Limits with Figma

50+ Figma solutions for advanced collaboration, prototyping, AI, and design systems in modern UX/UI

Šimon Jůn

Design Beyond Limits with Figma

Portfolio Director: Ashwin Nair

Relationship Lead: Nitin Nainani

Project Manager: Ruvika Rao

Content Engineer: Nithya Sadanandan

Technical Editor: Rohit Singh

Copy Editor: Safis Editing

Indexer: Manju Arasan

Proofreader: Nithya Sadanandan

Production Designer: Salma Patel

Growth Lead: Sohini Ghosh

First published: August 2025

Production reference: 2050925

Published by Packt Publishing Ltd.

Grosvenor House

11 St Paul's Square

Birmingham

B3 1RB, UK.

ISBN 978-1-83620-771-9

www.packtpub.com

I would like to express my heartfelt thanks to my wife for her unwavering support and encouragement throughout the writing of this book. I am especially grateful to my young children, who graciously allowed me to work through weekends and late nights to bring this project to life.

Huge thanks to my incredible beta readers for their invaluable insights and feedback. With over a hundred thoughtful comments, they helped shape this book from a minimum viable product into something truly complete. I'm deeply grateful to: Adam Sobotka, Ekaterina Pykhova, Jakub Sodomka, Jana Pavlanská, Klaudia Vavrinčík, Martin Laudát, Michaela Mojzisova, Michal Strnadel, Pavel Musinszkij, Tomáš Gluchman, Václav Kocián, Yana Abdulaeva, and Zdenek Zenger. Thank you all— this wouldn't be nearly as awesome without you.

Finally, my sincere thanks to the entire Packt team for their support and guidance throughout the process, making this an enriching and rewarding experience.

– Šimon Jůn

Contributors

About the author

Šimon Jůn is a design-led product leader and Chief Operating Officer at Dotidot, based in Prague, Czechia. Beginning his career as a product designer, he rose to the role of Chief Product Officer and now shapes company strategy as COO—giving him a unique perspective that spans hands-on design work and executive decision-making.

As the official Czech host of Friends of Figma, Šimon organizes community events and talks that foster open knowledge sharing. Through his workshops and online training programs, he has helped hundreds of teams streamline their Figma workflows and bridge the gap between designers and developers.

About the reviewer

Elena Gonci is a product leader and builder specializing in transforming complex systems through design thinking and team leadership. She has developed foundational design systems and pioneered AI-assisted development workflows that have redefined how products are conceived, designed, and delivered.

Renowned for her ability to bridge strategic vision with effective cross-functional leadership, Elena works across diverse sectors including fintech, hospitality, and emerging technologies. Her approach blends systems thinking with hands-on management and technical implementation—accelerating delivery timelines and producing scalable, production-ready solutions within complex organizational environments.

Table of Contents

Chapter 3: Harnessing AI in Figma and Beyond   51

Chapter 5: Scaling Design Systems for Consistency   93

Chapter 9: Elevating Stakeholder Engagement   **215**

Preface

Design collaboration has evolved from isolated creative work to dynamic, real-time teamwork spanning designers, developers, product managers and stakeholders. In today's fast-paced digital landscape, effective collaboration within design tools isn't just helpful—it's essential for shipping successful products.

Figma stands out as the most powerful collaboration platform because it was built for teams from the ground up. Beyond core design capabilities, Figma offers advanced features that transform how teams work: real-time co-editing, sophisticated permissions, robust version control, seamless developer handoffs, and integrations connecting design directly to code.

This cookbook guides you through advanced Figma techniques that go far beyond basic design skills. We'll explore sophisticated collaboration workflows, the plugin ecosystem, AI-powered design acceleration, scalable design systems, design tokens for consistency, and accessibility integration.

The second half focuses on design-to-development handoffs and stakeholder engagement strategies that eliminate miscommunication and reduce project friction. Each chapter follows a practical recipe format, presenting real problems and step-by-step solutions you can implement immediately.

These techniques come from years of working with design teams at companies of all sizes. Every recipe addresses challenges I've encountered while helping teams transform their Figma workflows from basic design creation to sophisticated collaboration systems.

Who this book is for

Are you a seasoned UI/UX designer, developer, or product manager who feels like you're only scratching the surface of what Figma can do? This book is for you. Whether you're struggling to get your design systems to scale properly, are tired of endless back-and-forth with developers during handoffs, or you're frustrated by stakeholder feedback loops that seem to go nowhere, we'll show you how to transform these challenges into streamlined workflows.

You'll get the most value from this book if you already know your way around Figma's basic features and work regularly with design teams. We assume you understand components, auto layout, and basic prototyping. What you might not know yet is how to leverage Figma's advanced capabilities to solve the complex collaboration challenges that emerge as teams and projects grow.

If you're ready to move beyond the basics and turn Figma into a true collaboration powerhouse for your team, this book will take you there.

What this book covers

Chapter 1, Advanced Collaborative Design with Figma, covers sophisticated collaboration techniques including real-time co-designing, advanced sharing settings, version control, and managing complex design projects to streamline team workflows and enhance productivity.

Chapter 2, Leveraging Figma's Plugin Ecosystem, explores how to discover, evaluate, and implement plugins that extend Figma's capabilities, automate routine tasks, and integrate with external tools to create more efficient design workflows.

Chapter 3, Harnessing AI in Figma and Beyond, shows you how to leverage Figma's built-in AI features, integrate external AI tools for faster prototyping, automate routine design tasks, and navigate the ethical considerations of AI-driven design processes.

Chapter 4, Enhancing Designer-Developer Synergy, details strategies for structuring design files for developer accessibility, creating clear design annotations, streamlining communication channels, and aligning design goals with development objectives.

Chapter 5, Scaling Design Systems for Consistency, explains how to build advanced component libraries, implement systematic documentation, manage evolving design systems for growing teams, and maintain brand coherence across extensive projects.

Chapter 6, Utilizing Design Tokens for Consistency, covers the implementation of design tokens as a bridge between design and code, version controlling tokens with GitHub or GitLab, and creating dynamic visual languages that maintain consistency across digital products.

Chapter 7, Building Accessible Design Systems, explores best practices for creating accessible components, maintaining proper color contrast ratios, ensuring keyboard navigation and screen reader compatibility, and integrating WCAG standards into your design process.

Chapter 8, Precision Handoff Techniques, demonstrates how to configure precise export settings, create detailed design specifications and annotations, optimize handoff processes, and establish feedback systems for continuous improvement between design and development teams.

Chapter 9, Elevating Stakeholder Engagement, shows you how to conduct impactful collaborative reviews, utilize interactive prototypes for live feedback, manage iterative design changes, and navigate complex feedback cycles to strengthen stakeholder relationships.

To get the most out of this book

Before diving into the advanced techniques covered in this book, you should be comfortable with Figma's core functionality. We assume you already know how to create and edit basic shapes, work with text layers, use components and variants, apply auto layout, and build simple prototypes. If you're still learning these fundamentals, we recommend getting familiar with them first through Figma's official documentation or beginner tutorials.

You should also have experience working in team-based design environments. The collaboration techniques we cover build on the assumption that you understand the challenges of working with multiple designers, developers, and stakeholders on shared projects.

Find the updated images

The updated color images for the book are placed on GitHub at `https://github.com/PacktPublishing/Design-Beyond-Limits-with-Figma`. We also have other code bundles from our rich catalog of books and videos available at `https://github.com/PacktPublishing`. Check them out!

Download the color images

We also provide a PDF file that has color images of the screenshots/diagrams used in this book. You can download it here: `https://packt.link/gbp/9781836207719`.

Conventions used

There are a number of text conventions used throughout this book.

`Code In Text`: Indicates code words in text, database table names, folder names, filenames, file extensions, pathnames, dummy URLs, user input, and Twitter handles. For example: "Organize your video library systematically to prevent chaos. Use a consistent naming convention, such as `YYYY - Area - Initiative Name`, for all your recordings (for example, `2025 - Onboarding - Mobile App Redesign`)."

A block of code is set as follows:

```
// Instead of this:
Figma: "Purple/500"
CSS: "primary-color"
iOS: "colorPurple"
Android: "color_purple_primary"

// Use a shared naming convention:
"color.primary.default": "#5C50E6"
```

When we wish to draw your attention to a particular part of a code block, the relevant lines or items are set in bold:

```
// Instead of this:
Figma: "Purple/500"
CSS: "primary-color"
iOS: "colorPurple"
Android: "color_purple_primary"

// Use a shared naming convention:
"color.primary.default": "#5C50E6"
```

Bold: Indicates a new term, an important word, or words that you see on the screen. For instance, words in menus or dialog boxes appear in the text like this. For example: "Figma's **Replace content** feature attempts to automate this often repetitive task, reducing the time spent manually inserting placeholder text and images."

Warnings or important notes appear like this.

Tips and tricks appear like this.

Get in touch

Feedback from our readers is always welcome.

General feedback: If you have questions about any aspect of this book or have any general feedback, please email us at customercare@packt.com and mention the book's title in the subject of your message.

Errata: Although we have taken every care to ensure the accuracy of our content, mistakes do happen. If you have found a mistake in this book, we would be grateful if you reported this to us. Please visit http://www.packt.com/submit-errata, click **Submit Errata**, and fill in the form.

Piracy: If you come across any illegal copies of our works in any form on the internet, we would be grateful if you would provide us with the location address or website name. Please contact us at copyright@packt.com with a link to the material.

If you are interested in becoming an author: If there is a topic that you have expertise in and you are interested in either writing or contributing to a book, please visit http://authors.packt.com/.

Share your thoughts

Once you've read *Design Beyond Limits with Figma*, we'd love to hear your thoughts! Scan the QR code below to go straight to the Amazon review page for this book and share your feedback.

https://packt.link/r/1836207719

Your review is important to us and the tech community and will help us make sure we're delivering excellent quality content.

1

Advanced Collaborative Design with Figma

The first time I used Figma in 2017, I was blown away by how seamlessly it supported collaboration. It was the first design tool truly built with teamwork at its core. While this approach might seem standard today, it was groundbreaking at the time. It shifted the mindset from isolated design work ("I'll work on this until the deadline and then share it") to a dynamic process of ongoing feedback and iteration. And as we all know, consistent feedback leads to better products. Figma excels at enabling this, but it's essential to understand the full range of collaborative features it offers.

This chapter dives into eight crucial areas of collaboration that will empower your team to create outstanding products by improving communication, streamlining workflows, and ensuring alignment between design and development. Mastering these areas will help you avoid common pitfalls, reduce inefficiencies, and deliver high-quality products faster, with fewer roadblocks along the way.

In this chapter, we will walk through the following topics:

- Communication gaps between designers and developers
- Repetitive design meetings waste time and delay progress
- Designers may not anticipate technical limitations, leading to missing details for developers
- Constant changes in the design
- Streamlining version control and iterations
- Unlocking advanced sharing and permissions settings

- Real-time co-designing for maximum team productivity
- Facilitating feedback loops in collaborative designs

Getting the most out of this book — get to know your free benefits

Unlock exclusive **free** benefits that come with your purchase, thoughtfully crafted to supercharge your learning journey and help you learn without limits.

Here's a quick overview of what you get with this book:

Next-gen reader

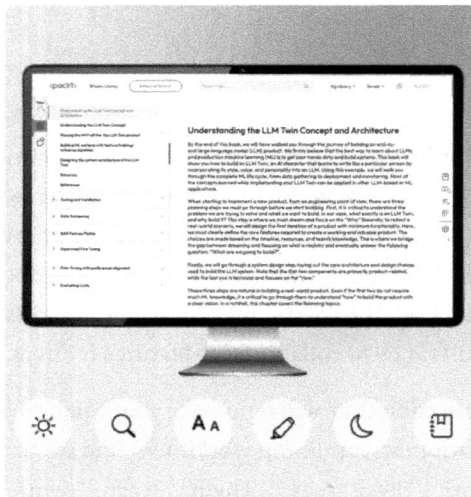

Figure 1.1: Illustration of the next-gen Packt Reader's features

Our web-based reader, designed to help you learn effectively, comes with the following features:

- ☁ Multi-device progress sync: Learn from any device with seamless progress sync.

- 📝 Highlighting and notetaking: Turn your reading into lasting knowledge.

- 🔖 Bookmarking: Revisit your most important learnings anytime.

- ☀ Dark mode: Focus with minimal eye strain by switching to dark or sepia mode.

Interactive AI assistant (beta)

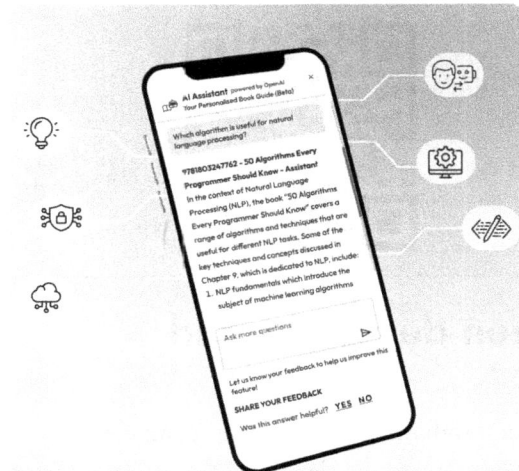

Our interactive AI assistant has been trained on the content of this book, to maximize your learning experience. It comes with the following features:

- ✦ Summarize it: Summarize key sections or an entire chapter.

- ✦ AI code explainers: In the next-gen Packt Reader, click the Explain button above each code block for AI-powered code explanations.

Figure 1.2: Illustration of Packt's AI assistant

Note: The AI assistant is part of next-gen Packt Reader and is still in beta.

DRM-free PDF or ePub version

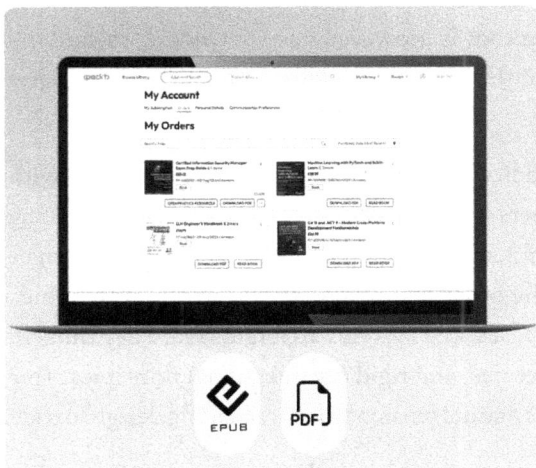

Learn without limits with the following perks included with your purchase:

- Learn from anywhere with a DRM-free PDF copy of this book.

- Use your favorite e-reader to learn using a DRM-free ePub version of this book.

Figure 1.3: Free PDF and ePub

Communication gaps between designers and developers

One of the most persistent challenges in product development is the interaction between designers and developers. While both disciplines work toward the same goal—creating functional, user-friendly products—they often approach problems from entirely different perspectives, leading to friction and miscommunication.

What's the problem?

Designers and developers are two essential forces in product development, but they often struggle to understand each other. As a designer, it's important to remember that what you create in Figma isn't the final product—the production code is. However, despite working toward the same goal, many teams face miscommunication that goes beyond just different terminologies and perspectives.

The challenges run much deeper than word choices. Designers and developers operate with fundamentally different mental models. Designers work with fluid, relational thinking, placing elements freely in space and considering visual hierarchy and flow—much like how Figma's free-canvas approach works. Developers, on the other hand, operate within structured, hierarchical frameworks shaped by how code, databases, and systems are organized. They think in terms of top-to-bottom sequences, nested structures, and rigid organizational principles. This fundamental difference in spatial thinking creates natural tension when translating design to code.

Additionally, there's often a knowledge gap around existing technical infrastructure. New designers, and even experienced ones joining a project, may lack the historical context of how current systems were built, what technical constraints exist, or what potential blockers might arise from legacy code. Understanding the production environment and existing technical architecture is crucial for creating designs that work within real-world constraints, not just in an ideal vacuum.

Here are some common terminology differences between Figma and code:

Figma	Code
Auto layout	Flexbox
Corner radius	Border-radius
Frames	Divs
Variables/design tokens	CSS variables
Prototypes	Clickable mockups (via JS/HTML)

Table 1.1 – Terminology difference between Figma and code

Understanding these differences is crucial to ensuring a smoother workflow and more effective collaboration between designers and developers.

How to fix it

To bridge this gap, designers and developers must actively work toward a common understanding:

- **Involve developers early:** Bringing developers into the design process from the start ensures technical feasibility and helps avoid late-stage surprises. Make sure everyone understands the purpose behind design decisions through clear design annotation. I highly recommend walking through the entire design with developers, explicitly describing each screen and interaction rather than assuming anything is "obvious." This serves two crucial purposes: developers can challenge your solutions and gain a deep understanding of user flows and interactions, while you, as a designer, can catch hidden flaws you might have missed during the design phase or that went unnoticed during design critiques.

- **Establish a shared vocabulary:** Document and define key terms that designers and developers use differently. This makes communication clearer and reduces misunderstandings. Consider using tools such as Storybook or similar documentation platforms to create a shared reference point where both teams can see how design components translate to code, helping establish common terminology and understanding.

- **Use Figma's Dev Mode:** Leverage Figma's developer handoff features to provide precise specifications and make it easier for developers to inspect design elements.

- **Encourage cross-team learning:** Designers should develop a basic understanding of development constraints, while developers should familiarize themselves with design principles.

- **Create a feedback loop**: Regularly review designs together to ensure alignment and address potential issues before they escalate. Remember that this loop goes both ways. Designers should also be involved in QA processes to verify that implementations match design intent, helping prevent details from getting lost in translation. Make sure everyone knows their roles and responsibilities, and establish clear points of contact so team members know who to reach out to when questions or ambiguities arise.

There are two primary ways to establish continuous feedback loops:

- **Scheduled weekly feedback sessions**: This is the most common approach, where teams set up recurring calendar meetings for feedback. Designers present their progress, and other designers and developers discuss any necessary changes or improvements.
- **Daily asynchronous feedback**: A more fluid approach, which I personally prefer, involves integrating feedback into the team's everyday workflow. At Dotidot, designers and developers provide feedback asynchronously at the end of each day using Loom recordings. This fosters a culture where feedback is a natural and ongoing part of collaboration, rather than being confined to structured meetings.

Even if your team lacks hybrid designer developers, following these practices will save significant time, reduce confusion, and create a more seamless workflow between both disciplines.

Repetitive design meetings waste time and delay progress

We've all been there. You sit in a meeting room (or on a video call) listening to someone explain what each screen does, what happens when you click this button, and why they chose that particular color. Meanwhile, you're thinking, "I could have understood this in half the time if it were properly documented." Design meetings are essential, but when they become repetitive explanation sessions rather than productive decision-making discussions, they drain energy and slow down progress.

What's the problem?

Endless design meetings often consume valuable time without adding significant value. While collaboration is essential, excessive discussions over the same design elements can lead to delays, frustration, and decision fatigue. Instead of refining and progressing, teams can get stuck in cycles of unnecessary revisions and redundant conversations.

A key difference between junior and senior designers is how they approach documentation and handoff. Experienced designers go beyond aesthetics—they consider functionality and development requirements upfront, reducing the need for excessive meetings. By structuring Figma files effectively and using built-in collaboration tools, teams can minimize disruptions and maximize efficiency.

How to fix it

To break free from the cycle of excessive design meetings, we can leverage screen annotations. Effectively using screen annotations helps convey the full story behind your design. It's important to note that these are custom-built components that we create and use in Figma, not built-in Figma features. You'll need to design and build these annotation components yourself or as a team to use them in your design files. Here's how to utilize them better:

- **Figma file structure**: Before diving into specific annotations, establish a consistent Figma file structure that serves as a single source of truth for your entire project. I use a standard seven-page structure in all my projects:

  - 01 – Getting Started
  - 02 – Project Name
  - 03 – Documentation
  - 04 – Components
  - 05 – Playground and Exploration
  - 06 – Archive
  - 07 – Cover

  This unchangeable structure helps me easily duplicate files and start new projects quickly, while developers know exactly where to find what they need. We'll dive much deeper into this file organization approach in *Chapter 4*, where I'll share the detailed methodology behind each page and how it enhances designer-developer collaboration.

- **Designer notes**: Add context directly next to your design with designer notes. Avoid using comments or Figma Dev Mode annotations, as Dev annotations require all users to have paid seats. Comments can be used even from viewer seats (free), but can be easily lost, and they aren't shown at first glance as easily as designer notes.

Instead, rely on prepared elements for clarity.

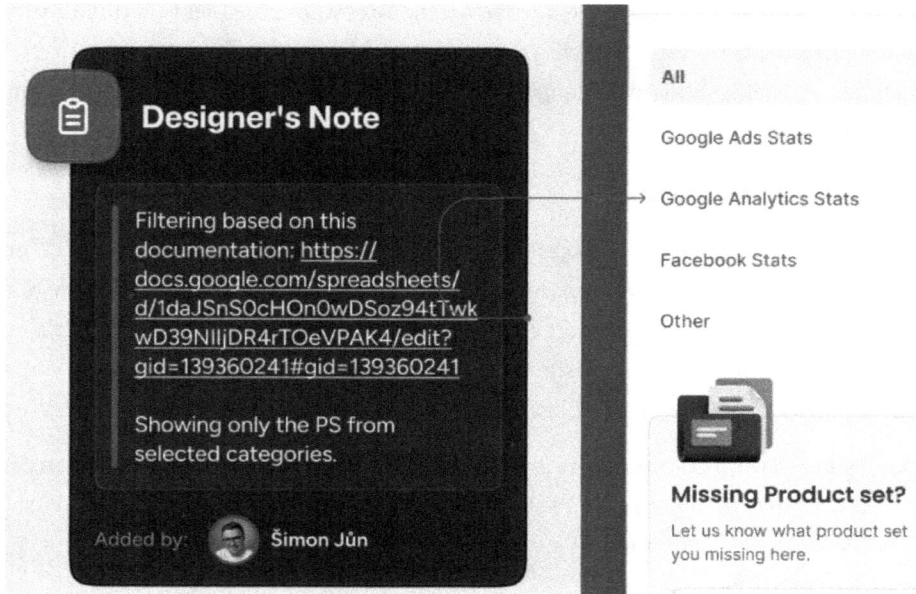

Figure 1.4 – An example designer note

This card demonstrates how to provide additional context within Figma designs. The note explains that filtering is based on the provided documentation and highlights specific parameters used in the project. Visual annotations direct attention to essential elements, ensuring clarity and fostering collaboration.

- **Copy note**: Provide specific copywriting instructions to ensure developers understand how to implement text accurately within the design.

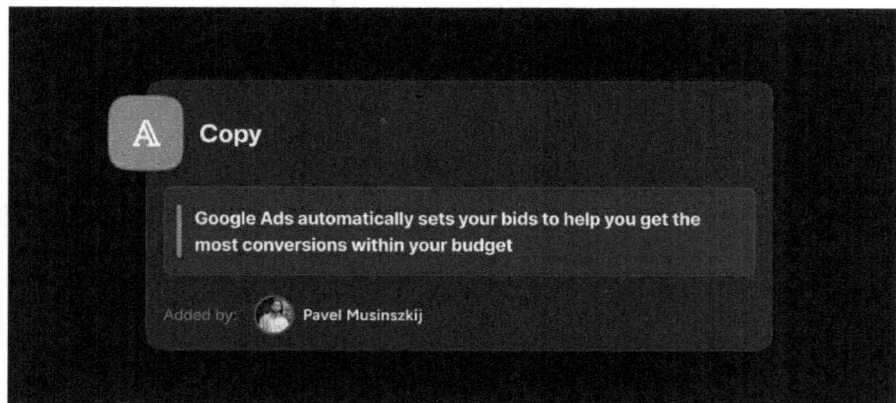

Figure 1.5 – An example copywriting instruction

- **Variant annotations**: Don't duplicate your design just to showcase small changes. Duplicating entire designs can create confusion about development complexity. At first glance, a project may seem much larger and more complex than it actually is. Additionally, excessive duplication can overwhelm developers, making it easier to miss crucial details buried within an abundance of similar-looking screens. Use variant cards to illustrate differences clearly and help developers grasp the full scope of adjustments. For example, opening a Figma file with 10 screens might appear overwhelming but could represent small changes on a few screens. Variants streamline first impressions, time estimation, and overall clarity. However, when variant logic becomes too complex to explain through annotations alone, consider using prototyping instead (if the budget and time allow), as interactive demonstrations can sometimes communicate functionality more effectively than extensive written explanations.

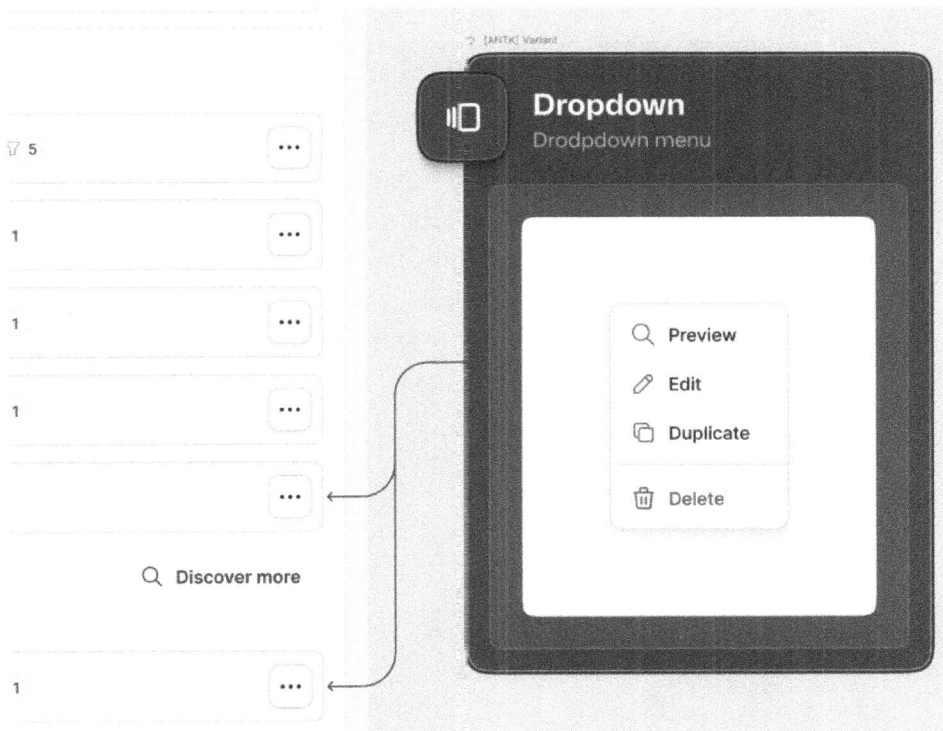

Figure 1.6 – Dropdown use case

Here's an alternate version of the tab variation case:

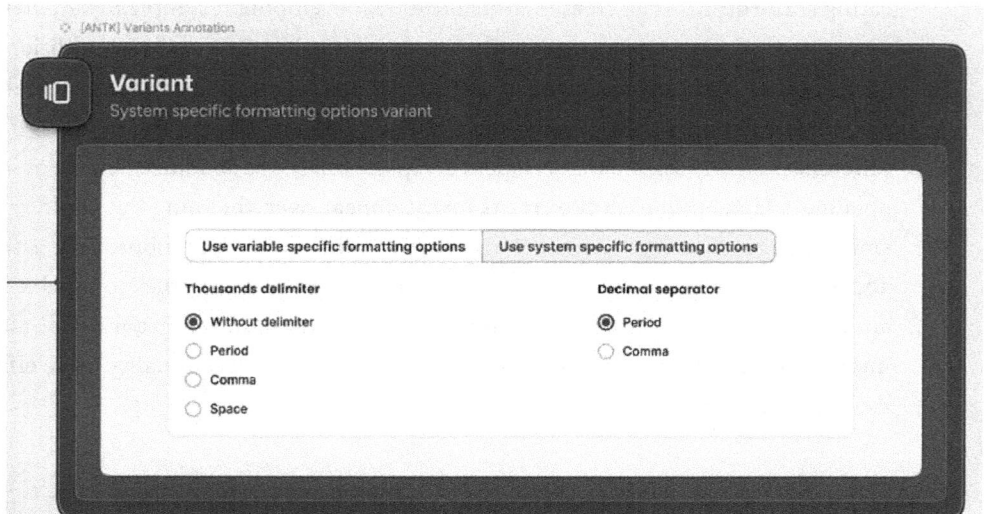

Figure 1.7 – Tab variation case

- **Highlight nice-to-have features**: While agile workflows prioritize speed, it's sometimes beneficial to design beyond the **Minimum Viable Product** (**MVP**), which is the simplest version of a product that includes only the core features needed to satisfy early users and gather feedback for future improvements, to showcase the broader idea. Use visually distinct elements to denote nice-to-have parts (for example, a feature such as **Search**).

This approach improves communication with stakeholders, ensuring they see the complete vision and grasp your intent more effectively.

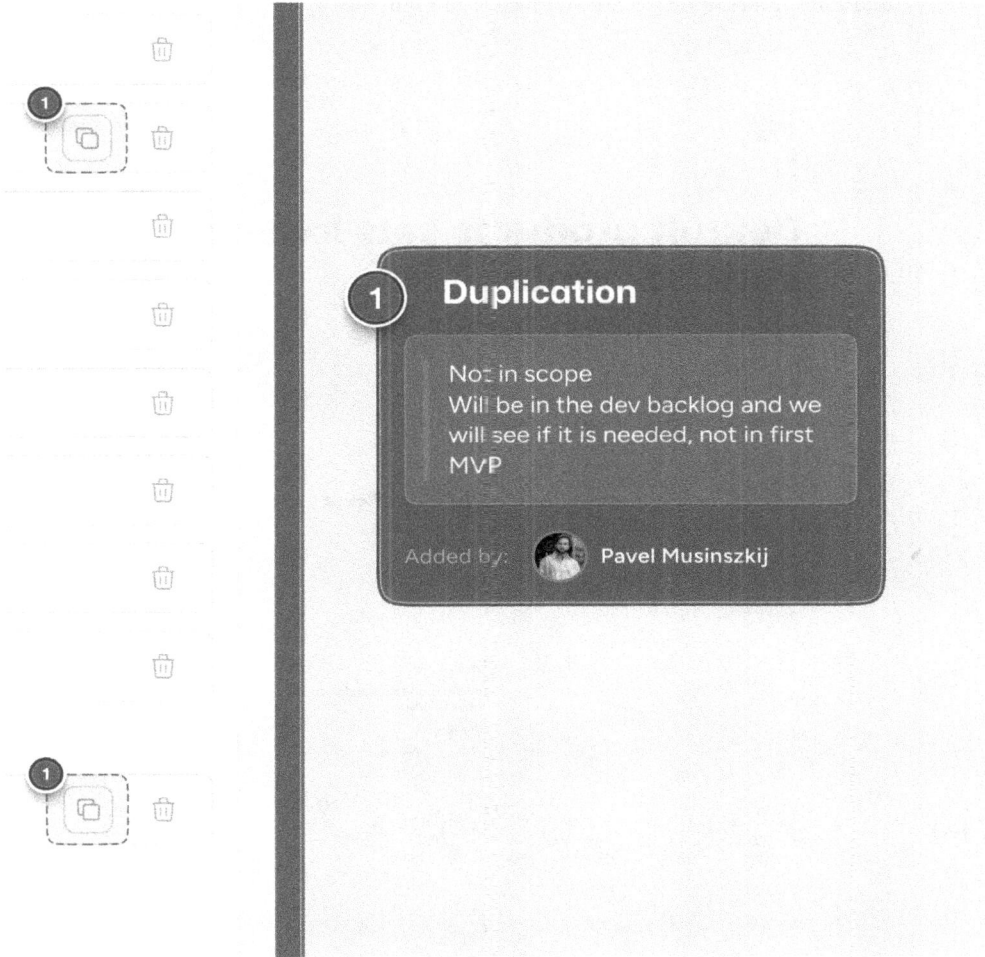

Figure 1.8 – Nice-to-have cards in a design

- **Ticket cards (Jira plugin for Figma)**: Link your Figma designs directly with project management tools such as Jira by adding ticket cards. These cards can display responsible team members and task statuses right in Figma.

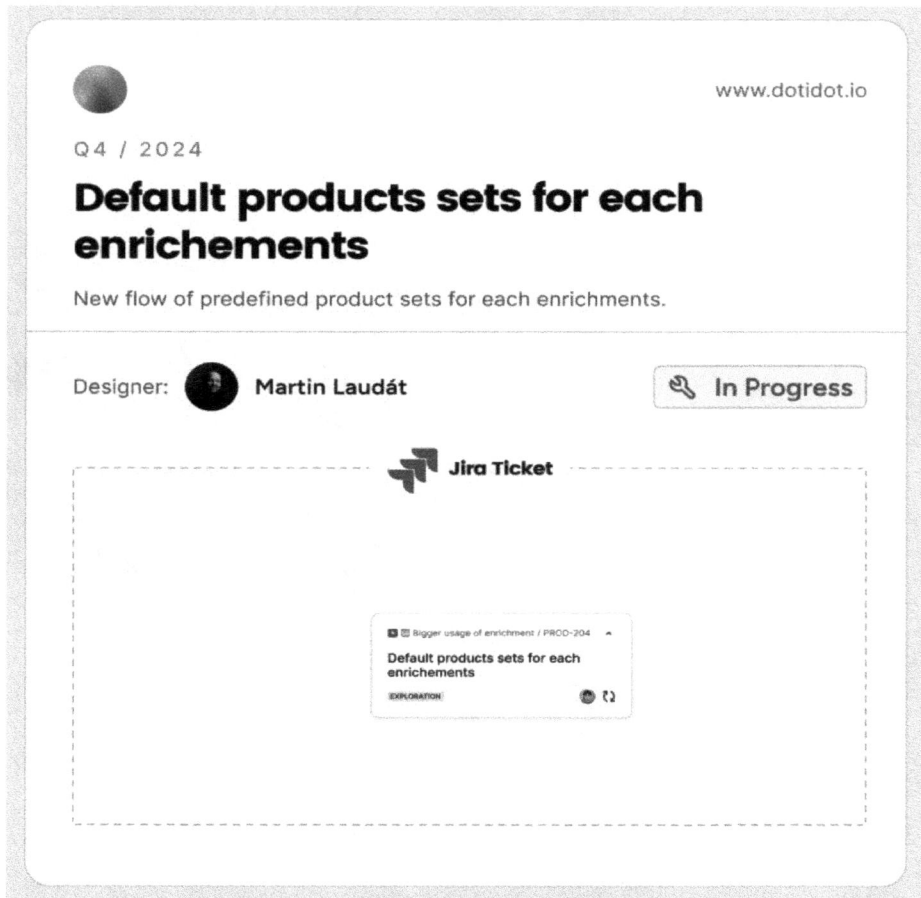

Figure 1.9 – Ticket card for new design project

- **Flow headings**: Include flow headings to outline logical sections of your design. This helps collaborators and developers understand the structure and implement the design as cohesive, story-driven blocks for quicker development.

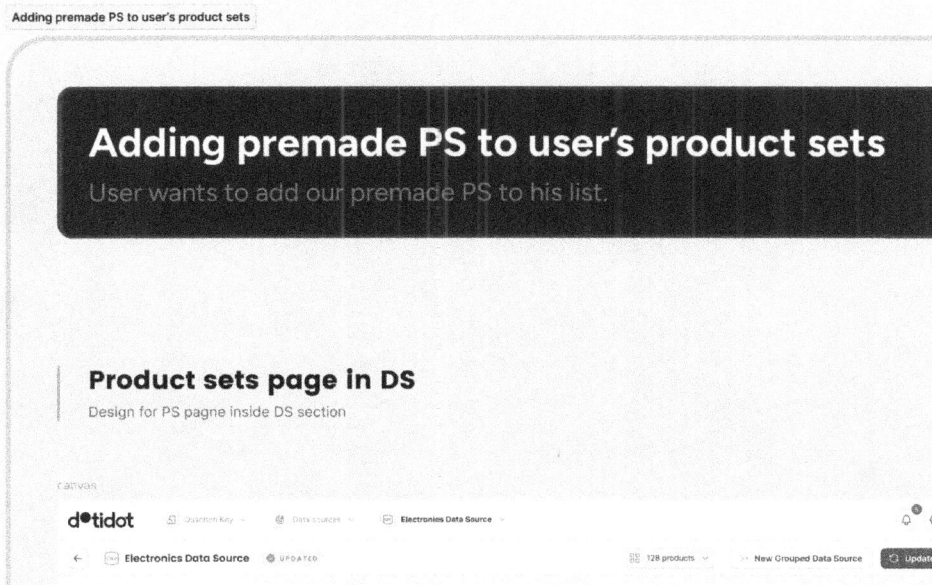

Figure 1.10 – Flow heading for a new section in a design file

All of these annotations are crucial for every Figma handoff. Remember, a good design file isn't just about frames with designs; it's about effectively transferring the right information from design to development, product owners, testers, and other stakeholders involved in the implementation process.

Loom video walk-through

Record videos for everything! Loom is an incredible tool—you just click and record, and your video is automatically uploaded to the cloud. You can then paste the link directly into Figma. Everything is clearly explained, and anyone can revisit the video as needed.

I shared my workflow on LinkedIn:

1. Record a short Loom video explaining the feedback or a new feature idea. I include examples and walk through our app directly in the video.

2. Loom AI automatically generates a transcript of the video.

3. I use the transcript as input for ChatGPT, paired with a custom prompt tailored to our Jira ticket structure (description, requirements, acceptance criteria, etc.).

4. Within seconds, I have a complete Jira ticket ready to go! I add the Loom video link to the ticket for reference, ensuring clarity for designers.

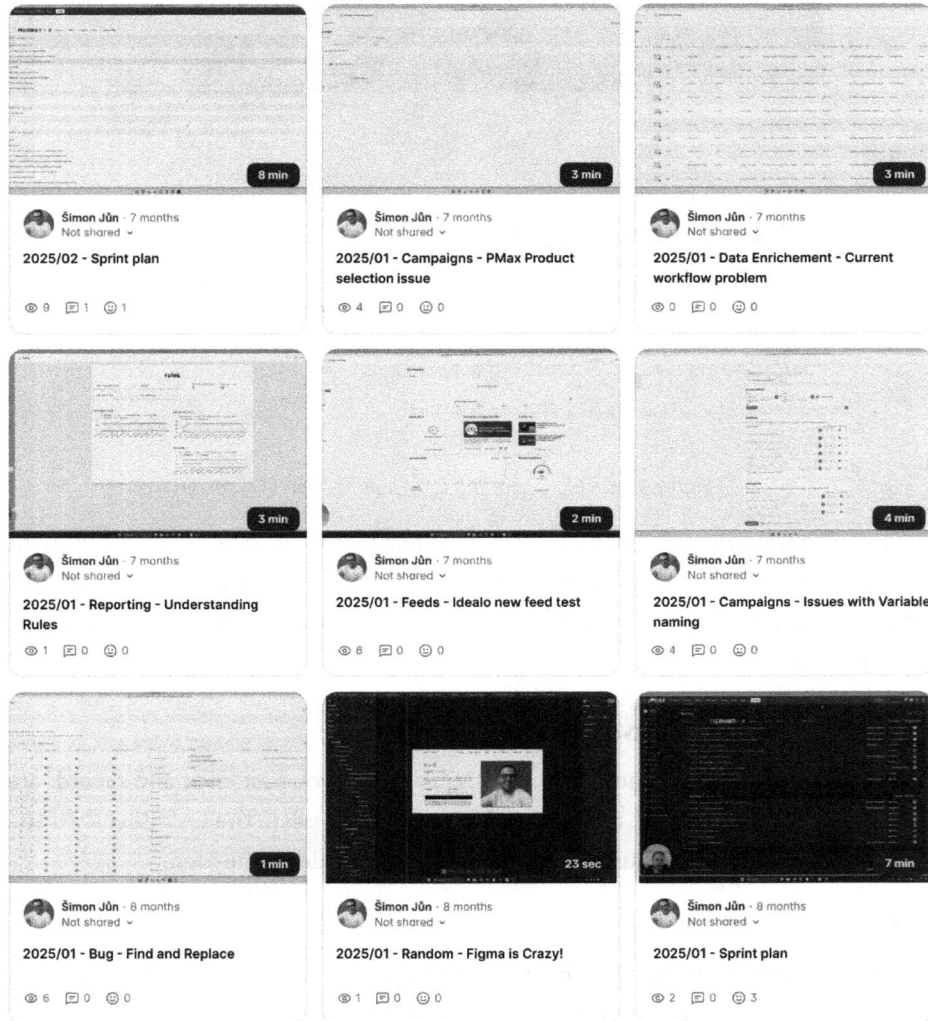

Figure 1.11 – Loom video gallery

Organize your video library systematically to prevent chaos. Use a consistent naming convention, such as `YYYY - Area - Initiative Name`, for all your recordings (for example, `2025 - Onboarding - Mobile App Redesign`). This makes videos easily searchable both in Loom and when referenced in tickets. Create a dedicated page or section in your Figma file specifically for important videos and links. Developers and team members are often pressed for time and want everything served in one convenient location rather than hunting through multiple tools. Having a **Video Library** or **Key Resources** page in your Figma file with all relevant Loom links ensures that critical context is always accessible without requiring people to search through chat histories or project management tools.

Designers may not anticipate technical limitations, leading to missing details for developers

Picture this: you've just finished what you believe is your best design yet. Every pixel is perfectly placed, the user flow is seamless, and the visual hierarchy guides users effortlessly through the experience. You hand it off to the development team, expecting them to be as excited as you are. Instead, you're met with concerns about API limitations, performance issues, or existing system constraints you never knew existed. Suddenly, your beautiful design needs significant compromises, or worse, a complete rethink. This disconnect between design vision and technical reality is one of the most common sources of friction in product teams.

What's the problem?

Designers often lack awareness of technical limitations, which can lead to missing details for developers. While designers excel at understanding user needs and business goals, gaps in technical knowledge can create challenges. Legacy tech debt, platform constraints, and performance considerations are often overlooked. Without early collaboration, these issues surface late in development, causing costly revisions.

How to fix it

The following steps will help designers to know and understand the technical limitations early in the design process, ensuring that the collaboration will be faster and smoother for both sides:

- **Involve developers early**: Bring developers into the design process from the start to identify technical constraints before they become blockers.
- **Assign a developer partner**: Designate a developer as a support resource for the project to provide real-time technical insights.

- **Use Figma's spotlight feature**: Leverage quick, real-time calls to align on design feasibility without unnecessary scheduling overhead.

- **Clarify technical needs**: Ask developers for input on system limitations, reusable components, and performance considerations upfront.

- **Document technical constraints**: Keep a shared space where designers, developers, and product managers can reference key limitations and best practices to avoid repetitive issues.

- **Leverage AI tools for technical understanding**: When in doubt, leverage AI tools that are fantastic at understanding technological limitations and try to understand why something can/cannot be done. There is no need to become a code expert, but becoming a design expert requires an understanding of code limitations.

By fostering an open dialogue between design and development, teams can avoid misalignment, reduce unnecessary rework, and build products more efficiently.

Constant changes in the design

You know the feeling. You've just finished explaining the latest design iteration to your development team, they've started coding, and then it happens. A stakeholder suggests "just a small change," or user testing reveals an insight that requires rethinking the entire flow. Meanwhile, your developers are caught in the middle, unsure whether to continue with the current version or wait for the next iteration. What should have been a straightforward development cycle turns into a confusing juggling act where everyone is working on different versions of the same product. Managing design changes effectively isn't just about version control; it's about maintaining team sanity and project momentum.

What's the problem?

Frequent design changes are inevitable in many projects, but they can create confusion and inefficiencies. A major challenge arises when development teams are already working on one version while designers are iterating on a newer one. This leads to uncertainty about what should be implemented, potential rework, and a frustrating experience for both designers and developers. In one project with a large insurance company, we faced this exact issue—multiple design iterations were being worked on simultaneously while the older version was still under development. Developers struggled to build a product that kept evolving beneath them.

How to fix it

To manage continuous design changes effectively, consider these two primary approaches:

- **Branching for isolated iterations**: This is an advanced feature that should only be used for big, complex projects where multiple people are working simultaneously on the same file. Think of branching like creating a separate workspace where you can experiment without affecting the main file that others are using, for example, if you're working on a design system component library with multiple designers, or developing a major feature for a large enterprise company where several team members need to contribute simultaneously. When you create a branch, you're essentially making a copy of the current file where you can make changes safely. Once your changes are finalized and approved, you can merge them back into the main file. This prevents your experimental work or iterations from disrupting the live version that developers or other team members are actively using.

  It prevents unnecessary changes from affecting the live version.

  Challenges: Requires Figma's Organization or Enterprise plan; designers may be unfamiliar with branching workflows. To overcome this, consider a developer-led training session on Git-based workflows.

- **Versioning for clear change management**:
  1. Manually create a version checkpoint before significant updates.
  2. Label versions clearly (for example, Onboarding_Flow_v1.2) to document progress and provide a stable reference.
  3. Use version descriptions to highlight key changes, reducing confusion for developers and stakeholders.

By adopting structured version control and branching techniques, you can reduce confusion, minimize rework, and create a smoother workflow between design and development teams.

Streamlining version control and iterations

How many times have you found yourself staring at a Figma file wondering, "Is this the latest version?" or "What exactly changed since yesterday?" Maybe you've been in a meeting where someone references "the version we discussed last week," but nobody can figure out which one that was. The difference between teams that struggle with version confusion and those that maintain a crystal-clear project history often comes down to understanding when and how to use manual versioning strategically.

What's the problem?

Many teams underutilize Figma's versioning features, missing out on its full potential. The tool offers two types of versioning—automatic (autosaves) and manual—but manual versioning, when used strategically, can significantly enhance workflows. However, teams often struggle with knowing when and how to create manual versions, leading to inefficiencies in sharing and collaboration. Without clear guidelines, this powerful feature becomes underused or misapplied, limiting its impact on productivity.

How to fix it

When you decide to create a manual version, it should be at the end of a workflow cycle. This could be when you're preparing a version to send to stakeholders or clients, or when you're working in two-week sprints and need to hand off a stable version to development. The exact timing varies across different teams I've worked with, but understanding how to create effective versions is more important than the specific timing.

Here is how to create a version in Figma:

1. Click on the arrow next to the filename at the top left of your Figma interface.
2. Select **Show version history** from the drop-down menu.

Click the + button next to **Version history** in the right panel. Every version can have a name and description. Let's talk about naming first. You can use several naming structures to maintain consistency:

*   **By Milestones:** `ProjectName_MilestoneName_vX`

    Example: `Dashboard_v1` or `Onboarding_Flow_v3`

*   **By Date:** `ProjectName_YYYY-MM-DD`

    Example: `Onboarding_Flow_2025-01-15`

*   **By Sprint or Release Cycle:** `ProjectName_SprintX` or `ProjectName_ReleaseX`

    Example: `Onboarding_Flow_Sprint12` or `Onboarding_Flow_Release2.1`

*   **By Stakeholder Review Stage:** `ProjectName_StakeholderType_Stage_vX`

    Example: `Onboarding_Flow_Review_v1` or `Onboarding_Flow_Feedback_v2`

Consistency is key—ensure the same structure is used across all your files to avoid confusion.

For descriptions, keep them concise but informative. Use them as a changelog to highlight differences from the previous version. Here's a quick tip: leverage emojis for clarity:

- ✅ Approved changes
- ➕ Additions
- ✖ Deletions

The following figure showcases the Figma version modal, where you can document and track all changes for future reference, ensuring clarity and seamless collaboration.

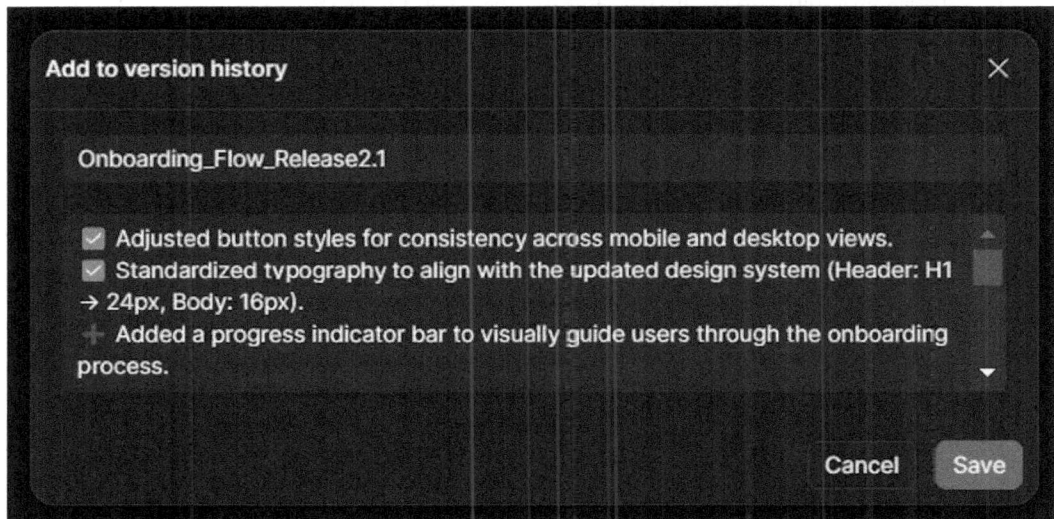

Figure 1.12 – Figma new version modal

Once you've established versions, you can easily copy the link for a specific version and share it with developers or stakeholders. However, note that older versions are view-only—people can't comment on them. A workaround for this limitation is duplicating the version into a separate file where comments and edits can continue. Meanwhile, keep the "hard" version as a separate file to maintain a clear record. Just remember to archive or close older versions to prevent an overflow of active files.

Versions that have been handed off to development or stakeholders should never be edited, even though technical workarounds exist. Editing defeats the entire purpose of version control. Once a version is shared, treat it as locked and create a new version for any subsequent changes. This maintains the integrity of your project timeline and ensures everyone is referencing the same stable point in your design history.

Unlocking advanced sharing and permissions settings

There's nothing quite like the panic that sets in when you realize you might have accidentally shared confidential client work with the wrong people. Or when you discover that your "quick internal mockup" with placeholder text saying "This feature sucks" somehow made its way to a stakeholder presentation. Figma's sharing settings seem straightforward at first glance, but the devil is in the details. One wrong click on **Anyone** instead of **only people you invite** and suddenly your private design exploration is discoverable by anyone online. Getting sharing permissions right isn't just about security; it's about maintaining professionalism, protecting sensitive information, and ensuring the right people have the right level of access at the right time.

What's the problem?

Managing sharing permissions in Figma can become a challenge, particularly when dealing with external collaborators or large teams. Improper settings, such as leaving files open to "anyone," can lead to unauthorized access, unintentional edits, or even the mishandling of sensitive content. Additionally, using group email addresses for collaboration can limit individual accountability in comments. Without a clear structure for separating internal and external files, informal content can unintentionally reach professional audiences, creating potential embarrassment or confusion.

How to fix it

Figma has a standard level of sharing permissions—not overly complex—but there are a couple of valuable tricks I've learned the hard way during my career:

1. If you open the file link to anyone, ensure that the **What can they do on View** setting and **Viewers can copy, share, and export this file** options are unchecked. This will save you from unnecessary problems caused by unintended editors accessing the file (trust me, it happened to me!) and provide some guardrails against unauthorized copying of your file by anyone online.

2. Understand Figma's different invitation levels to manage seats effectively. You can invite people at three different levels: directly to a specific file (most restrictive), to a project (moderate access), or to the entire team (full access). Each level has different implications for your seat count and billing. When sharing with external stakeholders or clients, consider inviting them only to the specific file rather than the entire project or team to maintain better control over access and costs.

There's more...

For better security, consider adding a password to the file or avoid using Anyone as an access setting altogether. Instead, add specific email addresses. When inviting a large number of people, you can copy and paste multiple email addresses at once, or use group email addresses such as marketing@company.com or figma@company.com. Group access works seamlessly, as Figma doesn't limit access from the same account being used by multiple people. The only downside is that comments from group accounts won't display individual names unless explicitly noted.

For Organization and Enterprise plans, you gain access to Activity Logs, providing a detailed overview of who accessed your files and what actions they performed.

Do a regular seats and activities check-in to uncover potential problems. If done regularly, this can take a half hour or less.

Enterprise users also benefit from the Password Protection Required feature, which enforces password use for all shared files—adding an extra layer of security.

Another smart approach is to establish a system where files shared externally, such as with clients or partners, are clearly separated from internal ones. This minimizes the risk of accidentally including informal content in professional files. Let's be honest—most of us have added memes or jokes in Figma files for team fun at some point. I once experienced the embarrassment of such a file being shared with a client's C-level executives. Luckily, they found it amusing, but it was a lesson learned! To avoid such situations, I recommend tagging shared files with an emoji and text in the name, such as [🔗 SHARED WITH CLIENT] File Name. This simple step can save you from potential awkwardness in the future.

Facilitating feedback loops in collaborative designs

Figma changed my perspective on design when I realized how deeply it integrates collaboration into the core of the experience. However, many designers still don't take full advantage of its potential. I've mentored numerous young designers who are hesitant to ask for feedback.

"What if someone finds out I'm not that good?" they often ask me. My response is always, "So what?"

Design is fundamentally about solving problems, and humans are naturally better at solving problems together. If we could hunt mammoths as a team, why can't we share an early Figma file? Here's the reality: designers aren't supposed to handle every single edge case of a product. That's what engineers excel at. Our role is to support and unblock when something is missing or unclear. The design-to-development process isn't always linear, where design ends and development starts. It's an ongoing collaboration where feedback becomes your best ally in design.

I frequently tell my team that having them to rely on allows me to work faster. I don't need everything to be perfect before sharing—it's through collaboration and early input that we achieve our ultimate goal: building the best possible product.

There are countless ways to foster this collaborative feedback process. While it takes experimentation to find what works best for you, I'll share a few methods to get you started.

What's the problem?

Many designers hesitate to fully embrace Figma's collaborative features, often avoiding feedback due to fear of judgment or exposing their skills. This reluctance hampers the potential of collaborative problem-solving and slows down design progress. The lack of early input leads to delayed iterations and missed opportunities for improvement. Establishing a culture of open and effective feedback is crucial for leveraging Figma's full potential and creating the best possible products.

How to fix it

Effective communication is crucial for a product's success. In recent years, the rise of remote teams and increasing workloads have made seamless communication even more critical. Teams must work proactively to ensure clarity and collaboration despite these challenges.

One way of doing this is by sharing feedback through a Slack, Teams, Webex, or other channel. Sometimes, you need feedback from people outside your design team. At Dotidot, for example, we often turn to our automation strategists or performance marketing geeks for their opinions—they align closely with our users' perspectives and often provide insights smarter than ChatGPT :D.

To streamline this, we created a dedicated Slack channel specifically for design feedback. It's crucial to make the request as straightforward as possible to keep people engaged over time. Every message should include the following:

- Title of the request.
- Brief description of the problem or assumption.
- Include a video explanation for more complex issues.

- Link to a specific section in Figma (not the entire file).

- Deadline for responses to help them plan their time.

- Mentions of all relevant team members for feedback, along with those who can contribute to the discussion in the thread below.

- Recording of every design critique. Yes, here it is again—Loom. You might think I own the company, given how often I mention it, but I genuinely love the tool. Whenever we have a quick call or live design critique, we always record the session and link it directly in Figma next to the design. This allows designers to focus on the discussion—thinking critically about the design—instead of scrambling to write comments or notes. After the meeting, you can revisit the recording and review specific parts as needed. Loom's AI-generated chapters make it easy to jump to the sections that matter most.

If you plan a long meeting (though in 99% of cases, long meetings aren't necessary), consider breaking it into multiple shorter videos instead of one lengthy Loom recording. This approach will help you move faster in the future and make it easier to revisit important points.

By the way, these video recordings also serve as excellent training materials for new team members. They can quickly learn from past challenges or *mistakes*, significantly speeding up the onboarding process.

Unlock this book's exclusive benefits now

Scan this QR code or go to packtpub.com/unlock, then search this book by name.

Note: Keep your purchase invoice ready before you start.

2

Leveraging Figma's Plugin Ecosystem

Plugins are an incredible addition to Figma, enabling users to accomplish much more. However, with tens of thousands of plugins available, it can be challenging to select the right ones. In this chapter, I will share my approach to choosing plugins, when to encourage your team to explore plugins, and finally, how to decide if developing your own plugin from scratch is the best solution.

Since the plugin ecosystem evolves rapidly and we can't update this book every week, I've created a curated list of recommended plugins that I update regularly. You can find the latest plugin recommendations at `simonjun.com/best-figma-plugins`.

We will discuss these six areas in this chapter:

- Selecting essential plugins for enhanced functionality
- Streamlining workflow efficiency with time-saving plugins
- Automating repetitive tasks with plugin integration
- Specific project needs solved by plugins
- Linking Figma to other software for cross-platform integration
- When to consider writing your own plugin

Selecting essential plugins for enhanced functionality

Before showcasing the selected plugins, it's important to discuss the process of selecting them. At first glance, choosing a plugin might seem simple—just pick one and test it. But what happens if you build your workflow around a plugin that later becomes unsupported or outdated? This could disrupt your processes. Selecting plugins shouldn't be a quick decision, much like choosing new design tools, website hosting, or any platform critical to your success. Here are the questions I always ask myself when selecting plugins:

- Am I the only user?
- Is this a one-time use?
- Is this plugin paid?
- Is it developed by a company?
- Are there any reliable alternatives?

These questions are important for ensuring the longevity of your decision.

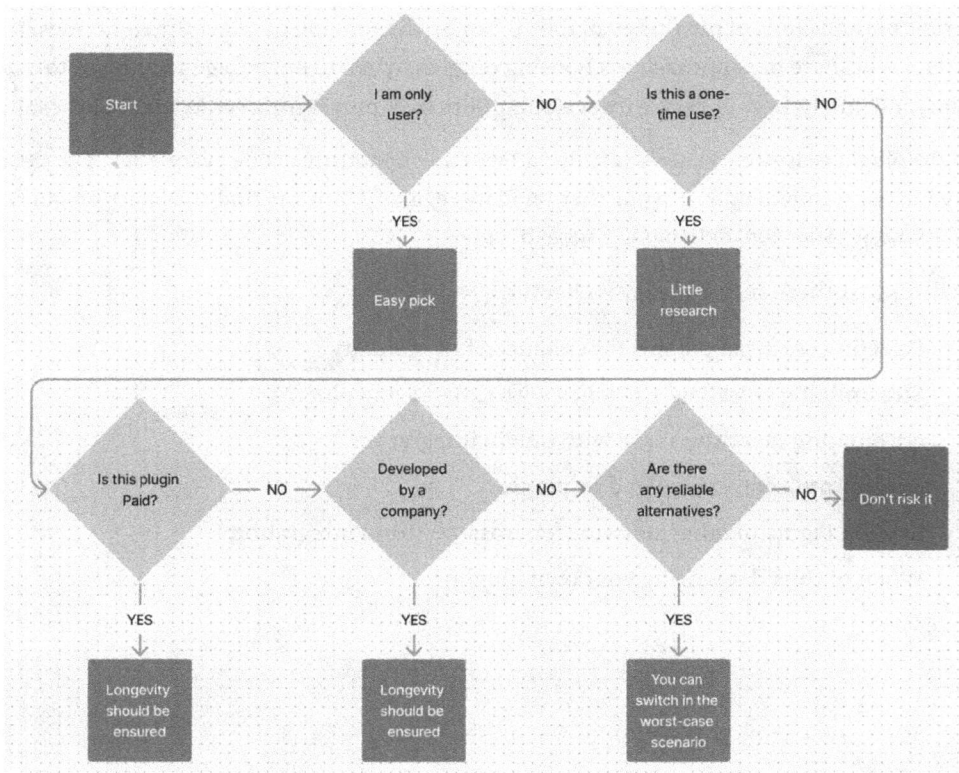

Figure 2.1 – My plugin decision workflow

Let's look at these questions in detail.

Am I the only user?

Let's look at our first question: the problem and its solution.

What's the problem?

Relying on a plugin that is used only by you might seem low-risk, but what happens if it stops working tomorrow? While your team's workflow won't be affected, your efficiency might take a hit, requiring time to find an alternative or adjust your process.

How to fix it

If a plugin is limited to your personal workflow, you have the flexibility to replace it or adjust your process if it becomes unsupported. Small productivity boosters, such as the CSV Data to Figma plugin, fall into this category. Before committing, always check for alternative plugins and ensure there are backups available to avoid unnecessary disruptions.

Plugin example—data.to.design

Review the Figma community plugin page, where you can read more and activate the plugin: `https://www.figma.com/community/plugin/1133729773197702197/data-to-design-by-divriots-google-sheets-csv-json-airtable-cr-notion-to-figma`.

One of the most impactful plugins I used during my consulting days helped bring prototypes to life with real data. Imagine this: you're presenting a new project to a client or the management team. These folks aren't designers—they don't speak the language of Figma prototypes or production code. But what they do understand is data that feels real and relevant.

Here's where these plugins shine. With just a few rows of data from the client's CRM, you can populate your prototypes with authentic information. Picture presenting an internal reporting dashboard that displays actual client names and real revenue figures instead of placeholders such as "John Doe" or "$11111." The impact? Game-changing. It fosters stronger connections with stakeholders and drives home the project's relevance.

You can easily map your data fields to your design and populate them in one click.

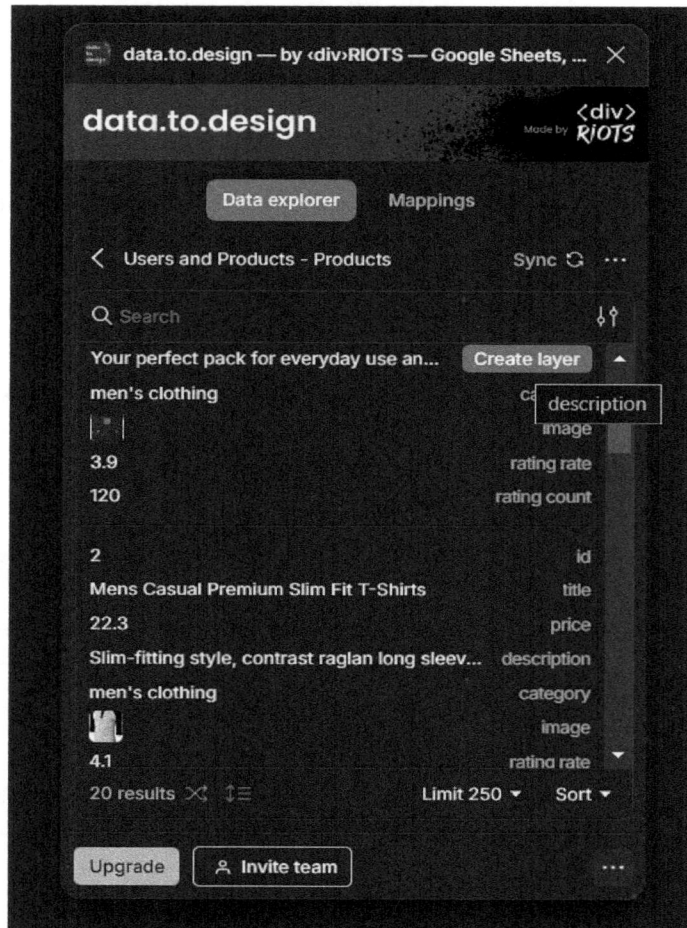

Figure 2.2 – Data explorer and data mapping in the plugin

While Figma now offers a native **Replace content** AI feature (which I'll cover in *Chapter 3*), this plugin excels because it lets you use actual data from your client's CRMs or ERPs—not AI-generated content, but real, meaningful information that truly reflects their business.

In an era where AI is rendering *lorem ipsum* obsolete, the mantra is simple: make it real. A design packed with genuine data delivers an entirely different experience—one that resonates.

Is this a one-time use?

Not every plugin is meant to be a long-term addition to your workflow.

What's the problem?

When selecting a plugin for a single-use task, long-term compatibility isn't a concern. But if you expect to use it repeatedly, you need to ensure that it will still function in the future. Will the plugin work the same way next year? If not, you might find yourself scrambling for alternatives.

How to fix it

If a plugin is intended for a one-time task, you can be more flexible in your selection. However, if it's something your team will depend on regularly, check its update history and ensure it has long-term support. A great example of a one-time-use plugin is Styles to Variable Converters, which helped many teams transition their styles into variables when Figma introduced the feature.

Another great example is Batch Styler by Jax Six, which simplifies managing multiple styles at once.

Plugin example—Batch Styler

Go to the Figma community plugin page, where you can read more and activate the plugin: `https://www.figma.com/community/plugin/818203235789864127/batch-styler`.

I used this plugin extensively in the past, so it deserves an honorable mention. As the name suggests, it works with styles. Nowadays, most workflows have shifted to Figma variables or Token Studio (which I'll cover shortly), so I don't use it as often. However, I know that some designers still rely on styles, especially for text formatting.

The plugin's main advantage is its ability to update multiple styles simultaneously, dramatically reducing the time needed for design system maintenance and updates.

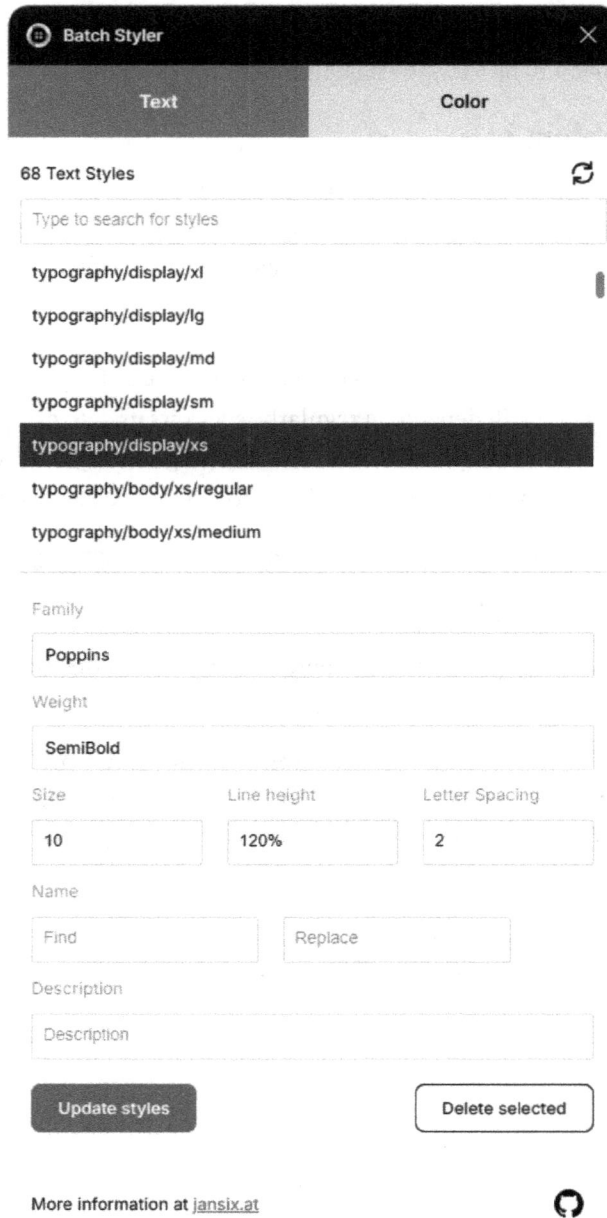

Figure 2.3 – Updating styles in bulk

There's more...

When browsing any plugin on the Figma community page, you can check the date of its last update. If a plugin hasn't been updated in over two years, it's wise to be cautious about integrating it into your long-term workflow, as it's unlikely to receive further updates. Another useful indicator is the comment section below the plugin, where you can gauge user feedback and recent experiences.

Is this plugin paid?

Not everything can be community-driven forever.

What's the problem?

Many plugins are developed as passion projects by independent designers or developers. While this contributes to a thriving design community—with hundreds of small, free plugins working perfectly fine—relying on unsupported plugins for long-term workflows can pose risks. For larger, more complex plugins where you expect continuous development and feature updates, you need to think long term. Without a monetization model or sustained company backing, these plugins may become outdated, break, or be abandoned, leaving users without support or updates.

How to fix it

To ensure reliability, prioritize plugins that have a sustainable business model or corporate backing. A well-maintained plugin is more likely to receive updates and ongoing support. A great example is Stark, which has a strong commercial foundation and continues to evolve with the needs of its users.

Plugin example—Stark

Visit the Figma community plugin page, where you can read more and activate the plugin: `https://www.figma.com/community/plugin/732603254453395948/stark-contrast-accessibility-checker`.

I'm happy to see that accessibility is becoming one of the key focuses for designers. One driving factor is the **European Accessibility Act** (**EAA**), which will take effect in June 2025. However, beyond compliance, I truly believe that when given the opportunity, we should aim to design inclusive experiences that benefit everyone.

In the past, I used Stark primarily for color contrast checks and vision impairment simulations. Today, the plugin offers even more—features such as **Typography Checker** and **Touch Targets (Area) Check** help ensure designs are both readable and user-friendly. These tools also assist developers by defining appropriate click zones, making accessibility a natural part of the design workflow.

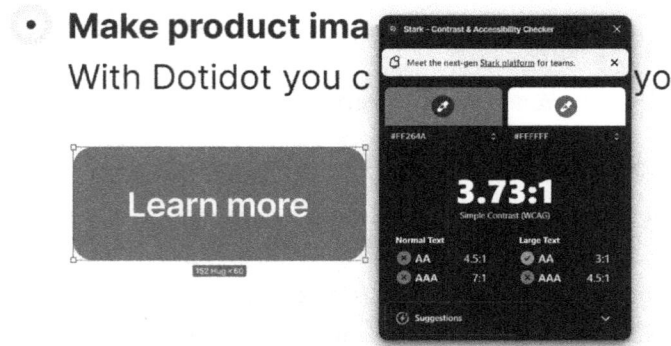

Figure 2.4 – Contrast Checker for selected button and text color

Testing your designs through vision impairment simulations takes only moments but provides invaluable insights into how your product will be experienced by users with different visual abilities.

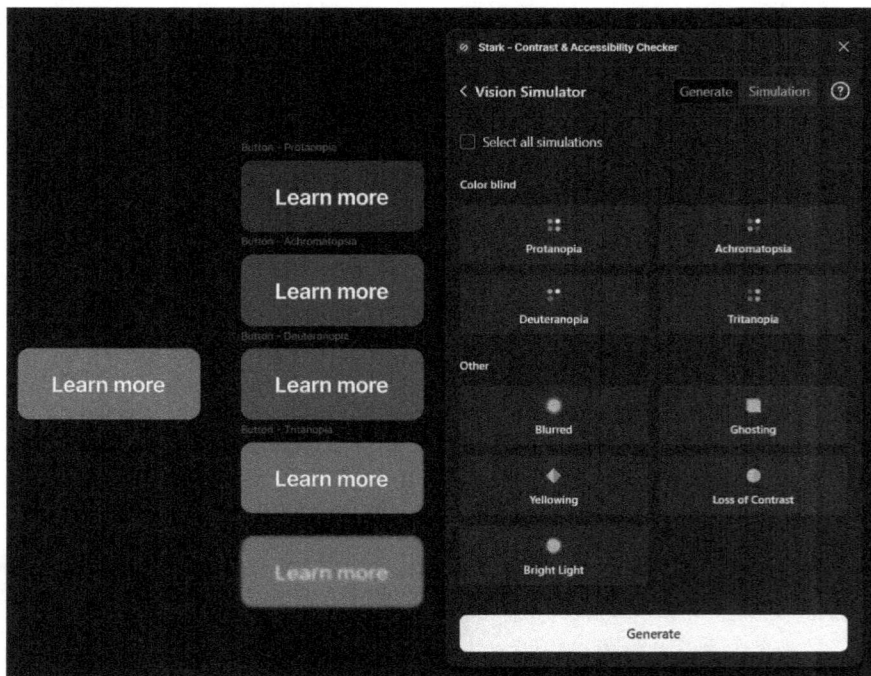

Figure 2.5 – Simulation of different vision disorders for you to see how your design will look

We should always keep accessibility at the forefront of our design process—it's not just a compliance checkbox but a fundamental principle that ensures our products serve everyone, regardless of their abilities.

Is it developed by a company?

The source of a plugin can tell you a lot about its long-term viability. While individual developers create amazing plugins, company-backed tools often have more resources behind them for maintenance and updates. However, keep in mind that company-developed plugins are typically designed to work best with their own workflows and ecosystems, which might not always be a one-size-fits-all solution for every team.

What's the problem?

Not all plugins are independently developed—some are backed by companies as part of their larger ecosystem. These plugins often come with greater reliability and long-term support compared to those developed by individual creators. A company has a vested interest in maintaining and updating its tools to ensure seamless integration with its core products. While there is always a risk that a plugin's functionality might shift in priority, businesses are generally more accountable for providing consistent updates and support, making them a more stable choice for long-term workflows.

How to fix it

To mitigate risks, prioritize plugins developed by companies with a vested interest in maintaining them. Plugins such as Figma to Webflow or Figma to Framer exist because these companies need smooth integration between their products. If a plugin is backed by a company that actively supports its product ecosystem, there's a higher likelihood it will be maintained. A strong example of this is Jira connectors and widgets, which are consistently updated and widely used in project management workflows.

Are there any reliable alternatives?

Every tool needs a backup plan. Before committing to a plugin that might become a critical part of your workflow, it's important to know whether there are viable alternatives you could switch to if needed.

What's the problem?

When selecting a plugin, it's crucial to consider whether there are reliable alternatives. While many CSV data-to-Figma plugins exist, making it easy to switch if one stops working, some plugins lack viable substitutes. If a plugin becomes unsupported, teams relying on it may struggle to find a replacement, causing workflow disruptions and additional development overhead.

How to fix it

To mitigate risks, always check whether alternative plugins exist before committing to one. If a plugin is critical to your workflow and has no direct competitors, consider its long-term sustainability. Assess the developer's track record, update frequency, and user community engagement. For example, Token Studio is a highly complex plugin for managing large design systems, and replacing it would require significant effort. In such cases, ensure you have a contingency plan or explore whether an in-house solution is feasible.

Streamlining workflow efficiency with time-saving plugins

Let's face it—design workflows can often get bogged down with repetitive tasks and inefficient handoff processes. The right plugins can transform these pain points into smooth, automated experiences. In this section, I'll share some of my favorite plugins that have saved my team countless hours and significantly improved our collaboration with developers.

What's the problem?

The handoff between design and development is one of the most time-consuming steps in any design project. Miscommunication and missing details can lead to inefficiencies, delays, and errors in implementation. Ensuring that developers receive the correct information is crucial for a smooth transition and to prevent unnecessary revisions.

How to fix it

Using Figma plugins designed for handoff can streamline this process and improve workflow efficiency. Tools such as Token Studio help manage design tokens, while Variables to CSS and Variables to JSON convert Figma variables into developer-friendly formats. These plugins ensure that developers have the necessary information at their fingertips, reducing friction and accelerating project timelines.

Plugin example—Token Studio

Go to the Figma community plugin page, where you can read more and activate the plugin: `https://www.figma.com/community/plugin/843461159747178978/tokens-studio-for-figma`.

Token Studio is an essential tool for teams managing and implementing design tokens within Figma. It acts as a bridge between design and development, converting tokens into code-ready formats. If your team handles large-scale design systems, Token Studio is indispensable for maintaining consistency across multiple projects.

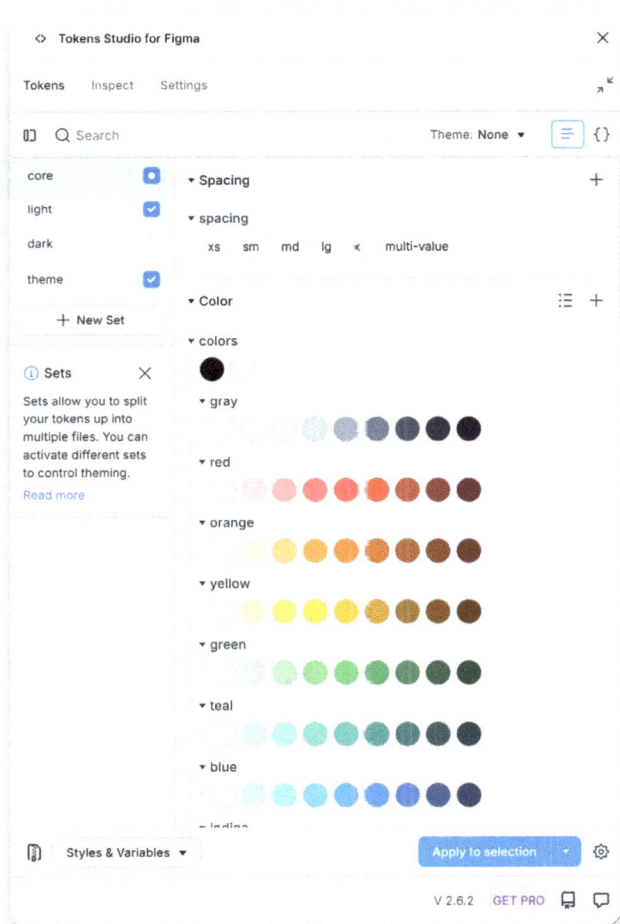

Figure 2.6 – Token Studio showcase in Figma. This is a demo project from the Token Studio team. Real structures are much more complex

Plugin example—Variables to CSS

Check out the Figma community plugin page, where you can read more and activate the plugin:
`https://www.figma.com/community/plugin/843461159747178978/tokens-studio-for-figma`.

Figma variables are powerful, but remember—your final product isn't the Figma file itself, but the production code. While variables in Figma enhance design consistency, they remain useful only if developers can easily access and implement them. Variables to CSS helps bridge this gap by exporting Figma variables into a developer-friendly CSS format, ensuring smooth handoff and better collaboration between designers and developers.

In the following screenshot, you can see the structured output of our design tokens exported to CSS, demonstrating how Figma variables are transformed into a code-ready format for developers.

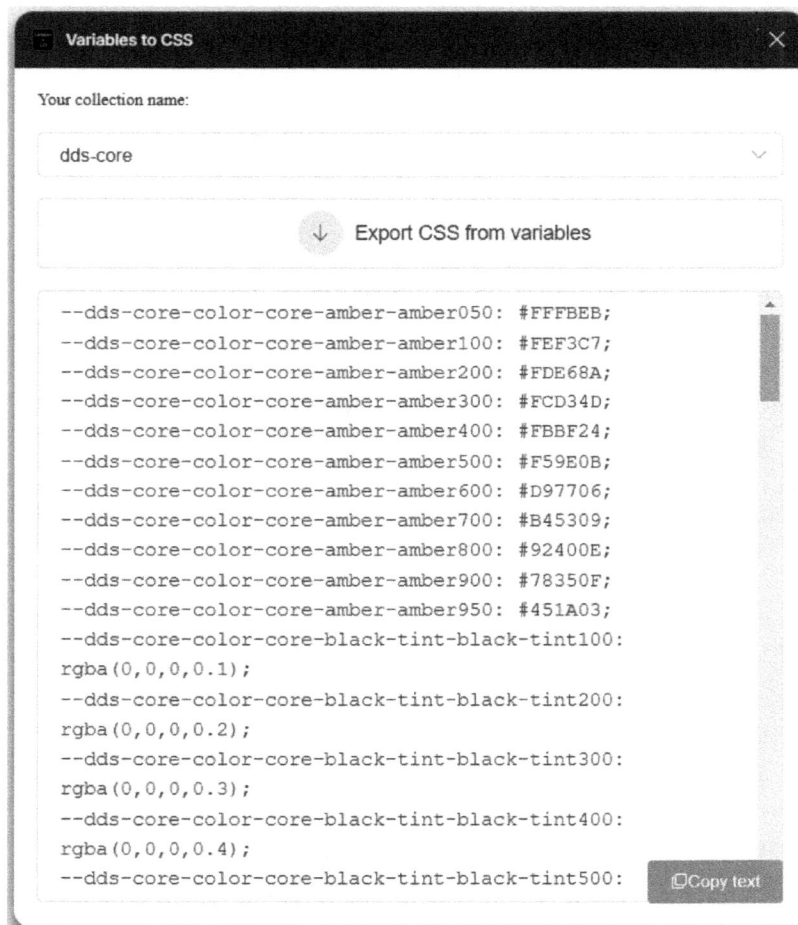

Figure 2.7 – Showcase of exported CSS code from Figma variables in the Dotidot design system

Plugin example—Variables to JSON

Check out the Figma community plugin page, where you can read more and activate the plugin: https://www.figma.com/community/plugin/1345399750040406570/figma-variables-to-json.

Similar to Variables to CSS, this plugin exports Figma variables in JSON format. The benefit? Developers can easily integrate design tokens into their workflows and even build custom export pipelines tailored to their project's needs. JSON-based exports provide flexibility, enabling teams to adjust naming conventions, value formats, and integration processes based on specific requirements.

Just like in the CSS example previously, you can see how Figma variables maintain their hierarchical structure when exported to JSON. The plugin offers customizable export settings, allowing you to adjust the output format to match your team's specific requirements.

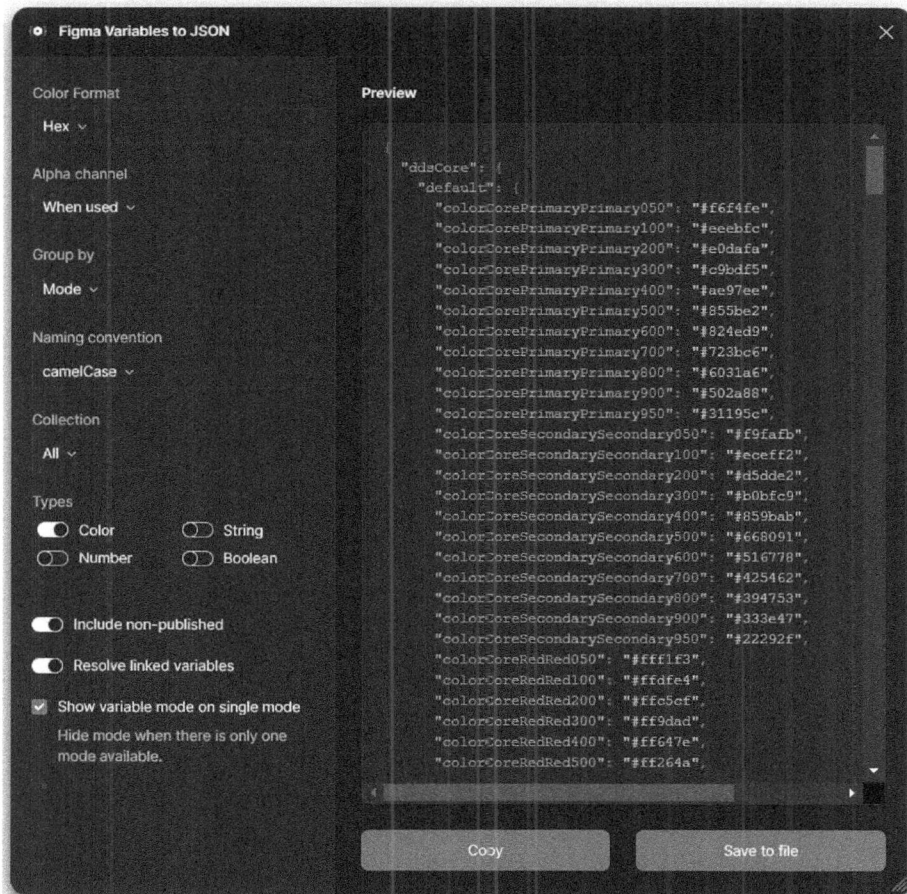

Figure 2.8 – Showcase of exported CSS code from Figma variables in the Dotidot design system

Plugin example—Builder.io

Visit the Figma community plugin page, where you can read more and activate the plugin: `https://www.figma.com/community/plugin/747985167520967365/builder-io-ai-powered-figma-to-code-react-vue-tailwind-more`.

Developers in my community highly recommend this AI-powered design-to-code plugin, which can accelerate the development process. It's not meant to replace developers but rather to enhance their efficiency and speed. If you're a developer, keep an open mind and give it a try—you might find it a valuable addition to your workflow.

Automating repetitive tasks with plugin integration

Every designer knows the feeling—you're deep in creative flow when suddenly you hit a roadblock of mundane, repetitive tasks. Whether it's populating designs with realistic content, organizing layers, or preparing assets for handoff, these necessary but tedious activities can drain your creative energy. This is where automation plugins truly shine.

What's the problem?

Designers and developers often find themselves repeating the same tasks, such as documentation, handoff preparation, and populating designs with real content. On larger projects, these tasks become time-consuming and, frankly, tedious. This repetition can slow down workflows, lead to inefficiencies, and take time away from more creative and strategic work.

How to fix it

I have prepared a few plugins for you that solve completely different problems, but all of them can automate your repetitive work so that you will have more time to focus on what truly matters—solving problems for your users.

Plugin example—Unsplash plugin

Go to the Figma community plugin page, where you can read more and activate the plugin: `https://www.figma.com/community/plugin/738454987945972471/unsplash`.

Every design should be presented or reviewed in its final form—essentially, how it will appear in production. However, in many cases, final assets, such as images, may not be readily available. Unsplash, one of the largest free image banks in the world, offers a dedicated Figma plugin that simplifies the process. If you're working on a large project with hundreds of images, this can save you valuable time by eliminating the need to switch between Figma and a browser, download images, and manually place them into your design. Instead, you can insert high-quality images directly, allowing you to focus on refining your design rather than handling repetitive asset management tasks.

Plugin example—Content Reel plugin

Check out the Figma community plugin page, where you can read more and activate the plugin: `https://www.figma.com/community/plugin/731627216655469013/content-reel`.

Content Reel is a powerful plugin that allows you to quickly populate your designs with real-world content. It is especially useful for different types of teams:

- **Agencies/freelancers**: When presenting designs to clients, realistic content can make a big difference. Content Reel provides instant access to diverse names, surnames, email addresses, phone numbers, country lists, and people's profile pictures. No more generic placeholder text or repeated `user@gmail.com` entries.

- **In-house teams**: When testing edge cases, Content Reel helps validate the design. By inserting real addresses, varied filenames, or long pieces of text, designers can stress-test components and identify UI issues, such as improper text truncation or input field overflow. This will help you save a huge amount of time in development.

Best of all, you can upload your own datasets and reuse them as needed. If your project requires specific types of content, such as long text in different languages, Content Reel ensures you can work with relevant information at all times.

As shown in the following screenshot, Content Reel provides an extensive library of pre-populated, realistic data categories that you can instantly drag and drop into your designs.

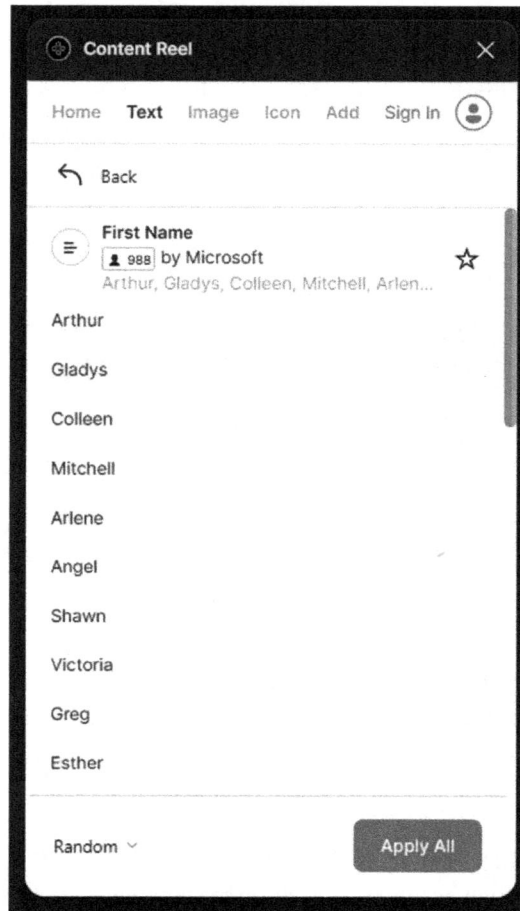

Figure 2.9 – Content Reel example of first names

Plugin example—Brandfetch

Check out the Figma community plugin page, where you can read more and activate the plugin: https://www.figma.com/community/plugin/733590967040604714/brandfetch.

When working with brand logos, you have two options: store a massive file containing logos from around the world or use Brandfetch to fetch them on demand. The choice seems simple, but if you find yourself googling *brand names + logos* repeatedly, it quickly becomes frustrating and inefficient. With Brandfetch, you can instantly access multiple versions of logos for major brands, ensuring consistency and saving valuable time in your workflow. One of the standout features is having multiple variations of logos in one place, as demonstrated in the Spotify example here.

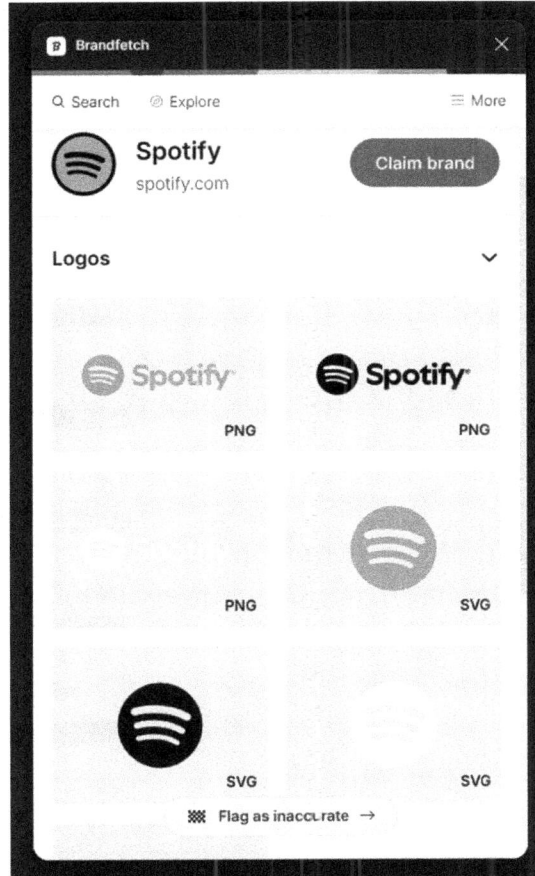

Figure 2.10 – All logos of popular brands in one place

Plugin example—Auto Documentation

Visit the Figma community plugin page, where you can read more and activate the plugin: https://www.figma.com/community/plugin/1134018716847999330/auto-documentation.

Design system documentation is essential. This plugin can generate a complete structure for your Figma variables or styles in seconds. For large systems with hundreds of tokens, this can save you an entire day—time better spent refining key design decisions rather than manually organizing styles.

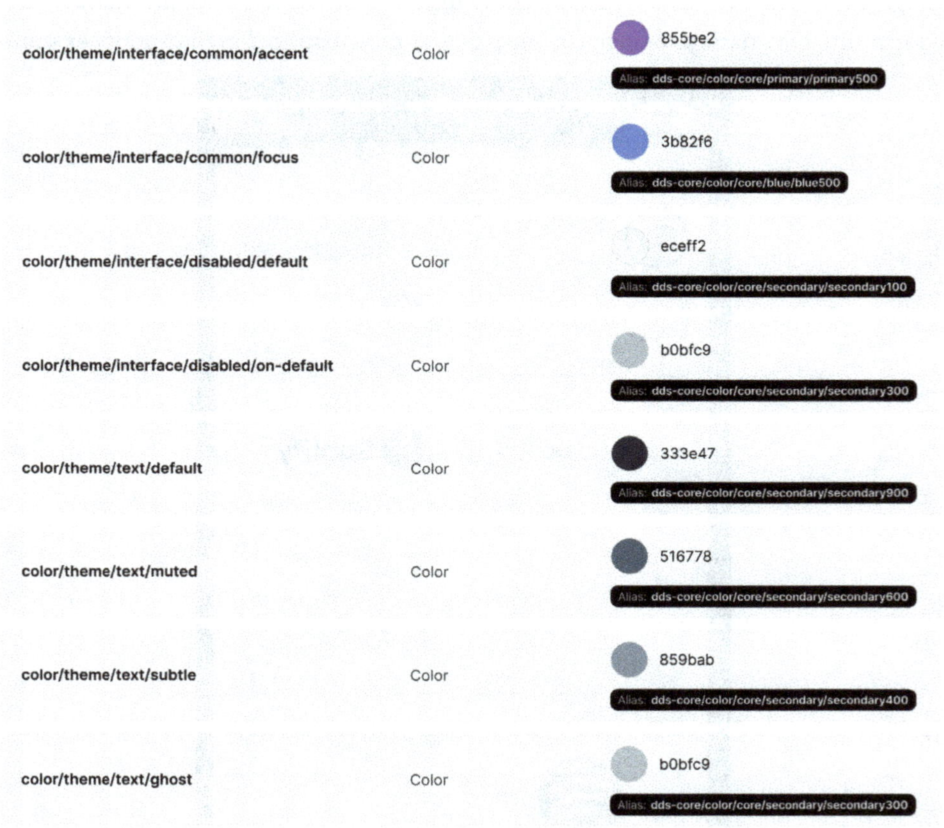

color/theme/interface/common/accent	Color	855be2 Alias: dds-core/color/core/primary/primary500
color/theme/interface/common/focus	Color	3b82f6 Alias: dds-core/color/core/blue/blue500
color/theme/interface/disabled/default	Color	eceff2 Alias: dds-core/color/core/secondary/secondary100
color/theme/interface/disabled/on-default	Color	b0bfc9 Alias: dds-core/color/core/secondary/secondary300
color/theme/text/default	Color	333e47 Alias: dds-core/color/core/secondary/secondary900
color/theme/text/muted	Color	516778 Alias: dds-core/color/core/secondary/secondary600
color/theme/text/subtle	Color	859bab Alias: dds-core/color/core/secondary/secondary400
color/theme/text/ghost	Color	b0bfc9 Alias: dds-core/color/core/secondary/secondary300

Figure 2.11 – Documentation of color design tokens/variables

Specific project needs solved by plugins

Every project comes with its unique challenges and requirements. While standard design tools cover the basics, specialized plugins can be the secret weapon that helps you tackle those project-specific hurdles with ease. Let's explore some plugins that solve particularly niche but important design problems.

What's the problem?

Some projects are highly specialized. I encountered this frequently during my freelancing days. One month, I was working on a large, multinational e-commerce store; the next, I was designing for a fintech start-up. These projects were exciting, but they often had unique requirements that needed to be solved at the design level. Unfortunately, you can't always copy and paste a solution from one project to another because each has its own constraints and challenges.

How to fix it

Over time, I discovered several plugins that helped me navigate these unique design challenges. While these tools may be niche, they can be invaluable if you find yourself in a similar situation.

Plugin example—Charts plugin

Go to the Figma community plugin page, where you can read more and activate the plugin: `https://www.figma.com/community/plugin/731451122947612104/charts`.

Designing charts can be challenging. If you've worked on complex dashboards before, you know the difficulties involved. Chart generation plugins were among the first I searched for and paid for because, without them, I wouldn't have been able to complete certain projects in the past. Always ensure you discuss charts with developers, as they are unlikely to build them from scratch. Instead, they will rely on existing libraries, so your chosen plugin should align with the functionality of the selected library to ensure seamless integration.

Alternatively, you can reverse-engineer this process—start by identifying which chart library your development team prefers, then find the plugin that best matches its capabilities and output format.

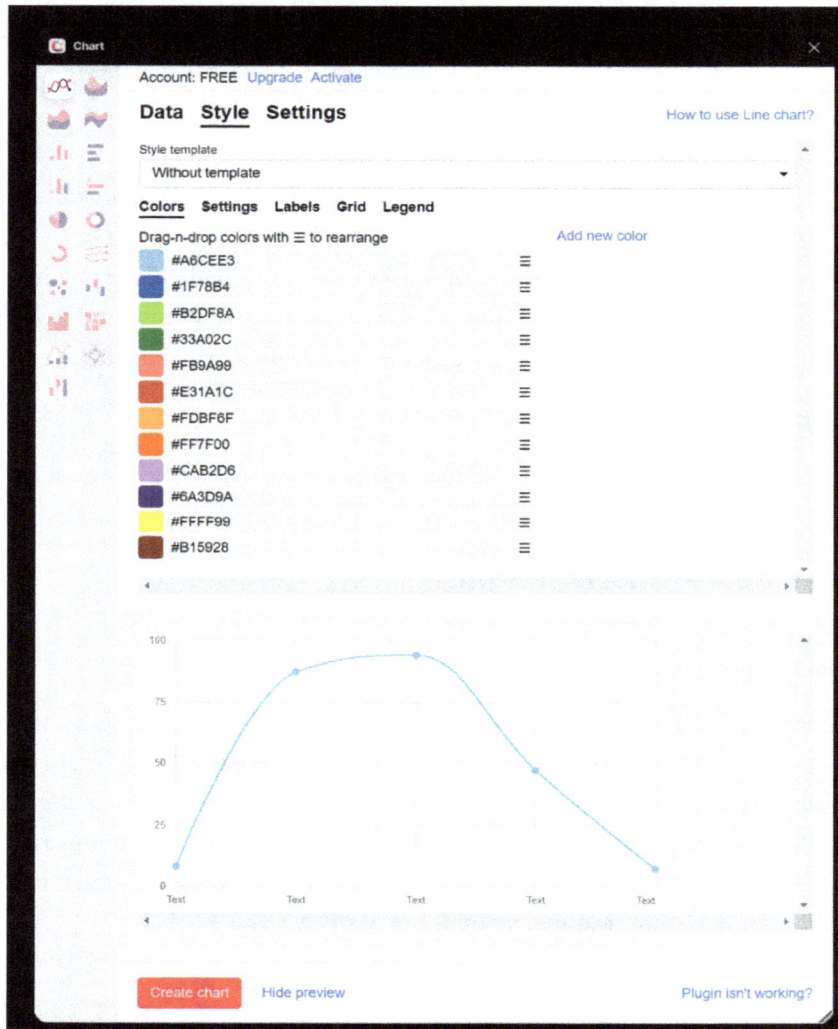

Figure 2.12 – Chart preview and settings before inserting into Figma

Plugin example—Downsize

Check out the Figma community plugin page, where you can read more and activate the plugin: `https://www.figma.com/community/plugin/869495400795251845/downsize`.

Large Figma files often contain numerous images, which can be particularly challenging for visually heavy projects such as brand websites. Figma's ability to save images in their original resolution provides a great starting point for design work. However, many developers fail to optimize images, simply downloading them from Figma as JPEG or PNG files and using them directly in their projects. This can lead to slow load times due to large asset sizes.

Downsize is a one-click solution for image optimization, ensuring that assets are properly compressed before they are exported and used in development. Another significant benefit of this plugin is improving Figma's performance. If your Figma files feel sluggish, optimizing images with Downsize can greatly enhance speed and responsiveness. I've personally found it to be an effective way to streamline workflows and improve project efficiency.

Linking Figma to other software for cross-platform integration

Design rarely exists in isolation. In today's interconnected workflow environments, your Figma designs need to communicate seamlessly with other tools in your tech stack. The right integration plugins can eliminate tedious manual transfers and keep your project information synchronized across platforms.

What's the problem?

Figma doesn't exist in a vacuum. It's part of a broader workflow involving multiple tools to transform designs into production-ready code. Through my mentoring sessions, I've often encountered teams that are highly skilled in Figma but struggle to integrate it seamlessly with their other tools, leading to inefficiencies in their workflow.

How to fix it

Take a step back and analyze your daily workflow. Identify the tools you and your team rely on and explore plugins that bridge the gap between Figma and those platforms. I will highlight some of the ones I use, but depending on your stack, you may find alternatives that better fit your needs. Since every team's toolset is unique, the key is finding integrations that streamline your specific workflow.

Plugin example—Jira

Go to the Figma community plugin page, where you can read more and activate the plugin:
`https://www.figma.com/community/plugin/1220802563996996107/jira`.

Easily integrate Jira issues in real time with your Figma file. If your team relies on Jira, this plugin
makes it much easier for designers, developers, and product managers to check specifications
directly within Figma. Since this is an official plugin, you can trust its reliability and long-term
support, ensuring a smooth workflow for your team.

Figure 2.13 – Jira widget in Figma

Plugin example—Asana

Check out the Figma community plugin page, where you can read more and activate the plugin:
`https://www.figma.com/community/widget/1098405969270214551/asana`.

Similar to the Jira integration, this official plugin connects Asana tasks in real time with your
Figma file. It streamlines collaboration by allowing designers, developers, and product managers
to access task details directly within Figma, reducing the need to switch between tools.

Plugin example—GitHub

Go to the Figma community plugin page, where you can read more and activate the plugin:
`https://www.figma.com/community/plugin/1220512233196109878/github`.

Seamlessly integrate GitHub issues into your design workflow. This plugin is particularly useful
for technical designers and developers, enabling them to access issues directly within Figma. By
consolidating everything in one place, it enhances efficiency and eliminates the need to switch
between platforms.

Plugin example—Figma to Webflow

Check out the Figma community plugin page, where you can read more and activate the plugin:
`https://www.figma.com/community/plugin/1164923964214525039/figma-to-webflow-html-css-and-website`.

Webflow is a low-code/no-code website-building platform that allows marketing teams to move faster without relying on developers. Many major brands use Webflow for its flexibility and ease of use, but it's also a great choice for personal projects. Having used Webflow alongside Figma for years, I was excited about this integration.

The plugin had a rough start, so if you've tried it before and dismissed it—like I did—it's worth giving it another shot. Now, you can sync variables, styles, and even entire components effortlessly. Grab a coffee and try it out!

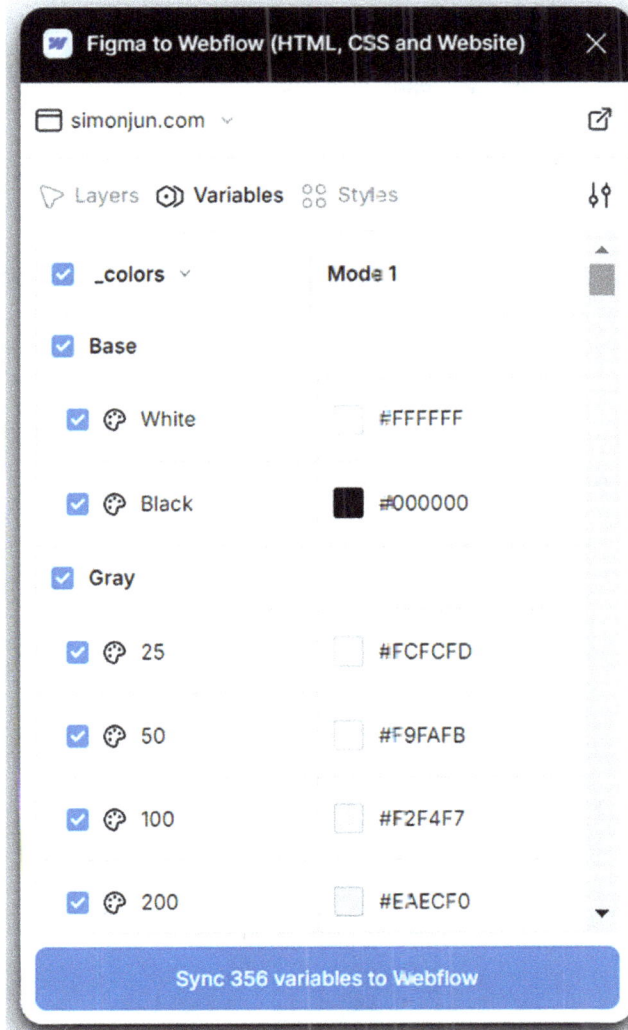

Figure 2.14 – Figma to Webflow variables sync

Plugin example—Figma to Framer

Figma community plugin page, where you can read more and activate the plugin: `https://www.figma.com/community/plugin/1037108608720448600/figma-to-html-with-framer`.

Similar to the Figma to Webflow integration, this plugin connects Figma with Framer. While I don't personally use Framer, I reached out to the community, and the feedback has been overwhelmingly positive. Given its strong reception, I wanted to highlight it as a valuable option for those working with Framer.

There's more...

The last point I want to highlight is Figma's integration with other tools. Figma has its own plugins within external platforms, enhancing connectivity and streamlining workflows. Two key use cases I rely on daily are Google Workspace and Jira, where these integrations make it much easier to link designs with documents or tickets, ensuring seamless collaboration across teams.

Figure 2.15 – In all Google documents, you will see this Figma filename pill instead of the whole link

The following figure demonstrates how seamlessly you can embed Figma into Jira tickets, allowing you to access designs directly without opening Figma separately.

⚡ PROD-322 / 🔗 PROD-530

Screen Rec....44.mov	Screenshot....38.png	Screenshot....0⁴.png	Screenshot....30.png
10 Jul, 2025	10 Jul, 2025	01 Jul, 2025	01 Jul, 2025

Designs (1)   + ∧

🅑 ⊙ Q3/2025 Design · Campaign Creation Flow   🔒 Edited 10 days ago

Expand in Jira   ⟲

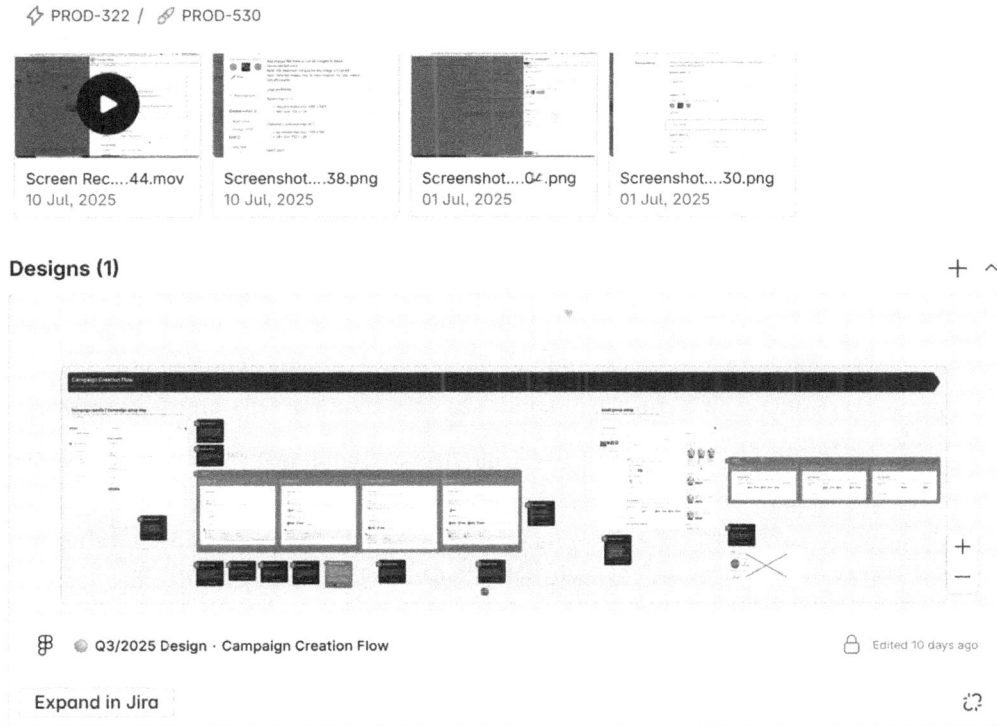

Figure 2.16 – An overview of a Jira ticket for Figma right inside Jira. No need to open up Figma

When to consider writing your own plugin

Sometimes, despite the vast plugin marketplace, you might find yourself thinking, "I wish there were a plugin that could…" That might be your cue to consider creating a custom solution. While it may sound intimidating, developing your own Figma plugin can be more accessible than you might think—and it could be the perfect answer to your specific workflow challenges.

What's the problem?

Sometimes, the available plugins on the market just don't meet your needs. What's the solution? Build your own! Before you turn the page, hear me out—I know most of you are designers, but many of my designer friends have successfully created their own plugins. Even my younger brother built one while still in high school!

How to fix it

While building your own plugin is one option, remember that you don't need to be a developer to create one. I've worked with several companies where designers approached plugin creation as simply another design task. They created the specifications and designs, then someone from the development team built it during their regular sprints, treating it like any other ticket.

If you want to create something simple, don't be afraid to try building it yourself. However, if you need something more complex—particularly if it needs to connect to your databases or other systems—don't hesitate to ask your development team for help. Figma provides excellent documentation, making it relatively straightforward for developers to implement your ideas efficiently.

This book isn't about plugin development, so I won't dive too deep into the technical details. But don't worry—it's easier than you think! Grab a coffee, fire up ChatGPT, and check out the following Figma tutorial. You've got this!

```
https://help.figma.com/hc/en-us/articles/4407260620823--BYFP-1-Overview.
```

Unlock this book's exclusive benefits now	
Scan this QR code or go to packtpub.com/ unlock, then search this book by name.	
Note: Keep your purchase invoice ready before you start.	

3

Harnessing AI in Figma and Beyond

AI is integrated into almost every tool nowadays—if a tool doesn't have AI, some might jokingly say it's already obsolete. Over the past few years, nearly every software has jumped on the AI bandwagon, often implementing features that feel experimental or lack a clear use case. In this chapter, I will explore Figma's AI capabilities and how I leverage other AI tools to enhance my productivity in Figma. We will cover these six key topics:

- Exploring Figma's built-in AI features
- Automating routine tasks with AI in Figma
- Integrating AI tools for faster prototyping
- Implementing AI into your design workflow
- Analyzing AI-enhanced design workflows—case studies
- Navigating ethical challenges in AI-driven design

Exploring Figma's built-in AI features

Figma includes several AI features, each aimed at addressing different challenges. We'll begin with the most useful ones before discussing those that feel less refined. Keep in mind that my perspectives are based on extensive experience using Figma in various teams. If you're a lighter user, some of these features might be more beneficial for you, as your expectations may differ.

Figma categorizes its AI features into three groups:

- Design tools

- Riffing and writing
- Image editing

Disclaimer

All insights into Figma's built-in AI features are based on my experience at the time of writing—mid-2025. If I express skepticism about a feature or state that it doesn't work well, the real question isn't *if* it will work, but *when*. If you're reading this later, check again—because right now, these features are at their least developed, and tomorrow they will be better, and the day after that, even better.

Design tools

Design tools have the most AI features, so we will start with them:

- Rename layers
- Search with image or selection
- Add interactions
- Replace content
- First draft

Rename layers

Let's start with a seemingly small feature that delivers massive impact in collaborative design environments. Layer naming might not be the most exciting topic, but any designer who's inherited a messy Figma file knows how crucial proper organization becomes during complex projects.

Keep in mind that most established companies have their own documented naming conventions for layers. While AI-generated names can be helpful, you may need to adjust them to match your team's specific standards and conventions.

What's the problem?

One of the biggest challenges in Figma collaboration is dealing with disorganized and poorly named layers. Many designers skip proper layer naming, leading to chaos in large team projects. Imagine a file filled with labels such as Frame236472—no one wants to waste time deciphering that. When multiple people collaborate on a project, unclear naming makes handoffs to developers and other stakeholders frustrating. Even solo designers need structured files because Figma designs often move into development or marketing assets.

How to fix it

Figma's **Rename layers** AI feature automates this process, making files easier to navigate and reducing errors. Here's how you can use it effectively:

1. **Select multiple layers**: Choose all the layers in your design that need renaming.

2. **Run the AI rename tool**: Let Figma analyze the structure and suggest logical names.

3. **Review and adjust**: While AI-generated names are often helpful, a quick review ensures they follow your team's conventions.

4. **Adopt naming standards**: If working in a team, define clear naming guidelines so AI-generated names remain consistent.

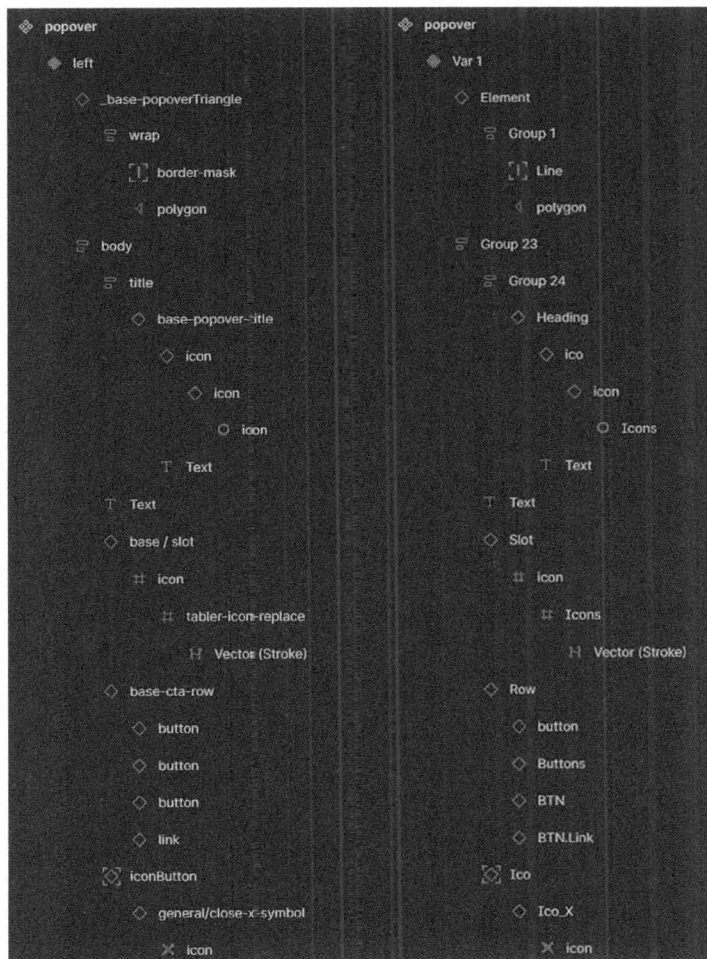

Figure 3.1 – The same component with the right naming (left side) and the wrong naming (right side)

Properly named layers improve workflow efficiency and enhance other Figma features such as **Smart Animate** and **Select Matching Layers**, making interactions smoother and troubleshooting easier.

Searching with image or selection

This feature might be one of my favorites that I use daily. Finding specific elements in large design systems used to be a major workflow bottleneck, but Figma's AI-powered search has transformed how we locate and reuse components across projects.

What's the problem?

Searching for specific elements across multiple Figma files can be incredibly time-consuming, especially when working on large-scale projects with extensive design libraries. Designers often waste valuable time scrolling through files or sending Slack messages asking for the correct link. This inefficiency disrupts workflow and slows down production. When dealing with complex design systems, finding the right asset at the right time is critical for maintaining consistency and efficiency.

How to fix it

Figma's search with image or selection feature simplifies asset retrieval by allowing users to find elements using a screenshot or selection. Here's how to leverage it effectively:

1. **Capture a screenshot**: If you come across an element in another project or on a live website/app, take a quick screenshot.
2. **Paste or select in Figma**: Upload the screenshot or choose an element directly within Figma.
3. **Run the AI search tool**: Figma scans its database and returns matching assets, streamlining the search process.

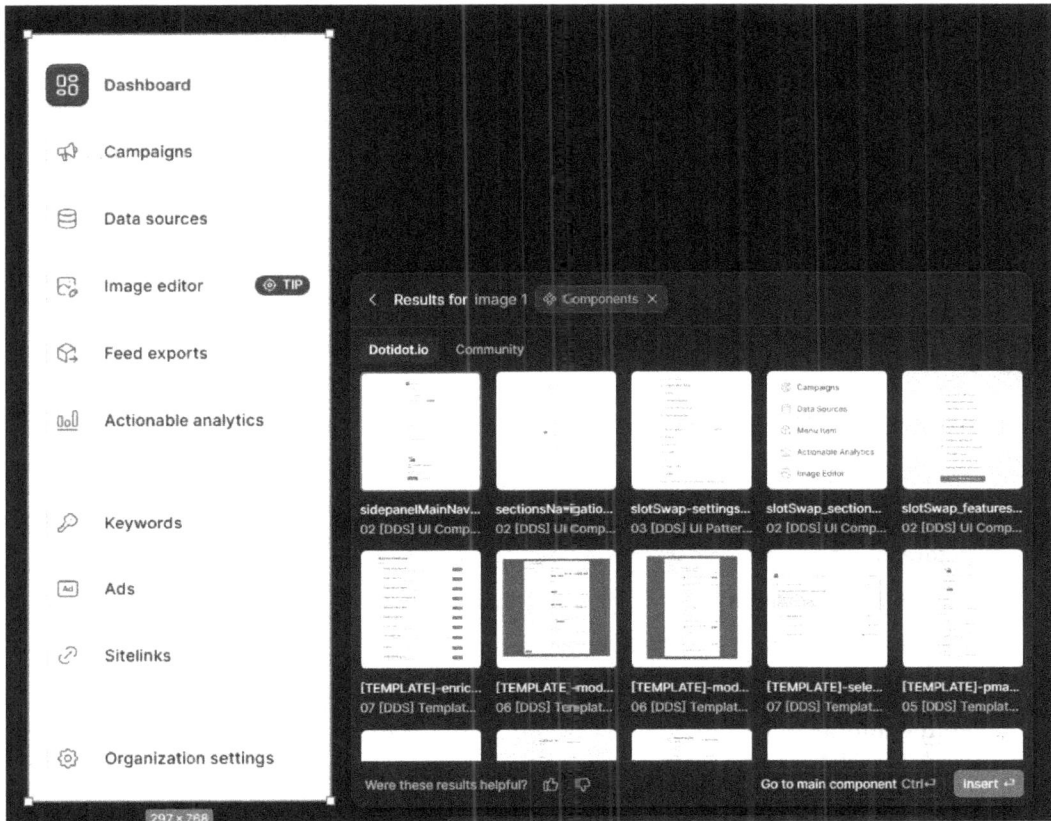

Figure 3.2 – Simple screenshot of Dotidot navigation from your live app – Figma finds the right components in seconds

For example, if I need to locate the navigation design from our Dotidot app, I can simply screenshot the live app, paste it into Figma, and instantly retrieve the relevant component. This feature works reliably in nearly every case, making it an invaluable tool for managing complex design systems.

Adding interactions

Creating prototypes manually can be tedious, especially for complex flows with multiple states and transitions. Figma's AI-powered interaction builder aims to streamline this process, though its success varies depending on the complexity of your design.

What's the problem?

Creating a complex prototype for user testing or showcasing can be a time-consuming and error-prone process. Manually setting up interactions between multiple screens requires careful planning and execution. While AI-driven prototyping aims to automate this process, its effectiveness depends heavily on understanding the design's intent. For simple user flows, AI-generated interactions work well, but for complex scenarios involving multiple user journeys, AI often falls short. Designers may find themselves spending more time fixing auto-generated interactions rather than benefiting from automation.

How to fix it

Figma's AI-powered interaction tool can assist in automating the prototyping process. Here's how to make the most of it:

1. **Start with a clear flow**: Define the user journey (positions of your frames on the artboard) beforehand to guide AI in setting up logical interactions.
2. **Enable AI-powered interactions**: Allow Figma to auto-generate connections between frames based on common user behaviors.
3. **Test the prototype**: Run the AI-generated interactions to check for accuracy.
4. **Refine and adjust:** Manually tweak the interactions to ensure they align with your intended user experience.

For simple interactions, this tool can save significant time. However, for more intricate workflows, manual refinement is often necessary to achieve the best results.

Replacing content

Populating designs with realistic content is essential for accurate testing and client presentations. Figma's **Replace content** feature attempts to automate this often repetitive task, reducing the time spent manually inserting placeholder text and images.

What's the problem?

When working with long lists, tables, or repetitive components in Figma, manually inserting diverse content can be tedious and time-consuming. Designers often struggle with maintaining variety in placeholders while ensuring a realistic representation of the final product. Without automation, this process can slow down workflows and lead to inconsistencies in design, such as using placeholder text that doesn't reflect realistic content lengths or mixing different content styles across similar components.

How to fix it

Figma's **Replace content** feature automates content population, helping designers quickly fill repetitive structures with varied text and images. Here's how to use it effectively:

1. **Prepare your layout:** Ensure you are using auto layout with properly structured structure (ideally components).

2. **Select multiple items:** Highlight the elements you want to populate with different content.

3. **Use the Replace content feature:** Let Figma's AI generate varied entries for your design.

4. **Review and refine:** Adjust or swap out any content that doesn't align with your intended output.

While this feature can speed up initial design iterations, it currently lacks contextual awareness, leading to less-than-ideal results. For more control and flexibility, dedicated plugins such as **data.to.design** or **Content Reel** (covered in *Chapter 2*) provide more reliable and customizable content generation options.

First Draft

The promise of generating entire interfaces with a simple text prompt is enticing. Figma's **First Draft** feature attempts to turn this vision into reality, though as you'll see, the results don't quite match the ambition—at least not yet. However, Figma Make does a far better job at this, even pulling from existing Figma design systems, instead of pulling the same generic UI wireframe kit that gets on everything generated through **First Draft**. I'll cover Figma Make in more detail in the *Integrating AI tools for faster prototyping* section later in this chapter.

What's the problem?

Generating a complete UI from a simple text prompt sounds like an incredible time-saver. In theory, this feature should allow designers to move from a blank canvas to a fully designed interface within seconds. However, after extensive testing in my online course, I found that the results were repetitive and lacked real usability. Regardless of the input prompt—whether "Budget app," "Bank app," or "Investment app"—the AI consistently produced nearly identical UI structures, heavily featuring cryptocurrency elements such as Bitcoin. This suggests that the AI is primarily trained on freely available Figma designs, following outdated trends rather than user needs.

While the idea is promising, its current execution is not practical for professional design work. The generated outputs are more suitable for quick visual placeholders than for fully functional products. Designing well-thought-out solutions involves more than arranging UI components— it requires user research, problem-solving, and contextual understanding, which AI-generated designs currently fail to deliver.

How to fix it

While Figma's **First Draft** feature is not yet refined for professional workflows, here's how you can experiment with it effectively:

- **Use it for ideation**: Treat AI-generated designs as rough starting points rather than final products.

- **Refine the structure**: Adjust layouts, replace irrelevant elements, and tailor components to your specific project needs.

- **Combine it with manual design work**: Leverage AI for inspiration, but rely on human insight for usability and UX improvements.

- **Supplement with design libraries**: If you need structured templates, consider using curated design libraries such as Material 3 from Google, UntitledUI (which I personally use), Figma's built-in UI kits, community-created template libraries, or premium resources such as UI8 or Creative Market instead of relying solely on AI-generated content.

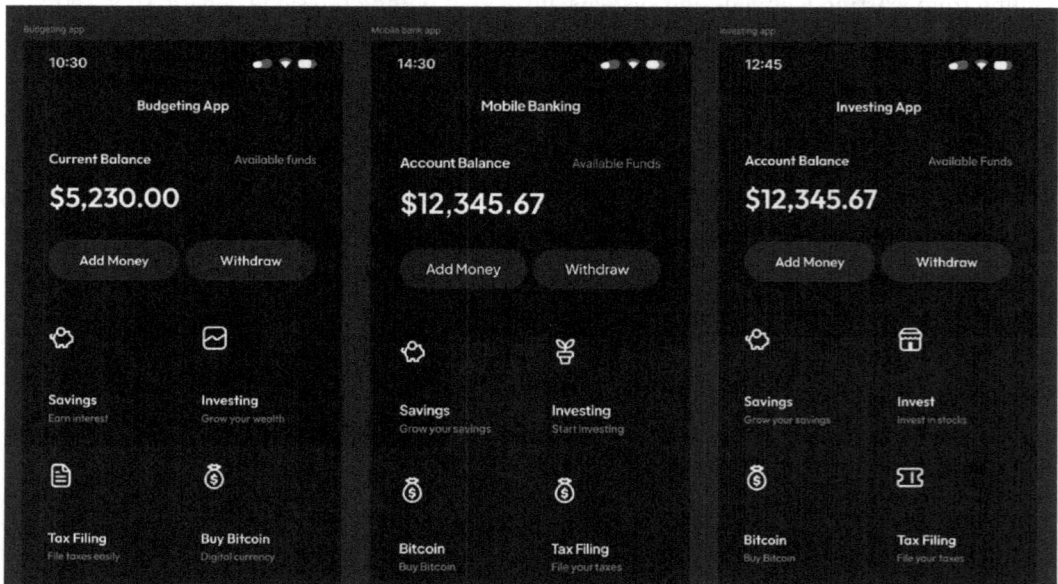

Figure 3.3 – Three different prompts, three same results

For now, this feature serves as a brainstorming tool rather than a reliable design assistant. However, as AI evolves, it could become a valuable asset for accelerating initial design drafts while still requiring human refinement.

Riffing and writing

Text is an essential part of every design. Thankfully, the days of relying on Lorem Ipsum are over, and AI has become a powerful tool in this field Figma offers three features to enhance text management in design:

- Rewrite this...
- Shorten
- Translate to...

Rewrite this...

Text quality can make or break a design. Figma's AI text rewriting capability helps designers improve copy directly within their workflow, without needing to switch between different tools or wait for copywriter feedback on every small text element.

What's the problem?

Ensuring consistent, high-quality text across a design can be challenging, especially when working with multiple stakeholders or large projects. Designers often struggle with refining placeholder text into something more meaningful while maintaining tone, clarity, and branding consistency. Without an efficient way to edit and optimize content within Figma, teams risk spending unnecessary time rewriting copy manually.

How to fix it

Figma's **Rewrite this...** feature simplifies the process by automatically refining and enhancing text. Here's how to make the most of it:

1. **Insert placeholder text**: Begin with a rough draft of the text you want to improve.
2. **Select the Rewrite this... option**: Let AI analyze and generate a more polished version.
3. **Adjust for tone and context**: Review and tweak the suggested copy to match the specific brand voice and project requirements.
4. **Use external AI for advanced editing**: For complex projects, integrate tools such as ChatGPT to train AI with specific guidelines, such as target audience, tone, and restricted words.

Additionally, ChatGPT works exceptionally well with design screenshots—simply take a snapshot of the design, provide context with placeholder text, and let AI generate refined content in seconds. This feature enhances productivity by reducing the manual effort required to refine design copy.

Shorten

Designing for multiple languages presents unique challenges, particularly when it comes to UI space constraints. This AI feature helps tackle text expansion issues that often arise in multilingual designs, especially for languages that typically require more characters than English.

What's the problem?

When designing for multiple languages, text expansion can quickly become an issue, especially in languages such as German or Hungarian, where words tend to be significantly longer than their English counterparts. This can cause layout breakages, misaligned elements, and readability issues. Without a proper way to test and adjust text dynamically, designers often struggle to ensure UI consistency across different languages.

For example, German or Hungarian text often requires more space, so shortening key labels can prevent UI misalignment. This feature is a valuable tool for ensuring multilingual designs remain visually consistent without excessive manual adjustments.

English	German	Hungarian
Login	Anmelden	Bejelentkezés
Accept all	Alle akzeptieren	Összes elfogadása

Table 3.1 – Showcase of various lengths of commonly used texts

How to fix it

Figma's **Shorten** feature helps solve this problem by providing more concise text alternatives while maintaining clarity. Here's how to use it effectively:

1. **Identify problematic text**: Check elements where text expansion may cause layout issues.
2. **Use the Shorten feature**: Let AI generate a more compact version of the text while preserving meaning.
3. **Compare and adjust**: Review the shortened text and ensure it fits within your design constraints.
4. **Test across languages**: If designing for multiple languages, compare different versions to confirm readability and alignment.

Translate to...

Expanding your product to global markets requires effective localization tools. Figma's translation feature aims to integrate language conversion directly into the design process, potentially saving rounds of back-and-forth with translation teams during the prototyping phase.

What's the problem?

Multilingual design is a necessity for many digital products, but ensuring accurate translations within the design workflow can be a challenge. While Figma's **Translate to...** feature aims to simplify this process, its current limitations make it less effective than dedicated translation plugins and professional localization solutions. Not all languages are supported, meaning designers working with less common languages may find the tool's usefulness limited for teams designing for global audiences. Some commonly used languages are still missing, limiting its usefulness for teams designing for global audiences.

How to fix it

Despite its limitations, the **Translate to...** feature can still be useful in streamlining multilingual design. Here's how to maximize its effectiveness:

1. **Check language availability**: Before relying on this feature, verify whether your target language is supported.

2. **Use it for common languages**: If your project includes widely used languages, the AI-generated translations can speed up the initial localization process.

3. **Integrate external tools**: For unsupported languages, consider using translation APIs or dedicated localization tools alongside Figma to ensure full coverage. Some plugins can help you with that.

While Figma's translation capabilities are promising, expanding language support would greatly improve its usefulness for designers working on truly international products.

Image editing

The last group of built-in AI features focuses on image editing. There are four in total—two that I find incredibly useful and one that frustrates me.

- Remove background
- Boost resolution
- Make an image
- Edit image

Remove background

Image editing was traditionally a task that required switching to dedicated software. Figma's background removal tool brings this essential capability directly into the design environment, streamlining what was once a multi-step, multi-tool process.

What's the problem?

Removing backgrounds from images has always been a tedious task for designers. Before Figma introduced this feature, many relied on third-party tools such as **remove.bg** to eliminate backgrounds with a single click. While effective, these external solutions required extra steps, disrupting workflow efficiency. Designers needed a seamless, built-in way to remove backgrounds without leaving Figma.

How to fix it

Figma's **Remove background** feature offers a quick and efficient way to isolate subjects from their backgrounds directly within the design tool. Here's how to use it effectively:

1. **Select an image:** Click on the image you want to edit.
2. **Apply the Remove background tool:** Use Figma's built-in AI to extract the subject.

Figure 3.4 – Showcase of Figma background removal

Leverage this feature for product images, marketing banners, or UI elements where background removal enhances the design. This streamlines workflows by eliminating the need for external tools. If you haven't tried it yet, I highly recommend giving it a go!

Boost resolution

Image quality issues are common when working with client-provided assets or legacy materials. This AI enhancement feature allows designers to improve low-resolution images right within Figma, eliminating the need for external image editing tools.

What's the problem?

Working with low-resolution assets has always been a major challenge for me when I was freelancing. Clients often insist on using outdated images or low-quality icons that look pixelated and unprofessional on modern high-resolution displays. Manually enhancing these assets was time-consuming, requiring external tools and meticulous adjustments to maintain quality without distortion.

How to fix it

Figma's **Boost resolution** feature provides a seamless way to upscale images while preserving clarity. Here's how to make the most of it:

1. **Select the image**: Choose the low-resolution asset you need to enhance.
2. **Apply the Boost resolution tool**: Let Figma's AI intelligently upscale the image.

Figure 3.5 – Figma Boost resolution on an old, pixelated icon

If this tool had existed during my freelance years, it would have saved me countless hours. Now, it's an essential feature for any designer handling legacy assets or repurposing outdated graphics for modern screens.

Make an image

AI image generation has been making waves across the design industry. Figma's implementation brings this capability directly into your design workflow, promising to create visuals based on text descriptions without leaving the design environment.

What's the problem?

AI-powered image generation promises to revolutionize design workflows by instantly creating high-quality visuals based on text prompts. The concept is simple: type a description and AI generates an image that seamlessly integrates into your design. However, in practice, the results often fall short. Many of the generated images are not usable.

Despite my experience as a heavy AI user, I found this feature unreliable, producing generic outputs that failed to meet expectations. While this tool has potential, it currently feels more experimental than practical.

How to fix it

If you want to experiment with AI-generated images in Figma, here's how to get the best possible results:

1. **Use simple, clear prompts**: AI performs best with concise and specific input, so structure your prompts carefully.
2. **Refine the output**: AI-generated images often require post-processing or manual adjustments to fit into a design.
3. **Combine AI with existing assets**: Use AI-generated images as a starting point rather than a final product.
4. **Test different prompts**: Small wording changes can yield significantly different results, so experiment with variations to get closer to what you need.

Although this feature is not yet reliable for production work, I am confident that it will continue to improve. AI image generation is evolving rapidly, and in the future, it could become an essential tool for designers.

Edit image

Figma's image editing capabilities extend beyond background removal and resolution enhancement. The **Edit image** feature provides additional AI-powered tools for adjusting and modifying images directly within your design workflow.

What's the problem?

Traditional image editing often requires switching between multiple applications, disrupting the design flow. Whether you need to adjust lighting, change colors, or make other modifications to images, having to jump to external photo editing software breaks your creative momentum and adds unnecessary complexity to simple tasks.

How to fix it

Figma's **Edit image** feature brings basic image editing functionality directly into the design environment. Here's how to make the most of it:

1. **Select your image**: Choose the image you want to modify in your Figma file.
2. **Access edit options**: Use Figma's AI-powered editing tools to make adjustments such as brightness, contrast, or color modifications.
3. **Apply changes iteratively**: Make incremental adjustments and preview them in real time within your design context.
4. **Maintain design consistency**: Keep your edited images consistent with your overall design aesthetic without losing the context of your project.

While these editing capabilities are useful for quick adjustments, they're best suited for basic modifications rather than complex photo manipulation. For more advanced editing needs, dedicated image editing software may still be necessary.

Automating routine tasks with AI in Figma

Beyond Figma's built-in AI features, there's tremendous potential in using AI to automate repetitive design tasks. The key is identifying which parts of your workflow can benefit from automation without sacrificing creative control or design quality.

What's the problem?

As a designer, you handle countless routine tasks daily. Over the years, as a mentor, I've met individuals who dedicate their evenings and weekends to automating not just their work but their entire lives. However, this level of thinking is rare. For the rest of you, here's my approach to thinking about automating routine tasks effectively.

How to fix it

To successfully automate routine tasks in Figma, follow this structured approach:

1. **Schedule a review**: Block a calendar slot every two weeks (or once a month) for two hours to analyze your workflow.

2. **Document repetitive tasks**: Create a simple sheet or document where you log time-consuming or repetitive tasks as you encounter them.

3. **Log in chronological order**: Write them down as they happen. If some tasks appear multiple times, that's a good indicator of where automation could help.

4. **Analyze trends**: During your scheduled review, assess your notes manually or with AI tools such as ChatGPT to identify the most repetitive tasks.

5. **Determine what can be automated**: Not everything can or should be automated, but recognize patterns where automation makes sense.

6. **Implement and iterate**: Apply automation techniques to the most frequent pain points and refine the process in your next scheduled session.

By incorporating this method, you can gradually optimize your workflow, eliminate redundant tasks, and free up more time for creative design work.

Integrating AI tools for faster prototyping

Not everything is possible in Figma, and sometimes it's better to use other tools. In the past, we would create prototypes in Figma, but now we can generate functional code in minutes.

What's the problem?

Static designs can't explain everything. Sometimes, for user testing or to help stakeholders understand the concept, you need a functional prototype. Creating a fully functional prototype can be straightforward for simple websites but extremely challenging or nearly impossible for complex applications (especially those with interactive elements such as tables).

The good news is that we now have AI tools that can quickly generate code from your designs. You can publish this ready-to-use code and send it to users, stakeholders, or developers, providing a much more interactive and realistic representation of the final product.

How to fix it

Since Config 2025, Figma has introduced Figma Make (currently in Beta), which transforms the prototyping workflow entirely. This AI-driven "prompt-to-code" tool turns static designs or simple text prompts into fully functional prototypes and web apps, all without leaving Figma.

Here's how to leverage Figma Make effectively:

1. **Start with existing designs**: Copy-paste any frame from your Figma file and use natural-language prompts such as "Make this into a login flow with email validation."
2. **Iterate conversationally**: Point at parts of the preview to tweak padding, replace assets, or adjust interactions—all through chat-based commands.
3. **Publish instantly**: One-click publish to a live URL for immediate stakeholder testing and feedback.

Here are some current limitations to consider:

- **Framework gaps**: Outputs vanilla HTML/CSS/JavaScript rather than React or Vue components
- **Beta maturity**: May have occasional UI quirks or imperfect CSS outputs
- **Limited backend scope**: Focused on frontend prototypes (though Supabase integration is coming soon)

Alternative tools for specific needs

While Figma Make covers most prototyping needs within Figma, external tools still offer unique advantages for specific situations:

- **lovable.dev** – best for full stack applications:
    - Provides an integrated Supabase backend, GitHub, and Vercel deployment
    - Outputs React code you can deploy immediately
    - Offers fine-grained **Select & Edit** UI tweaks
    - Trade-off: Requires leaving Figma, and code quality may need manual cleanup

- **v0.dev** – best for React ecosystem projects:

    - Deep integration with Vercel infrastructure

    - Outputs React/Next.js + Tailwind + shadcn/UI components

    - Strong developer controls over deployment

    - Trade-off: Focuses specifically on the React ecosystem rather than generic solutions

Tips for success with any tool

Regardless of which tool you choose, these tips will improve your results:

- **Provide comprehensive information upfront**: Give a complete picture of what you want to build rather than starting with minimal prompts and adding details later.

- **Leverage complementary AI tools**: When code generation tools create bugs they can't fix, sync the code with GitHub and use ChatGPT or Claude to resolve issues.

- **Don't hesitate to start fresh**: If your project isn't progressing, restart with an updated prompt that incorporates lessons learned along the way.

Implementing AI into your design workflow

While integrating AI as an individual designer is relatively straightforward, rolling out AI tools across an entire team requires a more structured approach. Success depends not just on the technology itself, but on how thoughtfully you introduce these new capabilities to your colleagues.

What's the problem?

Implementing AI into your design workflow is straightforward when working alone, but introducing AI across a team of designers and developers can be much more complex. Different team members have different needs, levels of experience, and concerns about AI's role in their work. While we've already covered how to use AI to automate individual tasks in *Automating routine tasks with AI in Figma*, this section focuses on integrating AI across an entire team workflow to improve efficiency and collaboration.

How to fix it

Approach this as you would any other design problem—treat it like a structured project with clear requirements and solutions. Here's a step-by-step guide to successfully implementing AI across your design team:

1. **Define your target audience**: Before implementing AI, understand who it will affect. Are you introducing AI to a small team of designers, or are you rolling it out to dozens of developers and product managers? Identifying your audience helps you craft a strategy that resonates with them and meets their specific needs.

2. **Find an ambassador**: Once you've identified your target audience, recruit an ambassador from each key group (e.g., designers, developers, marketing, or content). While you may lead the initiative, having a trusted advocate within each discipline ensures better adoption. For example, if you want developers to embrace AI, having a developer champion the cause will make communication and adoption smoother.

3. **Identify pain points:** AI should be a solution to real problems, not just a trendy addition. Identify pain points by talking to your team and gathering insights. Keep in mind that some pain points will originate from management rather than the team itself. For instance, leadership may push for faster delivery, but designers and developers may not see this as a personal issue.

4. **Workshop the strategy:** In Dotidot, we've eliminated most unnecessary meetings, keeping schedules clear for focused work. However, a well-structured workshop can be incredibly effective in defining an AI implementation strategy. Gather the ambassadors and key stakeholders, walk them through the identified problems, and guide them toward defining solutions themselves. A well-run workshop will lead to stronger buy-in and a more tailored strategy.

5. **Create a clear, concise plan:** After the workshop, document the findings in a simple, one- or two-page document outlining the following:

    - The target group
    - The specific problems they face
    - How AI can address these problems
    - Clear steps for implementation

6. **Run a pilot program:** Start with a pilot program rather than a full rollout. Set a strict evaluation deadline to assess whether the AI integration is actually improving workflows. Make it clear to the team that this isn't an after-hours side project—it's a structured initiative designed to improve efficiency and design quality.

By treating AI integration as a design challenge, rather than a forced technological shift, you can ensure smoother adoption, better team engagement, and ultimately, more impactful results in your design workflow.

Not every team or individual will immediately embrace these changes, and that's exactly why Ambassadors play a crucial role. If you're implementing improvements across multiple teams, begin with the most receptive group to build a strong, data-backed case for management. Ideally, every change would organically emerge from individual team members, but in reality, that's not always how things work. A solid proof of concept enables you to approach management and implement changes from the top down when necessary.

Analyzing AI-enhanced design workflows—case studies

At Dotidot, we're a small team that implemented AI in our design processes not as a trend, but as a necessity to work smarter and faster. I'd like to share three key use cases where we've trained ChatGPT to enhance our daily design workflows:

Marketing specialist assistant

This AI assistant embodies our target persona—automation strategists who work closely with clients to implement complex automation strategies. These specialists have limited availability but possess invaluable market knowledge that designers occasionally need to tap into.

Our actual marketing specialists use Dotidot for several hours daily to configure client setups. Since we make nearly all functions accessible to users, these power users have a deep understanding of the product experience. The AI assistant helps bridge the gap when the human specialists aren't available, allowing designers to get a perspective on user needs and market-specific knowledge without scheduling additional meetings.

UX writer assistant

As a B2B application, Dotidot contains numerous complex elements that require precise, clear wording. While we have an excellent UX writer on staff, their limited bandwidth meant they couldn't address every small copy request.

Our human UX writer became an excellent "teacher" for the AI assistant, continually helping us refine its capabilities. The assistant now handles routine copy tasks while maintaining our voice and standards, freeing our UX writer to focus on more strategic communication challenges and complex features.

Marketing content assistant

At Dotidot, our product team is also responsible for in-app marketing materials such as promotional banners, information boxes, and feature announcements. We trained a specialized AI assistant specifically for creating marketing copy that aligns with our brand voice.

This enables designers to simultaneously develop both the feature and its supporting marketing assets. Since the designers have the deepest knowledge of the new functionality, this integrated approach ensures marketing content accurately reflects the feature's capabilities and benefits while maintaining consistency across the product.

Navigating ethical challenges in AI-driven design

If you're a hardcore Figma user, you might remember when Figma announced the **Make Design AI** feature at Config 2024—only to pull it back within days after users noticed it generated designs strikingly similar to popular apps. I won't go too deep into this, but Figma claimed they didn't train the model on past Figma designs. Still, as a product person, I find it hard to believe that using existing Figma data wouldn't have been the logical starting point.

AI doesn't generate ideas from thin air—it builds on the data it's trained with. How much we integrate AI into our design process is a decision each of us has to make. For example, I see renaming layers as a no-brainer; it saves time without compromising creativity. However, using AI to generate the first version of an app design? That's where I draw the line. It may not be outright unethical, but it fundamentally changes the craft of design, replacing thoughtful decision-making with patterns pulled from who knows where on the internet.

Unlock this book's exclusive benefits now

Scan this QR code or go to packtpub.com/unlock, then search this book by name.

Note: Keep your purchase invoice ready before you start.

4

Enhancing Designer-Developer Synergy

As I discussed in previous chapters, successful collaboration between design and development teams should be a top priority if you want to optimize your processes and delivery speed. I've already mentioned some techniques, such as screen annotations, but in this chapter, we'll dive much deeper into bridging the gap between these two disciplines.

Every organization faces collaboration challenges, whether they're actively working to improve them or haven't addressed them yet. The approaches that work best depend heavily on your specific situation—business size, team maturity, whether teams are co-located or distributed, and even company culture (some lean more toward development, others toward design). There's no universal solution, but there are proven strategies you can adapt to your context.

We'll explore the following:

- Structuring design files for developer accessibility
- Creating interactive prototypes for developers
- Streamlining designer-developer communication
- Aligning design goals with development objectives
- Leveraging Figma's Dev Mode

Structuring design files for developer accessibility

Design files can quickly become a mess. While it's much better now than in the past—thanks to Figma's AI search feature that I explained in *Chapter 3*—finding specific elements is easier, but proper file organization should still be a fundamental part of your design process.

What's the problem?

Imagine you're in a new grocery store where everything is placed randomly. Next to milk are apples, next to those is orange juice, but the apple juice is on the other side of the store next to the shoes. That sounds crazy, but if you built that store yourself, you'd be fine with it. After all, you know where the apple juice is, right?

This is just an example, but many Figma files look exactly like that, and developers are the new shoppers in your store. If you spent the last week working on a file, you might think everything is in its place, but take another look. Would you be able to find everything after 3 months? That's a good exercise—try opening a 3–6-month-old file and see if you can immediately tell what the file is about and whether it contains everything developers need.

If developers are lost from the first minute of working with your file, they won't think highly of you or your design team. First impressions matter, and a well-organized file signals professionalism and consideration for your development partners.

This organization becomes even more critical when you're trying to scale—not just files, but entire design teams. The easier your files are to navigate for anyone, the easier they are to use and grow for everyone. When your team expands from 2 designers to 10, or when you need to onboard new developers quickly, clear organization becomes the foundation that allows your design system and processes to scale effectively.

How to fix it

I want to explain three possible solutions. All of them are viable, and the best choice depends on your situation and Figma plan:

- Quarterly files
- Project files
- Branching

Time-period files (quarterly files)

We started with this approach at Dotidot a few quarters ago, but you can adapt the time period to fit your company's workflow—some teams use monthly files, others prefer quarterly cycles. Our problem was that our Figma files didn't reflect reality—the production version of our app. When we worked on our application files, developers often didn't know which was the production version and which was the new design. It was communication ping-pong that led to a lot of confusion and forgotten changes.

So, we implemented quarterly files. We have two main groups of files in Figma:

- **Our application files (such as user dashboard, settings, product pages, checkout flow, etc.):** In these files, we have the latest version of the production design for these parts of our app. When you want to start making changes to campaigns, you know that everything there is on production 1:1, so it's easy to start

Figure 4.1 – Preview of all our application files

- **Our quarterly files:** One file per quarter, where each page is one ticket. We have all the tickets below each other, with each page containing a Jira widget that links to the corresponding ticket (if you want to know more, just check out *Chapter 2*, about plugins). Some pages are only one frame, some are huge, but everyone knows that each page represents a live ticket. When the ticket is released, you can see the updated status in the widget—though you'll need to click the **Update** button to refresh the information, which can be a bit annoying but it's a small detail in an otherwise smooth workflow.

Figure 4.2 – Preview of our quarterly files

At the end of the quarter, designers take all of the changes from the quarterly file that are in production (live) and implement them in the application files. This ensures that if you want to start making changes to something, you can start with the production version files. We leave the pages in the quarterly files and add a redirect to the application files, so you can always find the designs from links in Jira, Slack, and so on. This is crucial—don't delete the pages or files. The tickets that aren't completed stay in the quarterly file and are moved when they're in production.

This approach works great for smaller teams like ours because everything is clear, and it's super easy to explore ideas, even for product people, not just designers. Developers know that everything in the quarterly files is in one place, so they don't need to have dozens of files open—just one for the whole quarter.

Project files

This is ideal for mid-size teams that are working on multiple projects at once or agencies. You can duplicate the file structure for each project and then build in it. The fixed structure across projects will help designers, developers, and everyone else in the company know where they can find something, even across projects or clients. The structure is always the same, and you just delete the parts that you don't need.

I used this approach in the past as a contractor, and it helped me deliver projects with very high-standard handoffs, fast and easily.

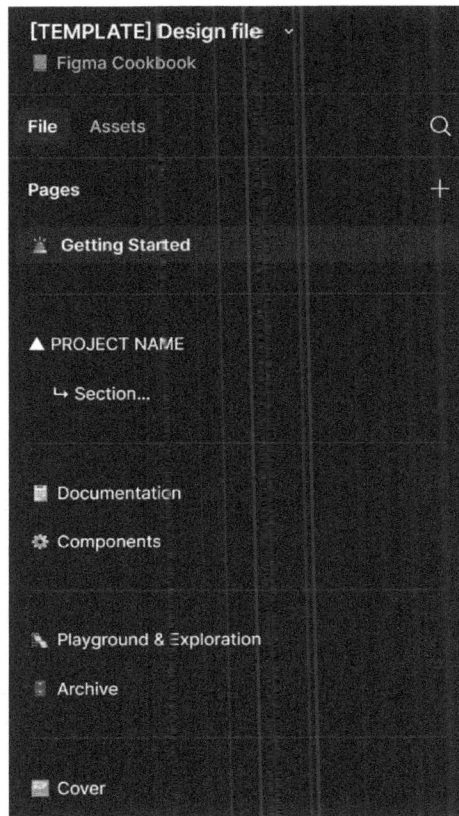

Figure 4.3 – Figma project file pages structure

Now I want to share my file structure and explain why I have certain elements in it. You can copy it directly or adapt it based on your specific needs.

My standard file structure

01 - Getting started

This is the landing page with all essential project information:

- Team members and contact details
- Project goals and timeline
- Resource downloads (fonts, assets)
- Links to relevant documents
- Client information

This page opens automatically when the file is first accessed.

02 - Project name

This is organized by logical sections of the product:

- For an e-commerce site: **Homepage, Product Listings, Product Detail, Checkout**

Each section gets its own dedicated page with all related screens.

03 - Documentation

This includes everything related to project requirements and references:

- Detailed project briefs and requirements with my notes
- Research findings
- Mood boards and inspiration
- Meeting notes
- User personas

Keeping this in Figma eliminates the need to search through emails.

04 - Components

- Local component library (when not using a design system)
- Component documentation

05 - Playground and exploration

There's space for experimentation here:

- Design explorations
- Alternative approaches
- Work-in-progress ideas
- Testing and iterations

06 - Archive

This is a repository for outdated but potentially useful designs:

- Previous versions
- Unused concepts
- Discarded approaches

Never delete work that might be valuable later.

07 - Cover

This is the professional project entry point:

- Project name and client
- Timeline and status
- Team members
- Brief description

A well-designed cover creates a professional first impression.

This unchangeable structure helped me easily duplicate the file and start a new project quickly

(Figma link – project template structure: `https://www.figma.com/design/ ZbHJ6n1slhkQYj0INDk3Vq/-TEMPLATE--Design-file?node-id=1-9&t=Frtj3FV4zVhBRQf7-1`).

Developers that I worked with were happy that every project had the same structure, and they knew where to find what they needed.

Branching

For teams with **Organization** or **Enterprise** Figma plans working on large, complex files, branching offers a third approach to file organization that mirrors developer workflows. While I covered the technical aspects of branching in *Chapter 1*, it's worth considering how this feature can enhance your file structure strategy.

Branching allows you to create separate versions of your design files for experimentation and iteration without affecting the main production file. This is particularly valuable when multiple designers are working on the same project simultaneously, or when you need to explore different design directions while keeping the main file stable for developer handoff.

If your team is already familiar with Git branching from the development side, implementing a similar approach in Figma can create consistency across your entire workflow. Consider speaking with your tech lead about how they use branching in code—this understanding can help you implement a parallel structure in your design files that developers will immediately recognize and appreciate.

Creating interactive prototypes for developers

Preparing an interactive prototype for developers can be fun, but first, really speak with them to find out whether they'll actually use it. I've met many designers who prepared elaborate prototypes that developers never used—they didn't even know how to run a prototype in Figma. Prototyping can be a powerful tool, but if the other side won't even run it, you're wasting your time.

What's the problem?

With complex flows or specific interactions, you need to give developers more than just a few frames next to each other with amazing annotations. You need to give them something clickable with proper transitions (and animations) for them to understand the goal that you want them to achieve.

But remember, prototypes are just one piece of the puzzle. Developers also need access to all component variants and states, whether in the prototype itself or the design file. Don't make them guess what the hover state of a button looks like or how an active focus state appears. Include links to design libraries, embed necessary assets directly in the file, and always follow up with a proper handover meeting where you can walk through the prototype together.

How to fix it

I'll start with the fastest and most "uncool" way: record a video with an explanation or showcase an example from somewhere else. Yes, this is the fastest way to do it, and in many cases, it's good enough. You can try to recreate some animation in Figma, but why bother if you can find the same one on CodePen and just record a short video with an explanation and link? All of this can be done in Loom and placed next to the design. Your time is valuable and probably expensive. Think about it. I know the C-level manager in me is speaking now, not the designer, but it will be okay. Trust me.

Figure 4.4 – CodePen showcase of drag and drop behavior

If you want to do it properly, you need to sit with developers and talk about the appropriate scope. Prototyping, like many things, isn't a *Yes* or *No* question—it's a scale of *How much?*

Creating a simple hover effect for buttons takes about 30 seconds in Figma, but creating a prototype of a table where you can add columns, rearrange them, and change values could take your whole lifetime. That's why you need to have a clear understanding of what's enough to convey the proper message, because beyond a certain point, more time won't give you better results.

So, simply speaking, you should do the following:

1. Talk with developers to find out whether they even need prototypes
2. Try to show interactions through examples with videos
3. Do as little as possible to transfer the message effectively

Quick tip—create user flow blueprints for maximum impact

While prototypes show how individual interactions work, developers often need to see the bigger picture first. Consider creating user flow diagrams that serve as blueprints – visual maps showing the complete user journey with final design screens attached to each step.

This approach works incredibly well because developers can quickly understand the entire solution before diving into specific screens. Combine user flows with prototypes and intro recordings, and it works like magic. The bonus? These flow blueprints also become invaluable for product managers during feature planning and QA teams when debugging issues.

Start with the flow, then add the prototype details. Think of it as giving developers a roadmap before asking them to build the individual roads.

Streamlining designer-developer communication

Communication is everything in every relationship, even between designers and developers.

What's the problem?

As I showed you earlier, designers and developers can both be speaking English but still not understand each other. These are different worlds, and we should spend more time in the developer's world to understand it better. But if you want to improve communication between you and your development team, I'll add some new tips.

How to fix it

Proper channels on Slack or in Teams are must-haves—every project should have one with a proper description and linked files. All project updates should be communicated there with proper links to Figma. Try to communicate only the necessary info and always use threads to go deeper.

Think about the search functionality in Slack, for example. You should be able to search quickly in the channel, so try to use headings for the start of announcements. Also, you can pin the main messages to the channel.

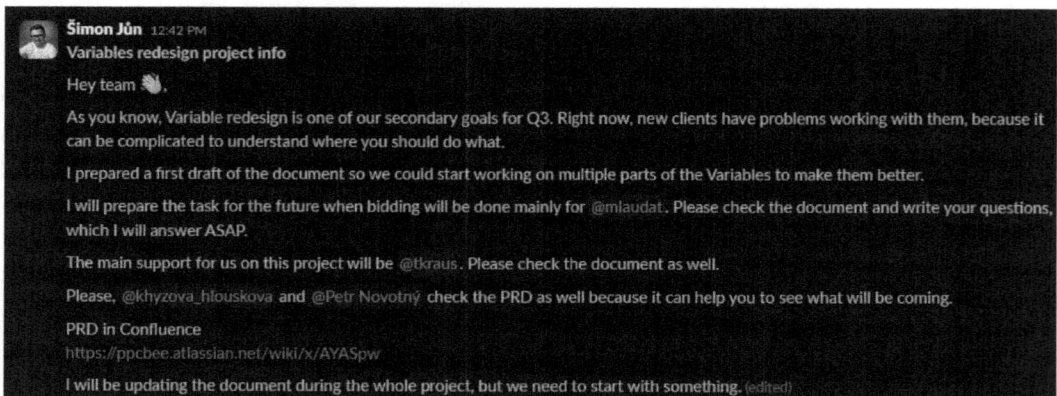

Figure 4.5 – Slack message at the start of our project

Try to go deeper into your communication tool's capabilities. At Dotidot, we use Slack, and we've found that many people don't understand its more advanced features beyond simple messages. Most team members don't have a proper workflow for how to use Slack effectively. That's why whenever a new team member joins, we always share our communication rules with them.

Remember, Slack isn't your personal messaging platform where you chat casually with family and friends, but many people use it the same way. This approach can cause problems in professional communication, especially between design and development teams. Here are some rules that you should follow:

- Always use headings for new topics or announcements. This makes messages scannable and searchable. Add an emoji at the beginning that reflects what's expected: 📣 for announcements, 🧠 for brainstorms and ideas, 👓 for design reviews, 🎬 for work in progress (sneak peeks).
- Always communicate in threads below the original message; never start a new message to continue a conversation. This keeps discussions organized, unlike WhatsApp and other consumer apps.
- Use the checkmark emoji ✅ to indicate when an issue is resolved. This visual cue helps everyone know what's still pending and what's completed.
- If you need something by a specific date, put this information at the beginning of your message with a calendar emoji 📅. This makes deadlines immediately visible.
- If you expect an answer from someone, mention them directly. Don't use @channel or leave messages without specific mentions, as this can lead to diffused responsibility.
- All Slack messages should be acknowledged by the end of the day. Never leave messages unanswered. Even a simple "I'll look into this on Thursday" is better than silence. Always communicate that you've seen the message and have a plan to address it.
- Always embed links within relevant words rather than pasting the entire URL. For example, write "Check the Figma design" or "Details in the Jira ticket" instead of dropping long, messy URLs into the conversation.

Quick tip—create communication cheat sheets for your team

Since communication guidelines can be repetitive to explain to new team members, consider documenting your team's communication standards in a dedicated space such as Confluence. Even better, create a small cheat sheet that becomes part of your project file template.

Make this cheat sheet specific and actionable – include guidelines for design reviews (what a good critique looks like), handover protocols (a combination of emojis, when to ask questions, where to post them), and team-specific communication standards. The real magic happens when you turn this cheat sheet into a Figma component that can be easily updated across all project files. Update it once, and every project automatically gets the latest communication guidelines.

This approach ensures consistency across projects and makes onboarding new team members much smoother.

Aligning design goals with development objectives

Even when designers and developers work on the same project with the same deadline, they often approach problems from completely different angles. This difference in perspective can lead to friction, misunderstandings, and solutions that don't fully serve either the user experience or technical requirements. The key is learning how to bridge these different approaches and create a collaborative environment where both perspectives strengthen the final outcome.

What's the problem?

For example, your overall goal might be to lower the drop-off rate in your application's onboarding process. Both designers and developers want this outcome, but will approach it differently. Developers will focus on aspects they can optimize, such as loading speed for certain steps in your onboarding flow. There are many studies that tie bounce rates (users exiting) directly to page speed. Designers, on the other hand, might focus on removing unnecessary steps to streamline the whole process.

You see? Both teams will work on completely different aspects, but they have the same underlying goal. That's why alignment is crucial.

How to fix it

I have multiple recommendations—go through them and pick the ones suitable for your situation:

- Understand different goals and plan around them. In some teams I mentor, they didn't even talk between departments or share goals. The teams worked in silos, which had a huge impact on the final result. So, ask questions and talk openly. If you're in the office, grab lunch with developers—it's much better than a formal meeting. As a designer, you should have some basic knowledge of research methodology. Use it during these informal conversations to learn more about their perspective.

- Involve developers as early as possible in the process. You want their feedback to help build a better product. Find developers who are happy to join the project early and share their opinions. Be aware that this should focus on the project in general, not just your design work. Sometimes you'll receive feedback that's purely about aesthetics rather than implementation, which isn't always helpful.

  This approach aligns with product trios, where a product manager, designer, and tech lead work closely together throughout the entire product development cycle. I'm a big believer in product trios and love this collaborative model, but in many cases, this isn't how organizations actually work. If you have a team where everyone wants to be involved and collaborate closely, push for implementing product trios. Teams that adopt this approach often see significantly better outcomes and fewer misalignments between design intent and final implementation.

- Be open to trade-offs, but ensure both sides are ready for this too. In the past, at Dotidot, we had a problem where design was always secondary to development's "how to do it as fast as possible" approach. There weren't true trade-offs—just the elimination of proper solutions in the name of speed. Often, the final result wasn't viable because we cut so many corners that users couldn't properly use the app. Trade-offs need to happen through discussion between equal partners. Neither designers nor developers are more important; your users and business goals should come first.

  When I was discussing this chapter with my beta reader, they suggested an interesting change of perspective that I hadn't considered before. They pointed out that many engineering teams are very sensitive to technical debt (whether it's increasing or reducing) or are keen on exploring new technologies and trends. Their suggestion was that building your trade-offs around supporting technical debt reduction or incorporating learning opportunities for new tech can be a way to achieve better outcomes for everyone.

- Be aware of past technical limitations (tech debt). This can be challenging for new designers or on new projects because people who have been with the company for some time often assume "everyone knows that." But many of these constraints aren't documented anywhere, so you need to explicitly ask about them.

  For example, you could propose a smooth animated transition between screens, but the existing navigation framework makes this technically impossible without rebuilding part of the system. These kinds of limitations significantly impact what you can design, but they're rarely written down anywhere.

- Establish shared naming conventions. I've mentioned this in previous chapters, but it bears repeating: you need to use the same terminology to understand each other. When designers talk about "cards" and developers call them "containers," miscommunication is inevitable.

Leveraging Figma's Dev Mode

Figma's Dev Mode is a powerful tool designed specifically to bridge the gap between designers and developers, yet many teams aren't taking full advantage of it. This feature transforms how developers interact with design files, but it requires both understanding and proper implementation to realize its benefits.

What's the problem?

Despite its potential, Dev Mode remains underutilized across many teams. The most common objection I hear is price—something I find perplexing. Dev Mode costs just a few dollars per month, while developer salaries in my region range from $4,000-8,000 per month—not including additional company costs. If you're in the United States, developer salaries are likely even higher, so a few dollars shouldn't be an obstacle to efficiency.

Beyond cost concerns, there's often a knowledge gap. Many teams simply don't understand what Dev Mode offers or how to integrate it into their workflow. This means they continue using less efficient methods for design handoff, costing valuable development time and introducing opportunities for misinterpretation.

How to fix it

Here are some amazing features that Dev Mode provides and how to leverage them effectively.

Reading tokens and variables made simple

One of the biggest sources of implementation errors comes from developers trying to guess or manually measure design values. In a regular Figma view, a developer might see a button and try to estimate its padding, border radius, or color values. This leads to inconsistencies and time-consuming back-and-forth communication.

Dev Mode solves this by displaying exact token values directly. When a developer clicks on any element, they immediately see the precise measurements, color hex codes, font sizes, and spacing values. If you're using Figma's variables feature for your design tokens, developers can see the variable names directly, making it easy to map design decisions to code implementations.

Use case

Instead of a developer asking "What's a text color?" or trying to eyeball measurements, they can instantly see "color/theme/text/default" and know exactly which design token to use in their code.

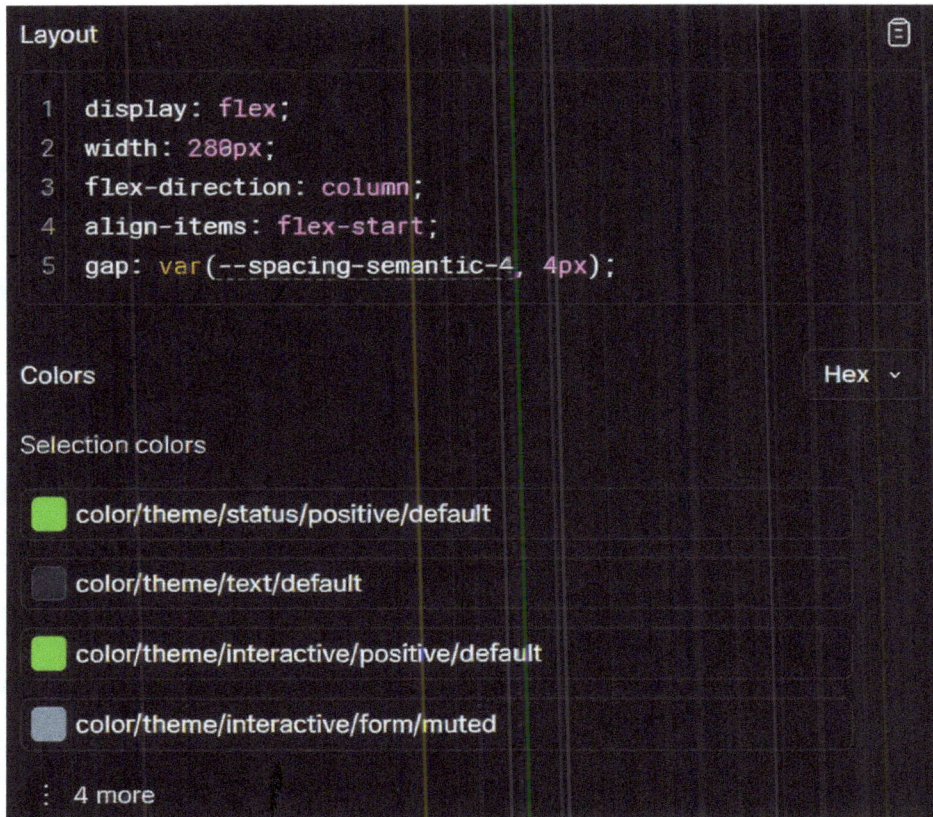

```
Layout                                                    🗐

 1  display: flex;
 2  width: 280px;
 3  flex-direction: column;
 4  align-items: flex-start;
 5  gap: var(--spacing-semantic-4, 4px);


Colors                                                 Hex ⌄

Selection colors

 ▢  color/theme/status/positive/default

 ▢  color/theme/text/default

 ▢  color/theme/interactive/positive/default

 ▢  color/theme/interactive/form/muted

 ⋮  4 more
```

Figure 4.6 – You can easily see the token/variable name for every element

Component playground for better understanding

The component playground is like a sandbox where developers can interact with your components without worrying about breaking anything in your design file. This feature shows all available variants, properties, and states of a component in one organized view.

When you create components with multiple variants (such as different button sizes, states, or styles), the playground displays them all systematically. Developers can click through different combinations to understand how the component should behave in various scenarios. This is especially valuable for complex components with multiple properties.

Use case

A button component might have variants for different states (default, hover, disabled) and configurations (with icon at start, with icon at end, text only). Instead of hunting through your design file for examples of each combination, developers can see all possibilities organized in the playground and understand how the button should behave with different icon placements and states.

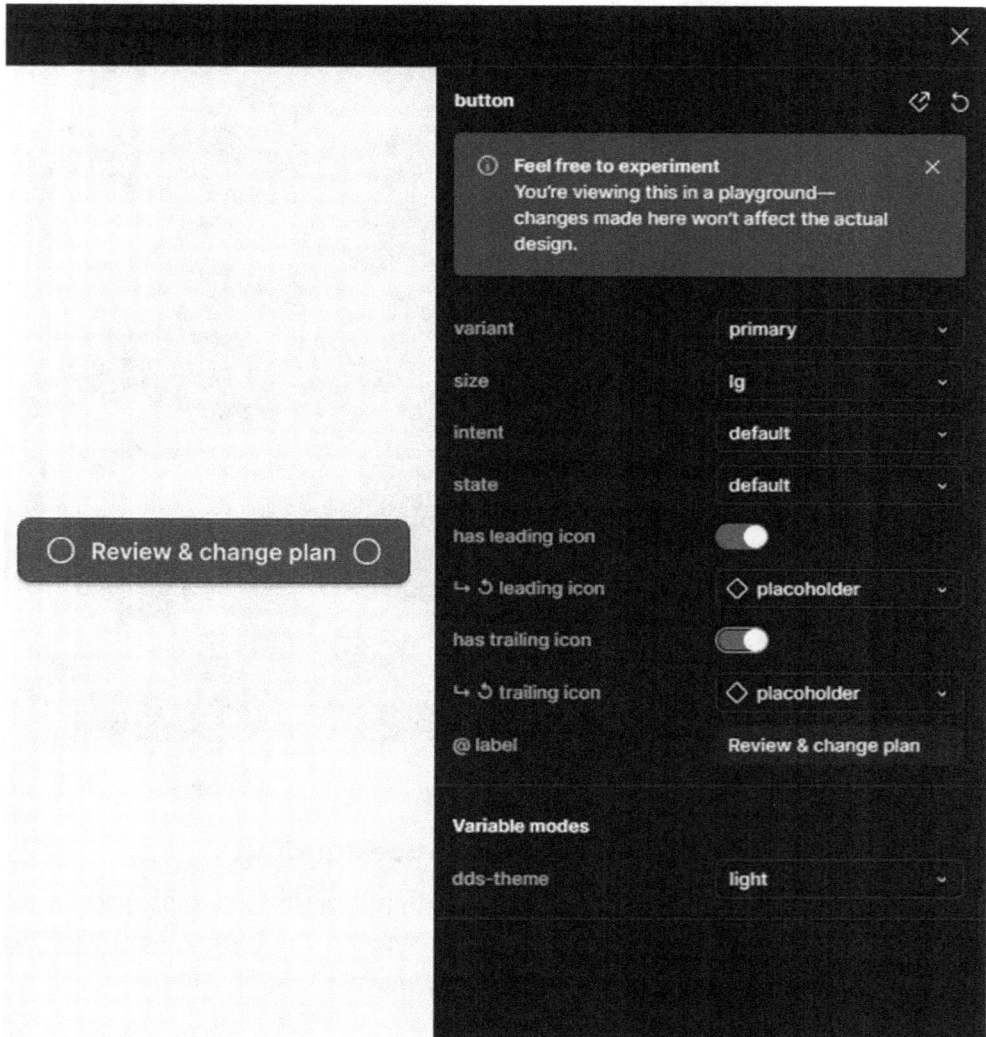

Figure 4.7 – Every component has this robust playground that you can use to test everything

Comparing changes efficiently

Design iteration is natural, but communicating changes to developers can be challenging. Traditionally, designers would take screenshots, draw circles around changes, or write long descriptions trying to explain what's different between versions.

Dev Mode's **Compare** feature shows design iterations side by side automatically. Developers can see exactly what changed between versions without needing detective skills. The system highlights differences visually, making it immediately clear what needs to be updated in the code.

Use case

If you update a card component's spacing and add a new icon, developers can see both changes highlighted in the comparison view instead of trying to spot differences themselves or waiting for you to explain what changed.

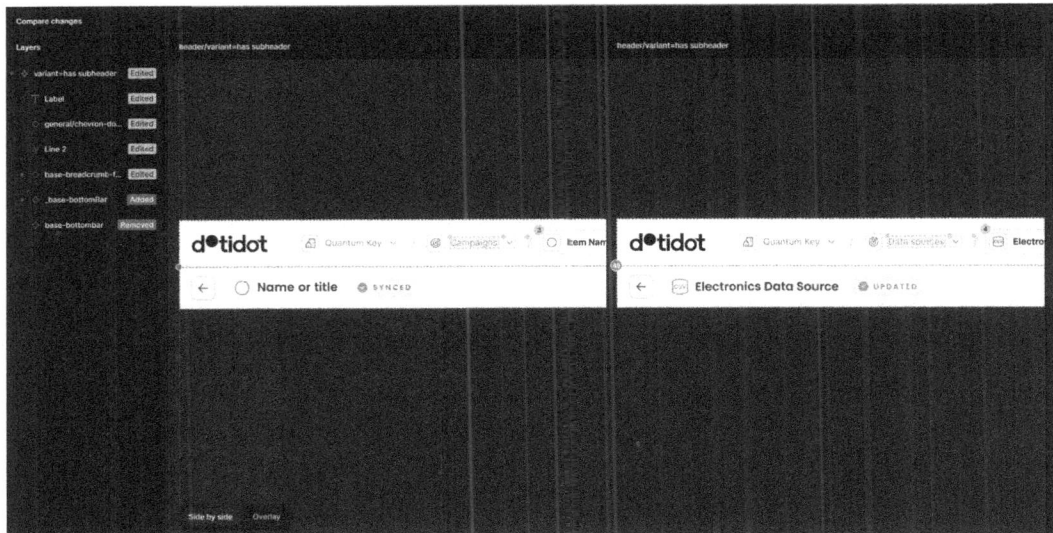

Figure 4.8 – You can see all changes in one place

The Ready for Dev filter keeps everyone focused

One of the biggest frustrations for developers is not knowing which designs are final and which are still being explored. They might spend time implementing something that's actually just a rough concept, or they might avoid implementing something that's actually ready to go.

The **Ready for dev** filter solves this by showing developers only the designs you've marked as finalized. When they switch to Dev Mode, they primarily see production-ready designs rather than getting distracted by work-in-progress explorations. This keeps development focused on the right priorities.

Use case

During an active design sprint, you might have 20 different screens in various stages. Instead of developers wondering which version of the checkout flow to implement, they can filter to see only the designs marked **Ready for dev** and know exactly what to build.

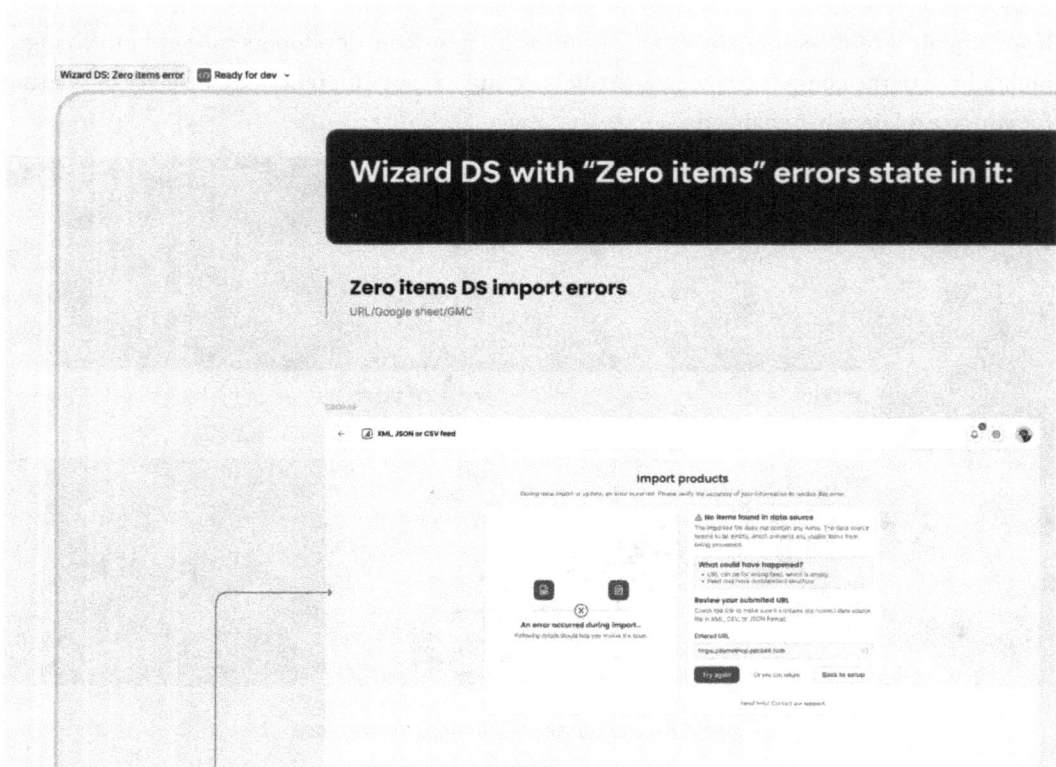

Figure 4.9 – Section with Ready for Dev status

Code Connect bridges the final gap

This is one of the most powerful features for bridging design and development, and the major feature that I push teams to upgrade from the **Professional** to **Organization** plan for. Code Connect allows you to link your actual production component code directly to Figma components, creating a seamless connection between design and implementation.

How it works

Developers can select any component instance in your design and immediately see the exact code needed to implement it, including all the correct props, variants, and configurations. For example, if you have a button with specific styling, size, and an icon, Code Connect will show the developer the exact React component code (or whatever framework you're using) with all the right parameters already filled in.

The setup requires some initial work from your development team to connect the code repository to Figma, but once it's configured, it eliminates the guesswork entirely. Developers no longer need to interpret design specs or figure out which props to use—they can simply copy the pre-configured code directly from Figma.

Use case

A developer sees a complex data visualization component in your design. Instead of trying to recreate it from scratch or asking multiple questions about implementation details, they click on it and get the exact code: `<Chart type="bar" data={salesData} colors={['primary', 'secondary']} showLegend={true} />`. The efficiency gains and reduction in design-development miscommunication make the plan upgrade cost negligible compared to the time saved.

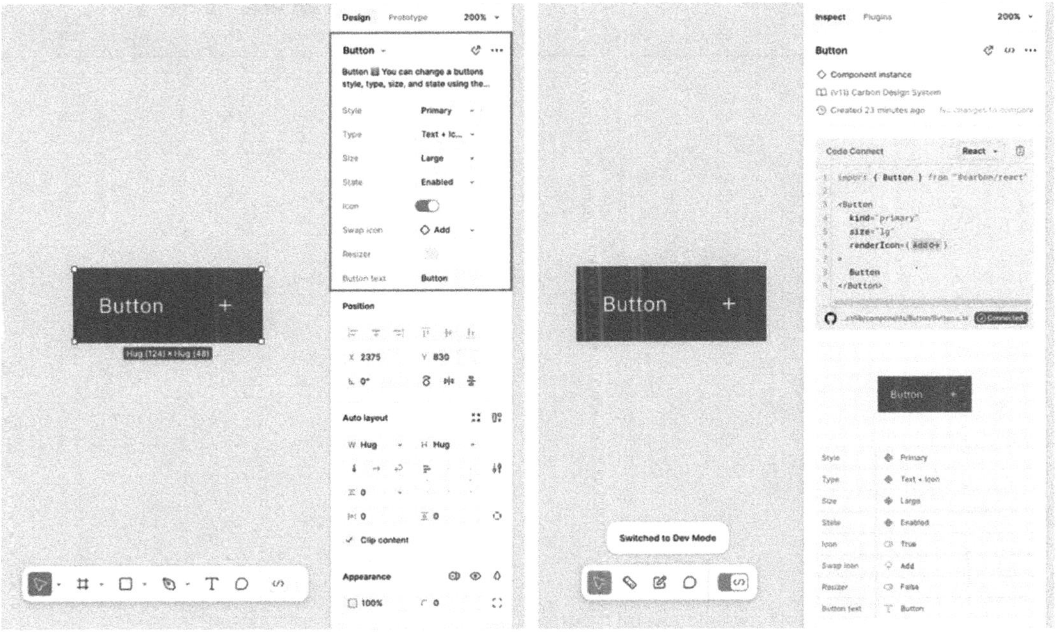

source: https://medium.com/carbondesign/carbon-and-figma-code-connect-redefining-the-design-to-code-experience-836eb3f454fc

Figure 4.10 – Connect your production code with Figma

Dev Mode is continuously being improved—funny name considering it's always in development itself. New features might be available now or coming soon that could help your workflow even more. Just grab a coffee and spend an afternoon exploring it. The time investment will pay off significantly in smoother designer-developer collaboration.

Quick tip—become the Dev Mode educator

Designers often know more about changes and updates in Dev Mode than developers because Figma is still primarily a design tool. Don't skip the dev announcements at Config and other Figma announcements. Take the role of educator on yourself if needed, and teach your developers about new features, tips, and tricks. You'll likely be the first to discover useful updates that could improve your collaboration, so share that knowledge proactively with your development team.

Unlock this book's exclusive benefits now Scan this QR code or go to packtpub.com/ unlock, then search this book by name.	
Note: Keep your purchase invoice ready before you start.	

5

Scaling Design Systems for Consistency

Design systems have been a hot topic for the past few years—perhaps even hotter than AI, but jokes aside, many designers mistakenly believe that design systems are a creation of Figma. They're not. Systems have been with us forever. We naturally look for ways to structure our work and establish rules that help us move faster. Components and systems have existed in the development world for decades, and I'm thrilled that designers, with encouragement from companies such as Figma, are now investing (not spending, but truly investing) time in design systems.

In this chapter, I'll share insights from my experience building design systems of all sizes—from small ones for one-time projects to massive systems for multinational corporations. A design system isn't a binary yes-or-no question; it's a spectrum. The real question is: how much do you want to invest to make that investment worthwhile? We'll explore six key topics:

- Design system creation planning
- Building advanced component libraries
- Ensuring systematic documentation and standards
- Managing design systems for growing teams
- Utilizing Figma's design system tools
- Dynamic system scaling to accommodate product iterations

Let's start with the first topic.

Design system creation planning

Building a design system can be challenging. Where do you start, and what is enough? When you look at established design systems such as Atlassian Design System, Shopify's Polaris, or IBM's Carbon, you see massive libraries with dozens of components, each with numerous variants and states. This can be intimidating—and honestly, it is—but it's wrong to use these as your benchmark. These systems were built by teams of designers over many years. If you're just starting or looking to invest more time in your design system, view these examples as inspiration, not as requirements.

What's the problem?

Many teams dive into building components without proper planning, only to realize later that their system doesn't meet actual needs or lacks scalability. Without a strategic approach, you risk creating something that looks impressive but doesn't serve your organization's unique requirements. The most beautiful design system is worthless if it doesn't solve real problems for your team.

When mentoring teams that are beginning with design systems, I always recommend checking established systems for inspiration and as external validation of your thinking about structure and naming—not as a direct template to copy. It's like looking at marathon runners before your first jog outside. They're good for inspiration and validating your approach, but not as a benchmark for where you should be.

Important exception

This advice works well when you're starting fresh. But I've seen a different scenario many times—when you join a company where the development team has already been using component libraries for months or years. In this situation, your strategy should flip completely. Instead of building something new, look for design systems that mirror what developers are already using. Libraries such as Shadcn and UntitledUI often have Figma counterparts, and using them can save you months of work while ensuring perfect alignment between design and code from day one.

The real challenge is building a *good enough* component library with the right level of complexity, something that serves your current needs while allowing for growth, without overengineering.

How to fix it

Before you start building, you need to sit and plan. I know—building is much more fun, but planning is essential. When building design systems, we always ask questions such as the following:

- What is the goal of the design system?
- Where will the system be used?
- How much time (and money) do we have?
- Do we have any historic systems to build from?
- Can we use something pre-built?
- Are there technical limitations to consider?
- Do we have time to work on it consistently?
- Who will be using the design system?
- How many designers will work with it?
- How often do we need to onboard new people?
- How many developers will work with it?

These are key questions that everyone should answer. Let's examine them one by one.

What is the goal of the design system?

A simple question, right? But you can spend a lot of time on it. It's very important to speak with all stakeholders about this topic because I can guarantee there will be multiple perspectives. Let me share two real-world cases from completely different environments: one from my start-up Dotidot—a fast-moving company with a small team and limited resources—and another from a large multinational corporation with significantly more time, people, and budget at their disposal. These contrasting examples will show how the same fundamental question leads to different approaches based on context.

Dotidot case

At Dotidot, the main push came from me and other designers. Our primary motivation was to reduce delivery time—which is one of the main reasons why design systems are built in the first place. We built our design system to completely skip wireframing and create designs in their final form from the start. This cut our time significantly (approximately 30-50% for many features). Another motivation was to make our lives in Figma much easier. Consistency was also important, but honestly, it wasn't our main driver.

Dotidot has significant technical debt—it's a 10-year-old start-up, and you can see it in the code base. Not every component in our design system is fully implemented, and many components exist in two variants: React and Ruby on Rails. These components often look similar but work differently, so you might use one component in Figma, but in the products, it can appear different on each page. This is our reality. Our goal is to eventually have a fully developed design system, but that's still in our future.

Multinational company case

This company had never had a design system and started building one alongside a new internal system. With hundreds of people working on it, they invited me as an interim leader to build both the system and the team around it. They faced a completely different problem: many development teams were building the same components repeatedly—similar but different—because no one spent time building them properly with all features. Each team built minimal versions of components only for their specific use, which meant other teams couldn't reuse them due to unfamiliarity with the code base and missing functionality.

This approach was incredibly expensive, so the main problems their design system needed to solve were cost reduction, increased development speed, and improved component UX. With a proper system, their UX team could invest time in user testing each component and optimize them much more effectively than before.

As you can see, they're two companies with two entirely different worlds. It's crucial to think about your specific goals because everything else will be built on the foundation of this question.

Where will the system be used?

Your design system can be used in many places, some of which might not be obvious initially. When I ask "where?" I mean across different platforms (website versus app, iOS versus Android), different contexts (desktop versus mobile), different brands (Brand A versus Brand B), or even different company divisions. For example, with Figma Slides, you can easily use your components in presentations as well. A small use case? Sure, but it's amazing to have consistency and speed (since you already know the components) with this approach.

My main point is about anticipating future use cases. For instance, sometimes you build your system for your app, and then the marketing team realizes it's awesome and wants to use it on the website as well. Knowing these possibilities in advance is very important because then you can structure your system properly. For example, you might create one file with foundations (tokens/variables) and separate files with components for your app and website.

Dotidot case

In our start-up, the use case is straightforward—we use the design system exclusively for our web application. Our marketing website has its own system, and it only shares foundations (colors, fonts, etc.) with the main product.

Multinational company case

Here, the situation is much more complex. The system is used across multiple subsidiaries under the parent company. They need the same system but must brand it differently across the daughter companies—what we call **theming** in the design and developer world— so employees find it familiar and contextually appropriate. They also need to share foundations with external agencies working on marketing websites and landing pages, and they need to integrate new components into legacy systems that aren't being fully updated.

How much time (and money) do we have?

Let's be honest—we would love to polish everything to 100%. We're designers; it's in our blood. When I switched from design to C-level management, this was one of the hardest mindset shifts. It's not that I don't want to invest time in our design system, but sometimes we need to build something more important for the company.

You need to know how much time you can invest. Based on this, you can plan effectively. Do you have only a week to build solid foundations? Great—your process and scope will look very different than if you have a year. This is why it's sometimes challenging for new teams that look at Polaris or Carbon as inspiration; they see Mount Everest before them when they only have time for a quick hike. Understanding your time constraints helps you use that time efficiently.

Another challenge can be that you'll seemingly be working on it "all the time," and your stakeholders may grow tired of hearing about it repeatedly. In bigger teams, you'll have dedicated people working on design systems, but in smaller ones, this can be a real challenge.

Dotidot case

This was a problem at Dotidot, before I switched from design. We needed to work on our design system, but it wasn't a priority, so we often talked about it, and the C-level executives thought we were investing a lot of time in it. In reality, we were only investing mental time—thinking about it during dog walks—not actual design time building it.

That's why my first project when I became CPO was to dedicate 14 days to build the entire system for designers (development isn't finished yet), and we did it. We had spent so much free time thinking about it that we had clarity on what to build, so 14 dedicated days were enough.

Plan your time responsibly. If you have only a small window, as we had at Dotidot, consider putting one designer in "vacation mode"—no meetings, no other tickets, as if they were on vacation—allowing full focus on the design system with a clear deadline. Our designer built it in those 14 days. Martin, if you're reading this, you're amazing!

Multinational company case

Here, the time window was completely different—measured in years rather than weeks. Of course, you needed to show monthly progress, but it was monthly, not daily, as is normal in a start-up environment. It might appear less productive, but that's not an accurate assessment. In these large organizations, you need to synchronize many teams across internal and external departments. You want to work with all development teams to establish proper standards that will facilitate adoption.

Feedback gathering takes much longer because you aren't simply speaking with one person over lunch, but with dozens across multiple countries. This significantly impacts planning and the time invested in each decision. When you make a mistake in a start-up, the impact is relatively small, but in a multinational company, it affects hundreds of developers. The stakes are higher, and the process necessarily more deliberate.

Do we have any historic systems to build from?

Sometimes you need to build on a historic system, which can significantly impact your planning. You need to know whether you're building on a clean sheet of paper or on top of something old.

If you're building on top of something old, you really need to understand it or have a developer who understands it working with you throughout the process.

Dotidot case

We had an existing system that we decided not to build upon but rather recreate from the ground up for two main reasons. First, Dotidot had undergone rebranding, so it was easier to implement all the changes at once. Second, the system wasn't properly maintained, making it more painful to repair than to rebuild. It's similar to an old building—sometimes it's faster and cheaper to tear it down and build something new than to repair it.

However, we faced a significant challenge with the development side of the system. We still haven't achieved 100% implementation because of some legacy components that can't be updated. In Figma, everything looks great, but remember: you're building design systems to speed up the entire process—particularly development—not just to have nice Figma files. This is a major consideration when building on top of something old.

Multinational company case

Here, it was a completely new project, so everything was built from the ground up. They didn't have any proper system, only UI kits, which actually helped tremendously in building everything as needed for the entire project. It was ideal because everything that was designed was immediately built and distributed to all development teams for implementation.

Can we use something pre-built?

Should you build a button again when there are millions of systems available with already created buttons? Good question.

Based on your answers from previous points, you should be able to decide whether there's a possibility to use or buy something already done and leverage it to your advantage. But be careful—these pre-built solutions have both advantages and disadvantages.

Here are the advantages:

- **Time savings**: It should save you time, at least in the short term.
- **Well-built structure**: Many of these systems are properly built in terms of naming, properties, variable/token usage, and so on. You can learn from them.
- **Code integration**: Some systems come with pre-built code components that mirror their Figma designs, which can save your development team significant time. Instead of developers building components from scratch, they can use ready-made React, Vue, or other framework components that match the design exactly. It's always great to have Figma and code working in tandem.

Here are the disadvantages:

- **Not an ideal fit**: If you build something from the ground up, you'll build it exactly as you need it. Pre-built systems often include features and complexity you don't need.
- **Performance in Figma**: I've worked with many pre-built systems; I even use UntitledUI for my personal website. These systems can be slow—very slow. They're complex because they aim to solve many use cases at once, which can make Figma sluggish.

- **Difficulty adding components**: Usually, you don't deeply understand the structure of variables/tokens or the naming conventions because you didn't build them. Adding something new in the same style can be challenging. You'll either spend a lot of time building to the same standard or won't respect it, creating problems for the future.
- **Future updates**: Updates can be challenging, especially if you've modified the system.
- **Cost**: Yes, it will probably cost something, but honestly, compared to typical design or developer salaries, this shouldn't be a dealbreaker. Yet, it's often the first objection people raise.

Using something pre-built isn't inherently bad, but if you have the time and resources to build something future-proof, I would always recommend building your own.

Are there technical limitations to consider?

Invite developers to the project as soon as possible. I mentioned this multiple times in previous chapters, and I'll emphasize it again here. Technical limitations are the biggest killers of design systems in my experience. If you design something that can't be built—no matter how amazing it looks in Figma—it's worthless. Remember, the final product isn't a Figma file but production code. You need to plan accordingly.

Talk with developers about these specific topics:

- Use of specific frameworks such as Bootstrap
- Use of certain libraries (for example, for complex components such as graphs or tables)
- Technical limitations from legacy code

Based on these conversations, you can design your system to ensure it will be developed as you intended.

It's also crucial to speak with every platform team in your company. Your design system might be used across the web, mobile apps, desktop applications, or even emerging platforms. Each platform has its own constraints, capabilities, and user expectations. Understanding all these environments upfront helps you create a system that benefits everyone rather than becoming a burden for some teams who have to work around limitations you didn't anticipate.

Do we have time to work on it consistently?

You need to know how much time you have to work on your design system, or if you'll have dedicated designers and developers assigned to it. In larger teams, it's typical to have dedicated people. In small teams, this can be a challenge.

My suggestion is this: if you don't have dedicated people who will work on the system, create explicit part-time roles for it. For example, a designer might spend 80% of their time on product work and 20% on the design system. Make this split explicit, because often the problem with unsuccessful design systems is the reality that we'll work on them "when we have time"—which, let's be honest, is never.

Create the split and then promote it within the company. When I consulted for a team building a large system without management buy-in, I pushed them to split the time of one designer. She worked 50% on the design system and 50% on website design. It was challenging, but they communicated that she was available for website work only on Monday, half of Wednesday, and Thursday. Other days, she was "off" and working solely on the design system. This hard split worked amazingly well, and they made significant progress.

Implement this type of split, because without it, people will push you to work on their "urgent" problems, and you'll end up working on the design system during evenings and weekends—which is unsustainable.

Dotidot case

At Dotidot, we can't have a dedicated team working on the design system because we have only two designers and two frontend developers. However, we do allocate specific time for making dedicated progress on it, with a separate backlog for all design system tickets. This approach ensures steady progress without overcommitting our limited resources.

Multinational company case

Here, there's a full team with designers, developers, and a dedicated owner working on the design system. This makes sense when you're building a system that will be distributed to hundreds of people. This reality completely changes how you can approach building design systems—it becomes its own product with proper workflows and dedicated time allocation.

Who will be using the design system?

This might seem obvious, but it's crucial to map out all the different roles that will interact with your design system. While designers and developers are the primary users, many other roles in your organization might need access to components, documentation, or system guidelines.

Consider these potential users: product managers who need to understand component capabilities for roadmap planning, QA testers who need to verify component behavior, content creators who might use components for marketing materials, customer support teams who need to reference UI elements when helping users, and even external consultants or agencies working on your projects.

Each user type has different needs and technical comfort levels. Product managers might need high-level component overviews, while developers need detailed technical specifications. This understanding directly impacts how you structure your documentation, what level of detail you provide, and what platforms you choose for sharing your system. The broader your user base, the more comprehensive and accessible your documentation needs to be.

How many designers will work with it?

You should know how many designers will use the system because that will significantly impact the complexity of the documentation. (Don't worry, we'll cover specific documentation approaches and what exactly to document later in this book.). If you have a small team like we do at Dotidot, you can get by with minimal documentation standards since it's relatively easy to quickly onboard someone and be available when they need help.

If you're building a large system for a company with high turnover (for example, with many external consultants), you should plan to invest more time in documentation. New people won't inherently know how to use your system, and you need to teach them without necessarily being available for calls. This point leads us to the next question.

How often do we need to onboard new people?

If you're frequently onboarding new people, you should invest in a proper process. Remember, this isn't just about onboarding designers but developers as well. In a large company I worked with, we built a comprehensive onboarding process with links, videos, and embedded Figma files in Confluence. We even created quizzes that designers and developers could take to test their understanding. This approach dramatically accelerated onboarding, especially for developers.

How many developers will work with it?

This question is similar to the one about designers, but I wanted to include it explicitly. The number of developers will impact documentation needs, onboarding processes, and knowledge dissemination throughout the team.

Remember, building the design system is actually the easiest part of the process. Company-wide adoption is the hardest challenge—but we'll talk more about that later.

Building advanced component libraries

Components are the building blocks of every design system, ranging from simple elements such as labels to complex ones such as navigation systems. In this section, we'll explore how to approach the challenge of growing your design system and building components properly.

What's the problem?

Many designers start with basic components that work for simple use cases but quickly run into limitations when real-world complexity emerges. Components become brittle, difficult to maintain, and eventually, designers start working around the system instead of with it. This leads to inconsistencies across products and ultimately defeats the purpose of having a design system in the first place.

How to fix it

Before diving into specific tips, let me emphasize the most critical aspect: solid foundations. The most important part of building component libraries is having perfect foundations—tokens, color naming, semantics, and all the underlying structure. For example, with the Dotidot design system, our designer spent much more time creating the foundation structure and tokens than actually creating components. It might seem like you're moving slowly at first, but having a solid base makes everything else much easier and faster later.

There are multiple tips I want to share with you. Unfortunately, I'm not sitting next to you to discuss them in your specific context, so you'll need to select the ones most relevant to your situation.

Create a clear component architecture

You should establish a system of component architecture and stick with it. Personally, I like to use the Atomic Design methodology with these levels:

- **Atoms:** The smallest building blocks (buttons, input fields, icons, labels)
- **Molecules:** Simple groups of atoms (search bars, form fields with labels)

- **Organisms**: Complex UI sections (navigation bars, forms, card layouts)
- **Templates**: Page-level structures
- **Pages**: Specific instances of templates (I rarely use these; in most cases, we stop at templates)

Alternative approach at Dotidot

While Brad Frost's Atomic Design is popular, our team at Dotidot uses a different structure that we find clearer and more understandable:

- **Primitives** (tokens, foundations)
- **Components** (individual UI elements)
- **Patterns** (combinations of components)
- **Templates** (page-level structures)

This approach eliminates some of the confusion around the atoms/molecules terminology and creates clearer distinctions between different levels of complexity. Choose whichever structure makes more sense for your team's mental model.

This system will help you organize your Figma files and improve performance, as Figma can have issues with files containing many complex components.

Leverage component properties

Figma has several component properties you can use. We developed a visual differentiation system that makes everything clearer at first glance:

Here's the component properties iconography:

- ◆ = Variant
- ↺ = Swap Instance
- ○ = Toggle ,
- @ = Content
- ↳ = Nested Property

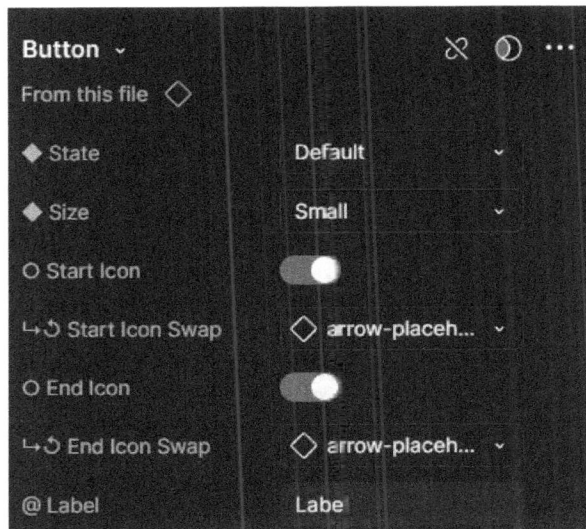

Figure 5.1 – Figma properties structure using Iconography

The second important aspect is sorting properties. Ensure you sort them consistently across components. For example, we always use this top-to-bottom sorting:

- Variants
- Toggles
- Swaps (under toggles)
- Content

Making sure every component follows the same hierarchy helps designers work faster because they know that content options, for instance, will always be at the bottom.

Manage nested properties carefully

When adding nested properties to nested components, only include those that will be changed most frequently. Otherwise, it can become very messy.

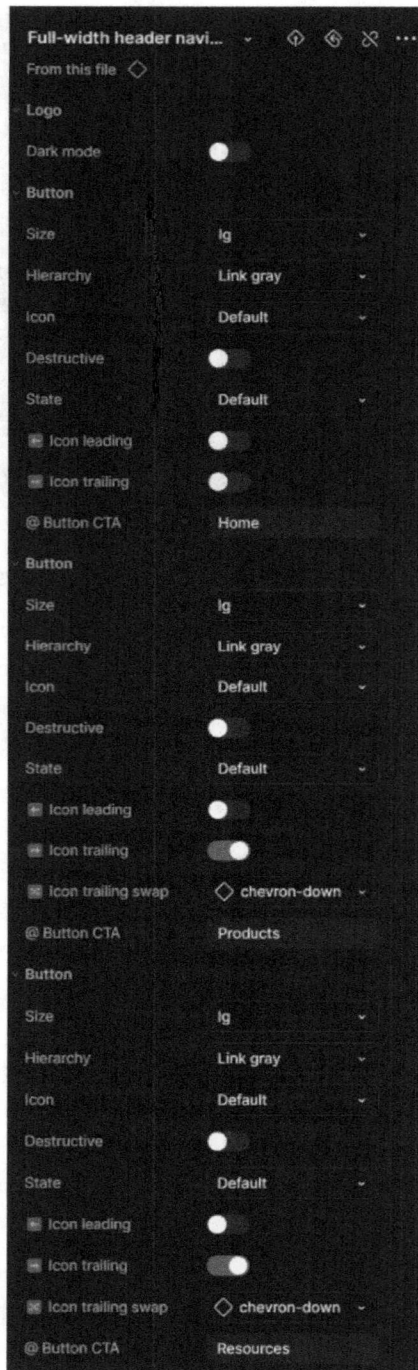

Figure 5.2 – If you add a lot of nested component properties, it can get messy very quickly

As you can see in the preceding screenshot, an overwhelming list of properties won't help anyone work faster. Properties that won't change often can remain accessible in the **Layers** panel inside the component.

Standardize property naming conventions

You should maintain consistent naming conventions for properties across all components. For example, will you use "Large," "Huge," or "Big" in size properties, or will you use T-shirt sizes such as "XXL"? This choice is up to you and your team, but apply it consistently to every component. (We'll dive deeper into naming conventions and platform-specific considerations in *Chapter 8*.)

Create interactive components

If you want to communicate information more effectively, you can create interactive components using prototypes. Of course, as you already know, I like to use the concept of scale, and this applies here too. Creating a hover effect on a button might take 15-30 seconds, while building a fully interactive navigation system takes much longer. You'll need to decide what warrants prototyping and what can be handled through documentation, as I discussed in *Chapter 4*.

Add brief descriptions

Each component can have a simple description that helps others understand it properly. Use this feature and document consistently. I recommend providing some details to ChatGPT and having it generate descriptions using the same template for consistency.

Use component background colors

Did you know that in the **Components** panel, you can see the background behind components? This is an excellent feature for indicating deprecated or utility components.

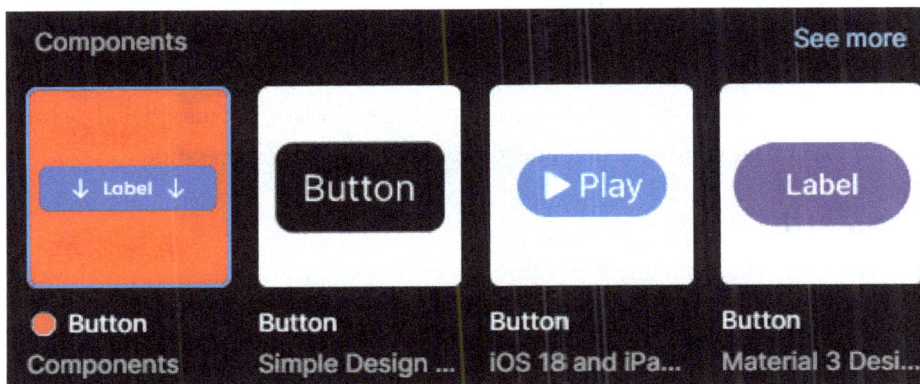

Figure 5.3 – Red background and icon 🔴 shows you deprecated components right away

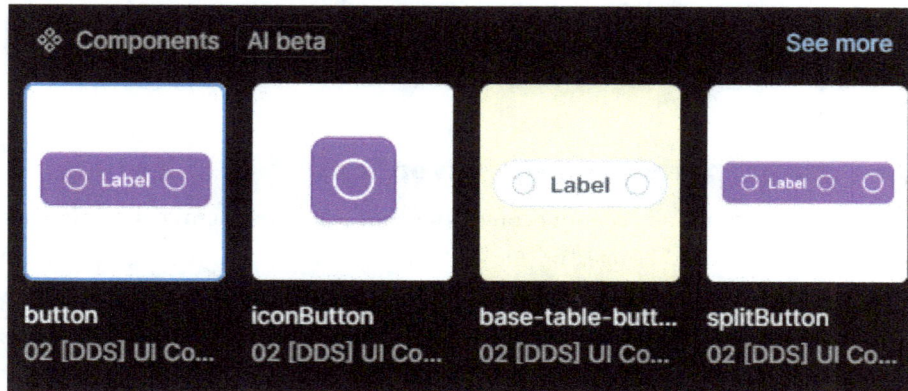

Figure 5.4 – Yellow background shows us utility (helper) components

You can see that we use red backgrounds for deprecated components and yellow for utility components. Simply add a fill to the component background.

Ensuring systematic documentation and standards

One of my friends told me in the past that, in every project, by the time they thought it was time to prepare documentation, it was already too late—and I believe it. As humans, we tend to forget things quickly, and this applies to design systems as well. We should document not only for ourselves but mainly for others. I mention documentation for ourselves because solo designers or small teams often argue they don't need to document because they know and remember everything. Yeah, sure…

What's the problem?

As your system grows and becomes part of your workflow, you'll start to onboard more and more people. As I wrote earlier, adoption is the tricky part, not the design itself. Documentation transforms a collection of components into a true system—a design system. Again, if you're looking at Polaris or Carbon, use them only as a reference, not as a benchmark, because their documentation is very complex, and you probably don't need even 10% of it to be successful.

How to fix it

You should consider the following key points.

Pick the right platform

I always start with a simple question before deciding how we should document: Who will be reading it? This is the fundamental question for you. If the documentation is only for designers, leave it in Figma, where the designers already work. If the documentation is also for developers (as it should be), I would prefer a platform that is more developer-friendly, since in most cases, there are more developers than designers, so you should make a concession. Storybook is an excellent choice, in my opinion. Some teams also use Notion with the ability to embed Figma files directly into it, which provides a nice middle ground between design and development accessibility.

Establish documentation standards

You need to agree on what the standard is at this specific time. Remember, you can always re-visit and make the documentation more robust if the system requires it in the future, but your goal isn't to spend an hour building a component and then a day documenting it. Agree with all stakeholders on the standards you'll deliver now.

Document component behavior and usage

I've mentioned behavior multiple times, but you need to document it properly when required. For example, here's some behavior documentation for our inputs at Dotidot:

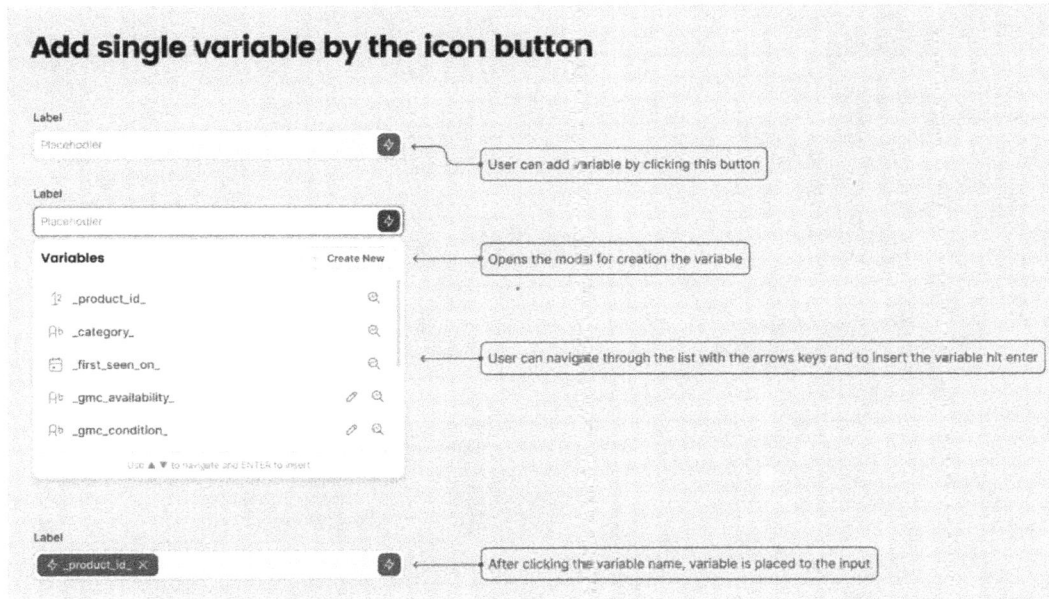

Figure 5.5 – Description for our developers on how this component should behave

Usage is another important part. For atomic components, it's often clear, but when you move to organisms and templates, you should definitely document usage guidelines. Without them, people either won't use these components or will use them incorrectly.

You can use plugins (for example, Auto Documentation, as I mentioned in *Chapter 2*) to handle part of this work.

Build a quick guide

At Dotidot, we had a problem with onboarding developers into our design system, so we created a simple quick guide on the first page of our Figma file and in Confluence with all the essential details that developers should know.

Dot App Design System

Owned by Martin Laudát · · ·
Oct 14, 2024 · 5 people viewed

Hello this page si dedicated to our design system. Here you can find the links for all the parts of our DS and more information.

Figma Files Links

File name	Status	Description	Link
00 - Getting started	Not Ready Yet	File which contains the getting started info how to start working with our design system	00 [DDS] Getting Started
01 - Tokens	Ready	Library with design tokens and styles of our design system	01 [DDS] Tokens v1.0
02 - Components & Patterns	Ready	Library with components and patterns that we are using in the App	02 [DDS] UI Components v 1.0
03 - Chart & Graphs	Ready	Library with chart and graphs components and patterns	04 [DDS] Charts v1.0
04 - Templates	Ready	Library with screen, modals, content blocks templates the help us designing product faster.	https://www.figma.com/de sign/6nYd3epGvhMBsjCCpZh Psn/04-%5BDDS%5D-Templat es-v0.0.1?m=auto&t=IfYNpq UILpeqcs2C-6 Can't find link
05 - Annotation Helpers	Ready	Our design team internal library with annotation helpers.	09 [DDS] Annotation Helpe rs v1.0

Figure 5.6 – Small and simple confluence page with all the links

As designers, you're probably very knowledgeable about something you've built, but always think about others who weren't part of the creation process.

Managing design systems for growing teams

If you're reading this, I want you to stop and congratulate yourself. If you need to deal with these problems, you've already succeeded in the sense that your design system is probably past its initial phases and is usable—but there are new challenges ahead.

What's the problem?

Scaling design systems across growing teams introduces new challenges, workflow bottlenecks, and communication gaps. Without proper management, your work won't have the impact you're looking for. What worked for 5 people won't work for 50, and you need to be ready for scaling.

How to fix it

Here are practical approaches that have worked well across different organizations. Adapt these strategies to fit your specific needs and constraints:

Implement monthly design system checks

Put in place regular meetings between designers and developers where you'll discuss all the sub-optimal things that need attention. If you have larger teams, include only the team leaders—you don't want to schedule meetings with dozens of people. Focus discussions on workflow optimization and how to make the design system easier to understand and use.

Establish governance

With bigger teams, you should dedicate specific people to work on your design system. In this phase, you should have three key roles filled:

- **Design system owner**: Handles planning, communicates with other teams using the system, argues about priorities, and works on adoption
- **Design system designer (aka Figma Magician)**: Builds and optimizes components, creates design documentation
- **Design system developer**: Builds the components and creates development documentation

Implement version control

As covered in *Chapter 1*, version control becomes critical for large teams. Use Figma's branching feature for design system changes. Create testing files where you can verify that nothing is "broken" by accident when releasing new versions. In these files, place all major designs next to the same frame as a screenshot. When you approve changes, you can easily compare the static screenshot with the dynamic frame to see if everything appears as it should.

Create multi-level access

Not everyone needs edit access to your design system:

- Set up projects and permissions to control who can edit the design system files
- Use Figma libraries to distribute components safely
- Create separate files for testing new components before they become part of your main design system files and are distributed to all teams

Build feedback loops

In larger teams, you need to establish proper feedback channels from other designers and developers to gather all input in one place. In bigger teams, it's good to approach this as you would normal product development: have a single location to collect all feedback from meetings, Slack, emails, and so on, and plan your roadmap accordingly. Each release of your design system should be treated like a product release—communicate about it, inform others, and ensure all teams understand the new components, just as you would ensure everyone understands new features in product development.

Another important aspect is to build easy channels for supporting designers and developers. Create separate Slack (or other communication platform) channels to help others with adoption and implementation. If they ask for help and you don't provide it, your adoption effort is a lost battle.

Utilizing Figma's design system tools

Figma is, in my opinion, the main reason why design systems have become such a hot topic for most teams. Design systems existed before Figma, but Figma has built many amazing tools that can help with their creation and adoption.

What's the problem?

Without utilizing Figma's specialized design system features, you're making your work more difficult than it needs to be. These tools are specifically designed to help you build, maintain, and analyze your design systems.

How to fix it

Figma offers several powerful tools specifically designed for design systems. Here are the most impactful ones that can significantly improve how your team builds and uses components:

Use Code Connect if you can

If your Figma plan allows it (Organization or Enterprise), use Code Connect—it's a game-changer for developer workflow. Here's how it works: you link your actual production component code directly to your Figma components. When developers inspect a component in dev mode, they see a **Code** tab next to the usual **Inspect** tab. Instead of manually writing code or copying CSS values, they can simply click and copy the exact component code they need.

For example, if a developer needs a button with a specific variant (such as **Primary** with an icon), they can click on that exact button in Figma and copy the complete React, Vue, or HTML code with all the right properties already set. No guessing, no manual translation from design to code—just copy and paste working components. This eliminates the back-and-forth between designers and developers about implementation details.

Leverage design system analytics in Figma

Figma has built complex analytics on top of your design system library. Unfortunately, this feature is also locked behind Organization or Enterprise plans. If you have access to it, dive deeper into it periodically—once a month is usually enough to spot trends. Look into these key points:

- **Check the Insert counts for components**: This metric shows how often a component was added to Figma files in the past 30 days. Is a major component missing from the list? Or, are new components barely used? This information signals that you need to better communicate with your teams. Sometimes teams simply miss information about new components and don't know they're available.

- **Monitor the Detach numbers**: If you see a large number of detached components, you have a problem. Try to find out why designers are detaching your components. Perhaps you're missing a variant—this should be a signal to reprioritize your roadmap and build it as soon as possible.

- **Review the file/team names**: In medium to large teams, you should know the main projects the company is working on. You should be able to see all file or team names in the analytics. If you're missing a team or file name, connect with the team and discuss why they aren't using the design system properly.

Implement design system analytics outside Figma

Of course, you already know that Figma isn't the final state—production code is. In this case, you should work with code analytics as well. You can use many third-party analytics tools to help you analyze component usage in code. Perhaps designers are using components in Figma, but development teams aren't implementing them. Work with your development team to find the most suitable option, but I can recommend Omlet. You can find out more at `https://omlet.dev/`.

Unpublish helper components

In your design system, you'll have many helper components—components that shouldn't be used by themselves but only in combination with other components (for example, a tooltip). A tooltip without any other component shouldn't be used, so unpublish it from your design system. You can do this easily by adding an underscore before the component name. So, it won't be "Tooltip," but "_Tooltip." You can also use a period, so it would be ".Tooltip."

Use branching for version control

As I've mentioned in previous chapters, branching becomes critical when working with design systems, especially for larger teams. If you have an Organization or Enterprise Figma plan, use the branching feature to manage design system changes safely. Create branches when you're making significant updates to components or adding new ones.

This approach lets you test changes without breaking the main design system that other teams are using. You can invite stakeholders to review changes in the branch, gather feedback, and make iterations before merging back to the main file. Think of it like code branching—you wouldn't push untested code directly to production, and you shouldn't push untested design system changes to your main library either.

Dynamic system scaling to accommodate product iterations

Every product changes over time, and your design system will need to adapt accordingly. A static system quickly becomes outdated and irrelevant.

What's the problem?

Many design systems become bottlenecks during rapid product development. If updating the system is too slow or cumbersome, teams work around it, creating inconsistencies and technical debt. Systems must evolve alongside products to remain relevant. Sometimes, company management thinks that design systems are a one-time investment, which doesn't help either.

How to fix it

Remember that a design system is a product, and every product needs iteration and optimization.

Implement modular architecture

You should plan the entire system to be modular. This ranges from simple decisions such as not keeping foundations and components in one file, to more complex choices such as avoiding intricate dependencies between components.

Establish update cycles

This sounds normal, and I've mentioned it previously, but in this case, I need you to work hard to establish this mindset from the stakeholders' (C-level management) point of view. You, as designers and developers, understand it, but now management needs to understand that you need to work on the system periodically to make it better for the rest of the company.

Try to align your updates with the rest of the product development in your company. Do they run in sprints? Great—run in them too, in parallel. Are you having company product team meetings for all product changes? Great—try to "steal" a minute or two to inform everyone about your updates and push the information to the product teams.

Plan for deprecation

Not every component should live forever. Sometimes you need to make the hard decision to deprecate components. Check the analytics I mentioned earlier to be sure which components are ready to retire.

Retiring components doesn't mean deleting them immediately—that would break all the old designs using them. Instead, mark them as deprecated (you can use the red background method I mentioned earlier), stop promoting their use, and gradually migrate existing designs to newer alternatives. Only remove deprecated components after you're certain no active projects depend on them.

Build experimentation spaces

Encourage all teams to experiment and help you build a better design system. Welcome their local components that you can build upon and bring to other teams. Create an environment where their work will be appreciated and built upon.

Unlock this book's exclusive benefits now	
Scan this QR code or go to `packtpub. com/unlock`, then search this book by name.	
Note: Keep your purchase invoice ready before you start.	

6

Utilizing Design Tokens for Consistency

Design tokens are one of the best helpers for consistency and transferring information between designers and developers. In this chapter, I want to dig deeper into them, explain the main difference between design tokens and Figma variables (because they aren't the same thing as many people think), and show you real-world cases of when to use what and why, and how to work on the versioning and documentation of your tokens.

Design tokens represent a fundamental shift in how we manage visual consistency across platforms, creating a true bridge between design and development.

We'll dive into how tokens serve as the "single source of truth" that both designers and developers can reference, ensuring that visual elements remain consistent across all products, regardless of platform or technology. By mastering these techniques, you'll establish a more efficient workflow that reduces errors, speeds up implementation, and creates truly cohesive digital experiences.

We will explore these topics in this chapter:

- Introducing design tokens as a design-code bridge
- When and how to introduce design tokens in your team
- Difference between design tokens and Figma variables
- Design token structure: how to build design tokens
- Implementing design tokens in Figma via Token Studio
- Implementing Figma variables

- Version controlling design tokens with GitHub or GitLab
- Maintaining token documentation for cross-team consistency

So let's jump into the first topic.

Introducing design tokens as a design-code bridge

Design tokens are decisions that you make as a designer, but unlike styles, you can transfer these decisions directly into code. What decisions? Things such as colors, typography, spacing, animation duration, sizing, opacity, and others. Without tokens, these decisions are simply rewritten by developers who look at your design and manually transfer values into code, introducing the potential for human error. With design tokens, developers work with the token itself rather than the underlying value, creating a shared language and bridge between designers and developers.

What's the problem?

Without design tokens, decisions exist in isolated environments. Designers work with styles, while developers implement these decisions in code using different naming conventions, structures, and sometimes even different values. This disconnect leads to inconsistencies, miscommunication, and tedious back-and-forth as teams try to stay aligned.

When a designer updates a color in Figma, developers have no automated way to know about or implement this change. Similarly, when developers need to adapt designs for different platforms, they often recreate values manually, introducing errors and variations. Without a shared system of record, maintaining visual consistency becomes increasingly difficult as products scale.

How to fix it

Design tokens are here for this reason. As with many things in this book, I like to look at solutions that scale. Design tokens are the same. When you google them, you'll find stories from Spotify or Adobe with thousands of tokens, but you don't need to have that many. You can start with even a small part of your design decisions and tokenize it step by step.

Here's how design tokens can help you bridge the gap:

1. **Single source of truth:** Design tokens give you a single source of truth because they're stored in code (mostly JSON), so both sides are using this instead of two separate sources (usually Figma styles and code). While developers use transformation tools to convert the JSON into their platform-specific formats, the key point is that everyone references the same source of truth.

2. **Consistent naming**: You'll establish the same naming across teams, so both teams will know what you're talking about, and changes can be implemented quickly.

```
// Instead of this:
Figma: "Purple/500"
CSS: "primary-color"
iOS: "colorPurple"
Android: "color_purple_primary"

// Use a shared naming convention:
"color.primary.default": "#5C50E6'
```

> 💡 **Quick tip**: Enhance your coding experience with the **AI Code Explainer** and **Quick Copy** features. Open this book in the next-gen Packt Reader. Click the **Copy** button **(1)** to quickly copy code into your coding environment, or click the **Explain** button **(2)** to get the AI assistant to explain a block of code to you.
>
> Copy   Explain
> ```
> function calculate(a, b) {           1        2
>     return {sum: a + b};
> };
> ```
>
> 🔒 **The next-gen Packt Reader** is included for free with the purchase of this book. Unlock it by scanning the QR code below or visiting https://www.packtpub.com/unlock/9781835083468.
>
>

3. **Separate design decisions from implementation**: Each platform can have different standards, and tokens are abstract values, so they can be transformed for platform needs very easily and quickly.

4.   **Clean hierarchy**: They use an easily connected system that helps you link multiple de-
     cisions as a chain. Changes are quick, and you avoid possible errors in the future (I'll
     explain more later).

```
// Primitive tokens (raw values)
"color.purple.500": "#5C50E6"

// Semantic tokens (usage-based)
"color.primary.default": "{color.purple.500}"
```

5.   **Multi-brand readiness**: This can be specific for certain businesses, but your system be-
     comes ready for multi-brand usage. Your development team can have just one component
     with many visual variations (amazing for white labeling systems or to brand the system
     for users' preferences).

6.   **Accessibility improvements**: With tokens, implementing accessibility needs becomes
     easier because developers won't need to manually adjust contrast, sizes, and other ele-
     ments throughout the code base.

Design tokens aren't just a new workflow, but a complete shift in how you think about collaboration between designers and developers across projects.

When and how to introduce design tokens in your team

Understanding design tokens is one thing—getting your team to adopt them is another challenge
entirely. The biggest mistake teams make is diving straight into technical implementation without considering the human element. Design tokens represent a fundamental shift in how teams
work together, and successful adoption requires a strategic approach.

What's the problem?

I once saw a team with a brilliant designer who understood the benefits of design tokens and
loved them. This was a few years back, when design tokens weren't as popular and Figma didn't
have variables yet. This designer prepared an amazing structure in Token Studio with everything
that a proper implementation of design tokens should have. He invested dozens of hours in the
structure, creation, and documentation of everything. The implementation and adoption in engineering and the rest of the design team were zero.

He had jumped to the finish line, investing enormous time into a technical solution without considering one big potential challenge: the human factor. Without buy-in from key stakeholders, even the most carefully crafted token system will be abandoned or inconsistently applied.

How to fix it

I love to say that we designers are good at solving problems—that's our job. But we don't always apply this amazing skill to other parts of our work. So, approach implementation and adoption of design tokens as another design problem that needs a structured solution:

1. Define your target audience.
2. Find ambassadors.
3. Identify pain points (why you're implementing them).
4. Start small with immediate impact.
5. Establish success metrics.
6. Plan onboarding of current and future team members.

Define your target audience

Like any project, design tokens have a target audience. The first group that comes to mind is designers, but don't forget developers, product managers, QA testers, and management. Each of these groups has different concerns with implementation:

- **Designers**: Fear of losing flexibility and creativity
- **Developers**: Worry about more work, especially if tokens are set up by designers who don't understand the development world, making them unusable
- **Product managers (PMs)**: Concern about pushing feature development to the side track, adding more maintenance, and requiring QA testing
- **Management**: Worry about a big project that won't have a real return in terms of money

Understanding these concerns upfront helps you address them proactively rather than reactively.

Find ambassadors

It's always good to find ambassadors in each of the groups described previously. These people can give you better insight into their concerns and pain points while helping you push for the project. In my experience, projects pushed from multiple roles have a much better chance of getting a green light from management. When leadership sees that designers, developers, and PMs are all calling for something, it's very hard to say no.

Try to find people who already understand design tokens or are willing to give you an afternoon when you can explain the benefits and why they should want them.

Identify pain points (why you're implementing them)

Each of your groups has different pain points that design tokens can solve when implemented correctly:

- **Designers**: Consistency across the whole product, and easier hand-off to developers.

- **Developers**: Easy UI changes that don't require implementation from scratch, theming (light and dark mode becomes super easy), and eliminating communication gaps.

- **Product managers**: Speed and consistency; developers can implement certain states without designers if they have semantic tokens (more about them later).

- **Management**: Speed equals money—that's the main argument for implementing design tokens. If your design and development teams work faster, you'll see better ROI.

Start small with immediate impact

Implementation of design tokens is about scale—it's not a yes or no question, but about how much you want to invest in them. Start small. Colors are an easy starting point because they're visual and open up theming (light and dark mode) that's easy to explain. Set a strict deadline for when you want to have some part implemented and where—this is crucial for the next steps.

Establish success metrics

Every manager will want to see success metrics that demonstrate that this is a successful project. In design token implementation projects, I like to talk about these:

- **Usage metrics**: How many components use tokens versus hardcoded values

- **Consistency**: Reduction of unique color/spacing/typography values that are now managed via tokens, making changes super easy and not time-consuming

- **Efficiency**: Time saved in design-to-development hand-off (this is honestly hard to measure, but in many cases, feedback from both teams that the process is much faster was enough for management)

- **Quality**: Reduction in visual inconsistencies (bugs) during QA

Plan onboarding of current and future team members

Creating design tokens is the easier part—the hard part is adoption. It's good to plan for it:

- Have a special communication channel for design system announcements (here you should talk about tokens as well)
- Have a dedicated support channel where you'll help people with implementation, explanations, and so on
- Celebrate wins and new ambassadors
- Have regular check-ins with all teams—this can be done by ambassadors in their roles, so developer ambassadors will check in with developers, PMs with PMs, and so on

These steps have helped me in the past with the implementation of design tokens and explaining their value to the whole company.

Difference between design tokens and Figma variables

When Figma announced variables at Config 2023, there was a slide showing **Design Tokens** crossed out with **Variables** next to it. This was the first indicator that Figma variables aren't the same as design tokens—and they truly aren't. Many designers without experience working with true design tokens (via Token Studio, for example) mistakenly think they're identical. Both variables and tokens have their strengths and limitations, and it's crucial to understand these differences before deciding which to use.

What's the problem?

Figma variables represent Figma's native interpretation of design tokens. While powerful, they have significant limitations. Token Studio (the most widely used plugin for working with design tokens in Figma) also has its own constraints. Choosing the wrong approach can cause problems later in your project, especially as it scales. Therefore, it's worth taking time to understand the differences to make the right, future-proof decision for your specific needs.

How to fix it

The simple answer is as follows:

- If you're building a small design system only in Figma with at most light and dark mode, use Figma variables
- If you're building something bigger, future-proof, and not locked into Figma, use Token Studio

But I understand you need more details, so let's break it down.

For designers or developers?

This should be your first consideration: Will the tokens be used only by designers or by developers, too? I always advocate for developer usage since that's the main benefit of tokens, but sometimes this is outside your control. If tokens will be used exclusively by designers, Figma variables work well. If developers are involved, I'd recommend Token Studio in 99% of cases. What about that 1%? I'll explain in the following points.

Figma versus other platforms

Figma variables can only be used within Figma—they're built natively into the tool, and that's it. Token Studio, however, can be used across different design applications.

Why is this important if you're reading a book about Figma, which has more than 80% market share? When I first started using Figma, I often heard, "That's nonsense, everyone designs in Photoshop or Sketch. Figma will never work." Well... that didn't age well. There was a time when Figma was the small player in the room. Now it's a giant, but this position can change. Something new might come along and dethrone Figma.

For example, Penpot (another small open source design tool) has native integration of design tokens and supports the W3C Design Tokens Community Group standard, and at Dotidot, we're testing it on a real project. I even know of some enterprises testing Penpot alongside Figma because Penpot can be self-hosted and is free.

Native versus plugin-based

Of course, Figma variables being native is a huge benefit. You don't need to open any plugin to use them. Variables are much faster than Token Studio and more designers understand them because they're built-in and, honestly, much easier to grasp.

Token Studio isn't just a plugin

It used to be just a plugin, but it's now a platform, with the plugin serving as the connector between Figma and the platform. Let me explain the key differences.

Token connection

With Token Studio, you can easily visualize how your tokens are connected to each other, which is crucial for larger design systems to see what will impact what. This visualization isn't available in Figma variables. For 100 tokens, this might not matter much, but with 500 or more, it becomes a significant issue.

Theming

Figma variables have modes, but they're very limiting: 4 modes in Professional and Organization plans, and 40 in Enterprise. This artificial limitation exists to encourage upgrades. In contrast, Token Studio's themes are unlimited—you can have as many as you need. However, the free version of Token Studio is quite limited and doesn't support themes or advanced folder structures, so you'll likely need the paid version for serious design system work.

Data structure

Figma variables are organized into collections and modes, which nobody outside of Figma designers will understand. Tokens in Token Studio are saved in a JSON structure that any developer will immediately comprehend.

Version control

Figma variables don't have a proper versioning system built in. They live in your file along with everything else. You can use the versioning techniques I explained in previous chapters, but that's not ideal.

Tokens in Token Studio can be synced with repositories such as GitHub or GitLab. This is fantastic because these developer platforms have robust version control, and developers are already familiar with them.

Types of tokens

Figma variables can do more than just design tokens—you can use them for advanced prototyping or text translation. That versatility is great, but it means they lack focus and specialized features for token management.

Figma variables offer just four basic token types:

- Color
- Number
- Boolean
- String (text)

What's notably missing are composite tokens, which Token Studio handles elegantly. Take typography as an example—in Token Studio, a single typography token can encapsulate font family, size, weight, line height, letter spacing, and more as one cohesive unit. This approach dramatically simplifies the management and application of complex token types across your design system.

This specialization is where Token Studio shines. By focusing exclusively on token management rather than trying to serve multiple purposes, it provides deeper functionality specifically tailored to the design system's needs.

Code use

Figma variables don't have a straightforward way to use them in code. You need a third-party plugin just to export them. You can use plugins such as **Variables to CSS** or **Variables to JSON** (which I mentioned in *Chapter 2*) to bridge this gap. In enterprise environments, the exported JSON is typically processed through **Style Dictionary**, the industry standard for transforming design tokens into platform-specific code formats such as CSS variables, iOS Swift, or Android XML.

Token Studio is built with developers in mind, so it assumes you'll use tokens in code. You can export them from the platform to any format your development teams need across various platforms (web, iOS, Android, etc.).

Design token structure—how to build design tokens

Now that you understand the difference between Figma variables and Token Studio, let's talk about the proper structure for your design tokens. This structure can be applied with either Token Studio or Figma variables—the principles remain the same regardless of which tool you choose.

What's the problem?

Design tokens can become messy very quickly. Without proper planning and structure, they'll devolve into an unusable collection of values that nobody will adopt. Think of it like a disorganized library—if books aren't properly categorized and you can't find what you need, you'll eventually stop going there altogether. The same applies to design tokens. Taking time to plan your token structure is crucial; otherwise, you risk creating a system that people avoid rather than embrace.

How to fix it

Remember that in most cases, other people (both designers and developers) will be using your design tokens. Their core purpose is to bridge the design and development worlds, so it's essential to create a system that's intuitive for everyone involved.

Proper hierarchy (structure)

One of the most powerful features of design tokens is the ability to connect/reference them (token alias) to each other, building a logical hierarchy that's easy to navigate and use. Let me explain with an example.

If I show you #007BFF and ask where and how this color is used, you wouldn't know. Neither would I.

What about color/blue/500? Now you have context—it's a blue color at the 500 level, likely the default blue in your system.

Let's go further: color/background/default. This tells you it's used for background elements in their default state.

Even more specific: button/primary/background. Now you know exactly where and how this color is applied—it's the background for primary buttons.

This hierarchy demonstrates the beauty of design tokens. You can start with primitive (core) tokens such as color/blue/500 and build up to more specific (semantic) tokens such as color/background/default or even component-level tokens such as button/primary/background.

The real power emerges when these tokens are connected. If developers implement your design tokens in code using button/primary/background and you later change the underlying value that this token connects to (perhaps from color/blue/500 to color/green/500), they won't need to modify any code where the component token is used. Instead, they only need to update the single core token value in one place, and the change propagates automatically through the token hierarchy, updating every component that uses the connected component tokens instantly.

This means changing a color across hundreds of components requires updating just one line of code instead of hunting down every instance manually.

Practical token planning

Now that you understand the hierarchy, you might be wondering: *How many tokens do I actually need to create?*. This is one of the most common questions from designers new to tokens, and the answer depends on your specific project, but here are some practical guidelines to get you started.

Start with an audit (if you have an existing project)

If you're working with an existing project that already has components and designs, start by auditing what you currently have. Open your Figma file and count the following:

- How many unique colors do you actually use?
- How many different spacing values appear in your designs?
- How many typography styles do you have?

You might be surprised to discover that many designers think they have many more colors than they actually use when they count unique values properly.

The "three uses" rule

A good rule of thumb is that if you use a value (color, spacing, or typography) in three or more places, it probably deserves a token. If it's only used once or twice, you might not need a specific token for it yet.

Some teams are very strict and require that everything must be a token, with no hardcoded values allowed. While this approach has merit for large, mature design systems, if you're just starting out, the bigger problem you'll face is managing thousands of tokens rather than having some values hardcoded. Start pragmatically and let your system grow naturally.

Semantic token examples for a typical website

For colors, you might need semantic tokens such as the following:

- `text/primary`: Main body text color
- `text/secondary`: Subtitle and secondary text color
- `text/error`: Error messages
- `text/success`: Success messages
- `surface/default`: Main page background
- `surface/raised`: Card or section backgrounds
- `border/default`: Standard border color
- `border/focus`: Focus state borders

Component token examples

For buttons, you might create the following:

- `button/primary/background`: Primary button background
- `button/primary/text`: Primary button text color
- `button/secondary/background`: Secondary button background
- `button/secondary/border`: Secondary button border

Start small and grow

Don't try to tokenize everything on day one. Start with the following:

1. **Colors first**: They're visual and easy to understand.
2. **Spacing second**: Usually, 4–6 values cover most use cases.
3. **Typography third**: Focus on the most common text styles.

Common beginner mistakes to avoid

The following are some beginner mistakes to avoid:

- **Over-tokenizing**: Creating tokens for values used only once
- **Under-tokenizing**: Using the same core token directly everywhere instead of creating semantic tokens
- **Inconsistent naming**: Mixing different naming conventions within the same system
- **Too many variations**: Creating 15 button variants when you really only need 3

Remember that tokens are meant to make your life easier, not more complicated. Start simple, and let your system grow naturally as your design needs become clearer.

Implementing design tokens in Figma via Token Studio

I want to start with implementing design tokens using Token Studio because it's my preferred approach. We'll talk about Figma variables in the next section, so if you don't want to use Token Studio, feel free to skip ahead and come back when you're ready to explore it.

First use of the plugin

Token Studio is a platform for complex design systems, but I'll focus on the Figma plugin and working with it. When you first open the plugin in a new Figma design file, you can explore their example by clicking **Load Example**. This provides a simple structure of design tokens to help you experiment with the plugin without needing a proper project. For our purposes, we'll click on **New empty file**.

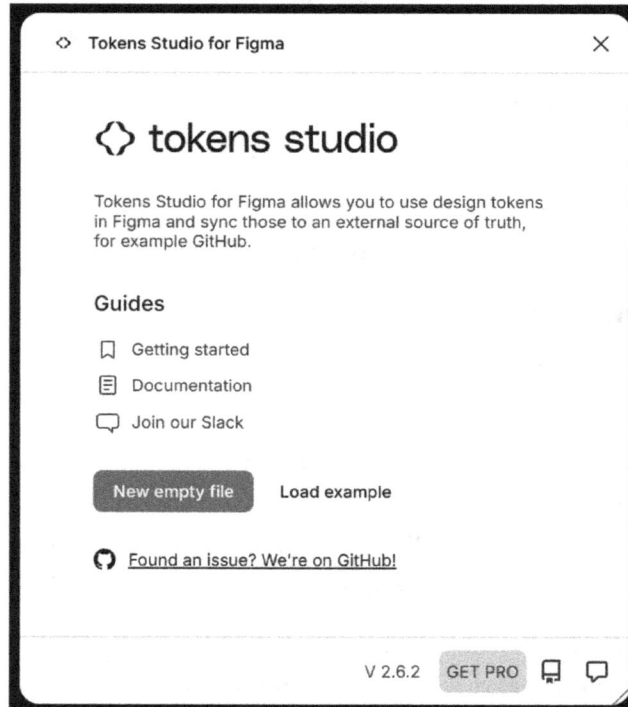

Figure 6.1 – The first page that you see when you open the Token Studio plugin

A new file without any tokens will appear, and you'll see the Token Studio UI for the first time. Let me introduce you to its main components.

Figure 6.2 – Token Studio navigation tabs

You have three main tabs:

- **Tokens**: This is where all your design tokens will live. Here, you can create new tokens, apply them to elements in Figma, and switch between different token sets (groups of tokens) or entire themes (for example, light and dark mode).
- **Inspect**: Click on any element in Figma, and you'll see what design tokens are applied there, whether there are any problems, and what needs fixing.
- **Settings**: This is a simple settings panel where you can add a license key for the Pro version and adjust minor preferences such as language and base font size. The most important function here is **Sync providers**, which we'll explore next.

Settings—Sync providers

Token Studio is a plugin in Figma, and because of that, it can't save design tokens automatically with the Figma file like Figma variables can. So, how do you share design tokens with other designers? That's where sync providers come in.

You can select from multiple options, but the most useful ones from my perspective are the following:

- **GitHub**: I'll demonstrate this approach in the next section.
- **GitLab**: This is similar to GitHub but preferred by some development teams. (I will show you how to connect GitHub; if you are using GitLab, follow this guide: `https://docs.tokens.studio/token-storage/remote/sync-git-gitlab`.)
- **Supernova**: This is an excellent Czech app for managing and documenting large design systems (`https://docs.tokens.studio/token-storage/remote/sync-cloud-supernova`).
- **Token Studio Cloud**: Remember when I mentioned that Token Studio is a platform and not just a simple plugin? This is one aspect of that platform (`https://docs.tokens.studio/token-storage/remote/sync-cloud-studio-platform`).

How to set up GitHub sync step by step

I'll show you the GitHub option because it was the first one I used and the one I use most frequently. Most developers I know use GitHub, and it's always better to be on the same platform as your development team. This eliminates the roadblock of explaining why your tokens aren't in their environment. If your development team uses GitLab, use that instead—the setup process is very similar:

1. Click on **GitHub** and you'll see the settings panel shown in the following figure:

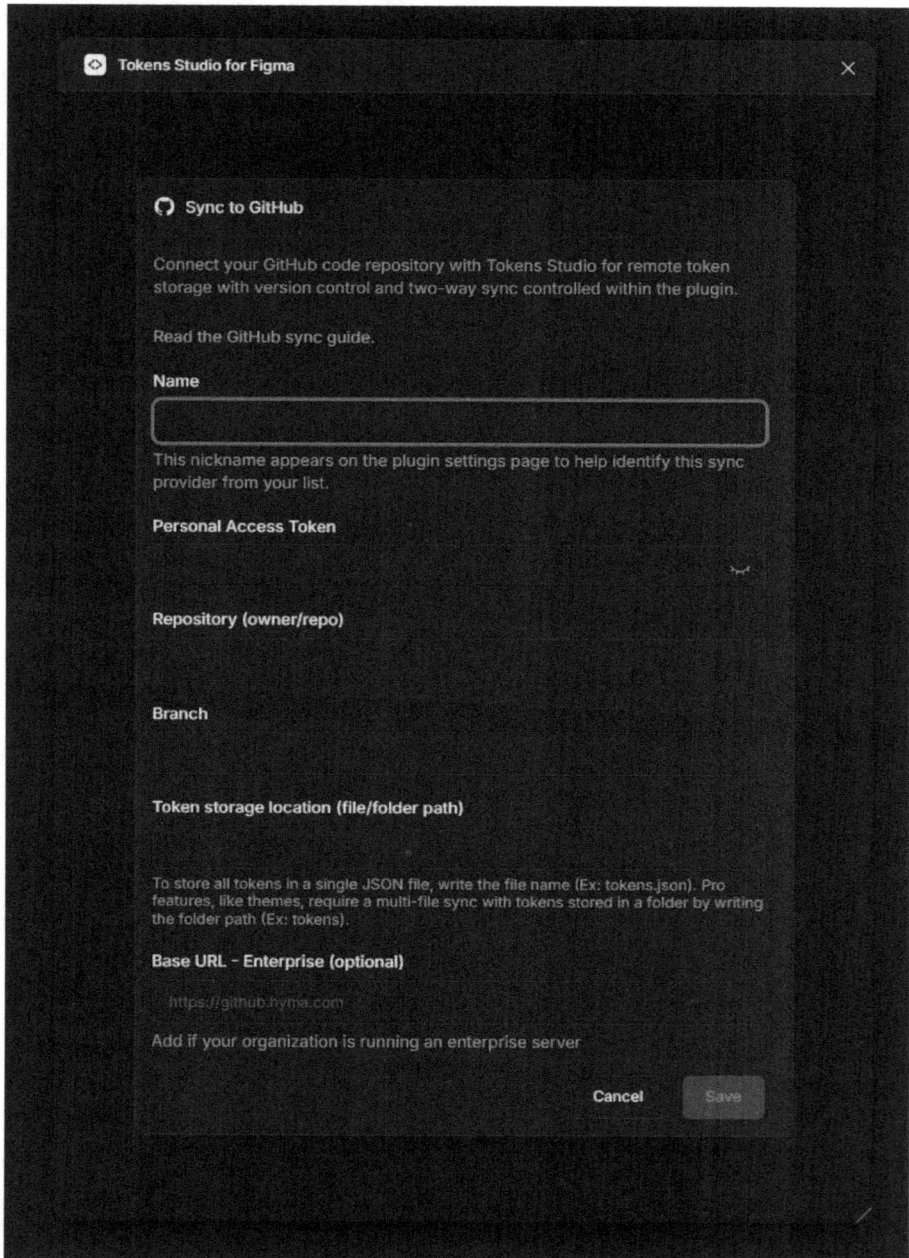

Figure 6.3 – GitHub sync settings in Token Studio

2. You'll need a GitHub account for this to work. Registration is free and straightforward—just go to https://github.com/signup and follow the wizard.

3. You'll need a personal access token to verify that Token Studio is authorized by you and allow the plugin to push (upload) design tokens to the repository we'll create.

4. Click on your profile picture and go to **Settings**.

5. At the bottom of the side settings menu, click on **Developer settings**.

6. Then, go to **Personal access tokens** and select **Tokens (classic)**, which works fine for new accounts.

7. Add a descriptive name (your choice).

8. Select the **repo** scope in **Select scopes** to give this token all the permissions it needs.

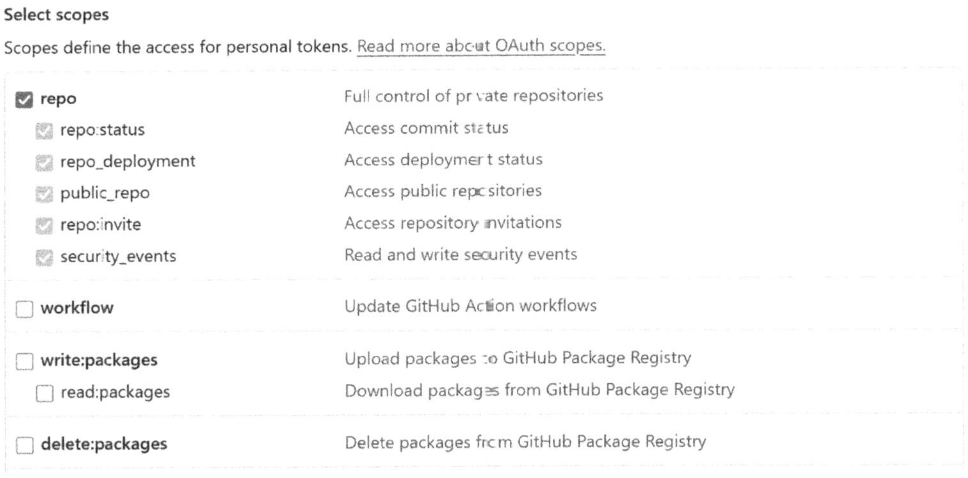

Select scopes

Scopes define the access for personal tokens. Read more about OAuth scopes.

☑ **repo**	Full control of private repositories
☑ repo:status	Access commit status
☑ repo_deployment	Access deployment status
☑ public_repo	Access public repositories
☑ repo:invite	Access repository invitations
☑ security_events	Read and write security events
☐ **workflow**	Update GitHub Action workflows
☐ **write:packages**	Upload packages to GitHub Package Registry
☐ read:packages	Download packages from GitHub Package Registry
☐ **delete:packages**	Delete packages from GitHub Package Registry

Figure 6.4 – Scope selection in GitHub

9. After creation, you'll receive a token similar to the one shown in the following figure. Copy this to Token Studio.

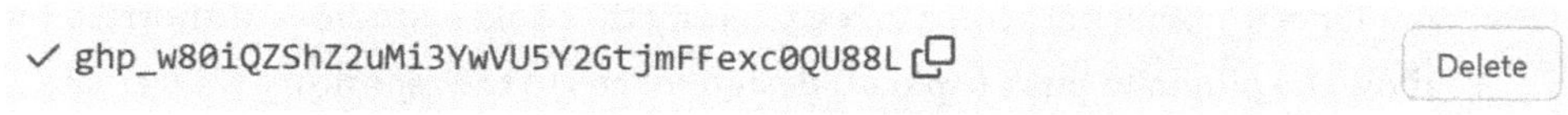

✓ 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 ⎘   Delete

Figure 6.5 – Personal access token from GitHub

10. Now, we need to create a *project* in GitHub where we can upload the file with design tokens. In the top navigation, click on the + icon and then **New repository**.

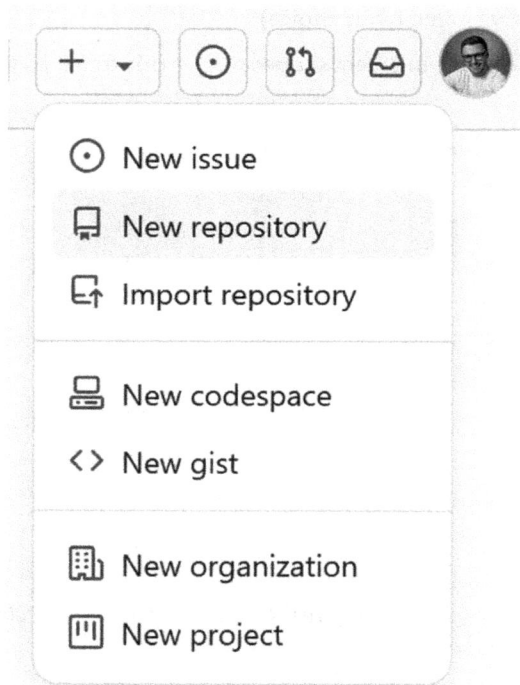

Figure 6.6 – Creation of repository in GitHub

11. Add a repository name
12. Change the visibility to **Private** (so you'll need to send invitations to team members to access it).
13. Check **Add a README file.**

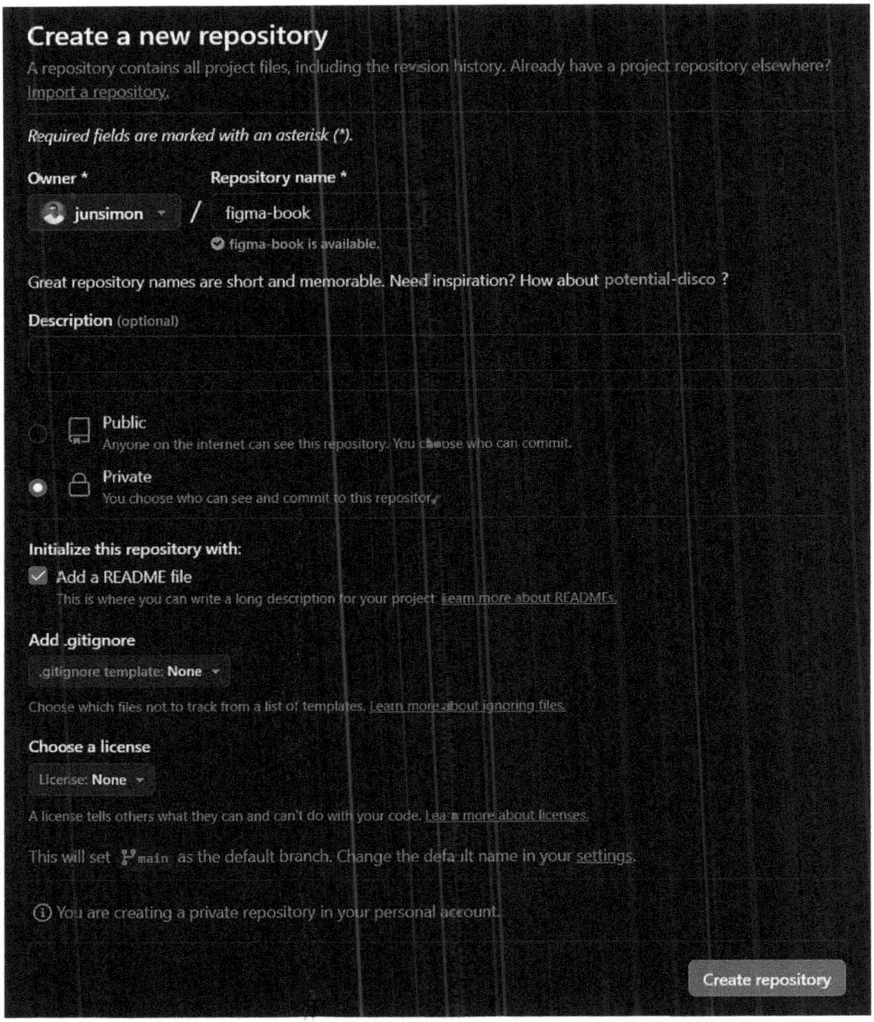

Figure 6.7 – Repository creation settings

14. Click **Create repository**.

15. Copy the owner name (account name) and repository name (from the URL) and enter them in Token Studio.

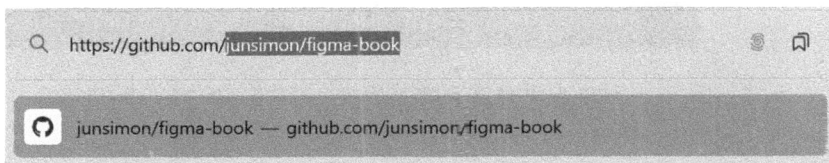

Figure 6.8 – Repository URL

16. In the **Branch** input, enter **main**.

17. **Token storage location** is the folder and filename on GitHub. For our case, we'll simply use tokens.json (it needs to be in .json format), so just enter your chosen name followed by .json.

    The remaining inputs can be left empty. Your Token Studio settings should now look like this:

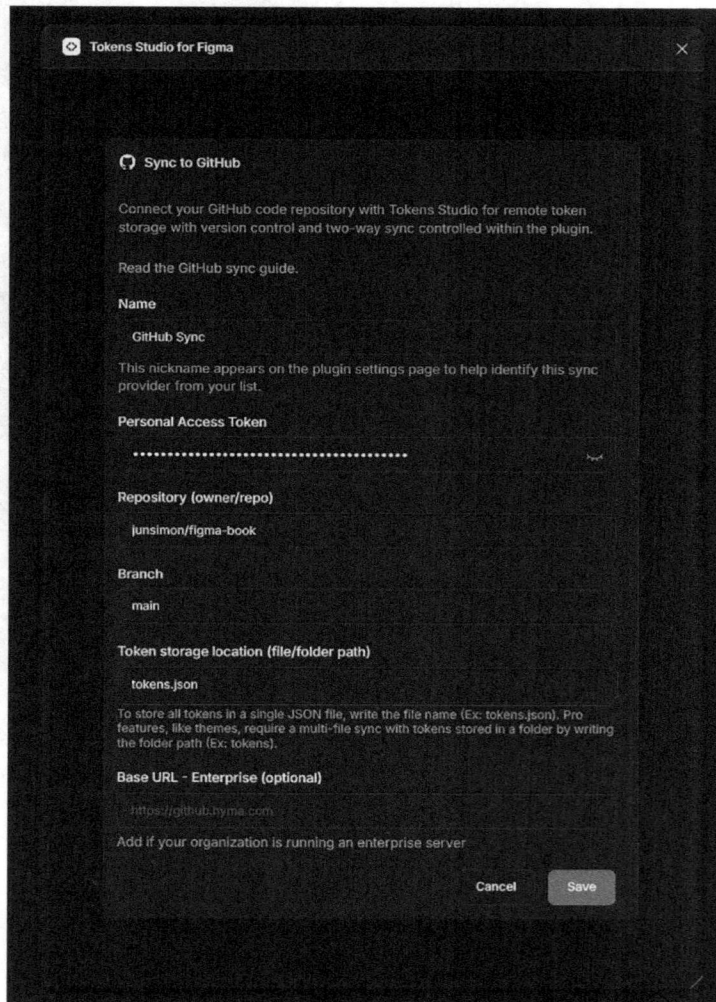

Figure 6.9 – Complete GitHub sync settings in Token Studio

18. Click **Save**.

19. If everything is configured correctly, you'll see a new popup asking for a commit message for the first sync:

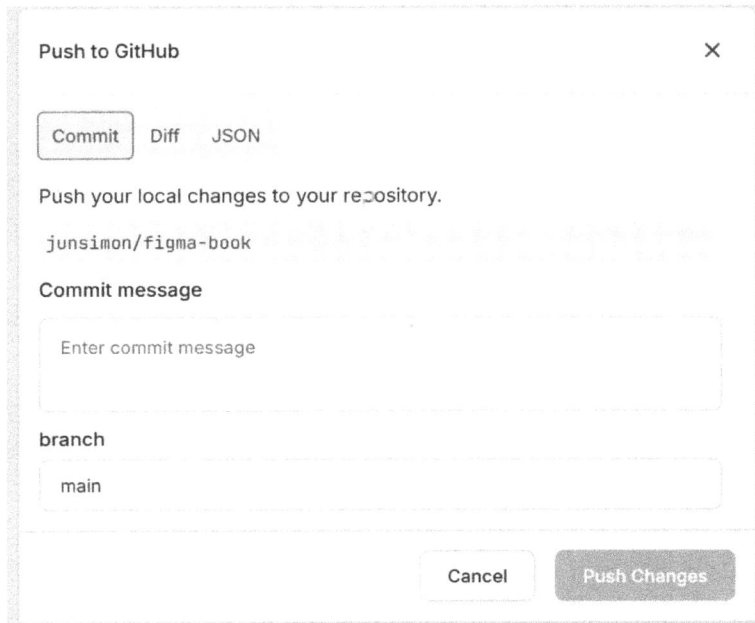

Figure 6.10 – Push changes modal

20. Push the changes (there aren't any yet since we haven't created tokens, but this will set up the file on GitHub). This process can take some time, so be patient and wait until it completes.

21. Return to GitHub, and you should see your new file with the specified filename.

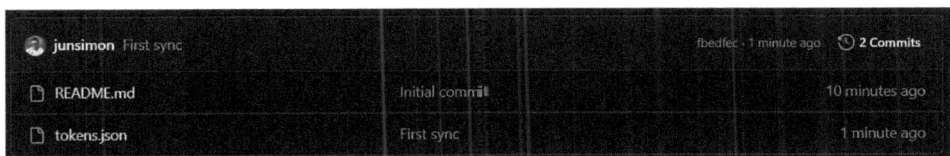

Figure 6.11 – New tokens.json file in GitHub created from Token Studio

You're all set! Now, you can easily push new changes to GitHub, and anyone with access to this repository can pull (download) them and work with them in their own Token Studio. They'll need to follow this guide as well, but can skip the repository creation part since you've already done that.

Creation of a new set

Now that you've handled the technical setup with GitHub, you can focus on creating design tokens. Return to the first tab in Token Studio labeled **Tokens**. Let's start building a proper structure and tokens.

Proper structure

There are many approaches to creating an effective token structure, and yours should be tailored to your specific needs. While you can find various methodologies online, we'll start with a simple, three-tier approach:

- **Core:** These are your foundational tokens, such as `Blue500` (color), `Primary500` (color), `Poppins` (font family), `2px` (dimensions), `Underline` (text decoration), and so on.
- **Semantic:** These use purpose-based naming so everyone knows exactly where to apply them. Examples include tokens such as `Heading1`, `color.action.default`, `border-radius.none`, and so on.
- **Component:** These are specific to individual components, when needed. Examples include tokens such as `button.primary.border-radius.default`.

To begin, click on **+ New Set** and create a **Core** set.

After creating it, you should notice a new blue bubble at the bottom of the Token Studio plugin. This icon indicates that there are unsynchronized changes that haven't been pushed to GitHub yet, which is expected since we just created a new token set.

Figure 6.12 – Indicator of new unsync changes

Creation of design tokens

Let's create our first design token in the new **Core** set. We'll start with colors because they're easier to understand:

1. Click on the + icon next to **Color**.

2. You need to add a name. It's important to understand how you can nest tokens. You have two options:

    -   Use just the name of the token, for example, `Primary500`.
    -   Use a group structure that will nest tokens, for example, `Red/500`. If you include a slash (/) in your token name, Token Studio will automatically create a group. This grouping is one of the most important structural decisions you'll make to keep everything properly organized and easy to find.

3. Add values. This is up to you—simply add a hex code for your color.

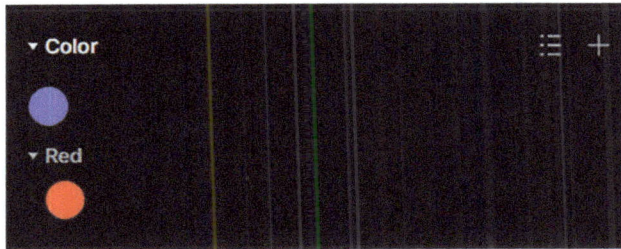

Figure 6.13 – Your first two color tokens

Congratulations! You've now created your first design tokens. The preceding figure illustrates what your tokens should look like at this stage.

Creation of alias (semantic) tokens

For better usability, you need to create semantic tokens, because knowing where to use tokens such as `Primary500` or `Red/500` isn't always intuitive. Let's create some semantic tokens:

1. Start with a new token set. Click on **+ New Set** and create a **Semantic** set. This will be empty initially since all your existing tokens are in the **Core** set.
2. Let's create new color tokens in the semantic set. Click on the + icon next to **Color**.
3. We'll use semantic token names that reference our `Red/500` token. Here are two examples that will use the same core token as a reference:

    -   `text/error`: For error messages in our design
    -   `background/discount`: For discount badges in our design

    Notice how two different use cases can reference the same core token.

4. In the **Value** field, instead of adding another hex code, we'll connect it to the core tokens we created earlier. Click on the little arrow next to the input field and select the `Red/500` token.

Repeat this process for the next semantic token.

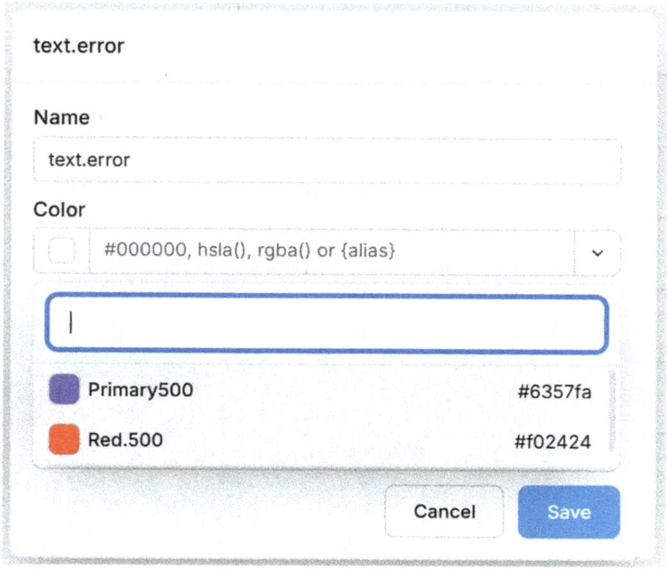

Figure 6.14 – Reference tokens selection

5.   When you select your desired design token, you will see the token name in brackets.

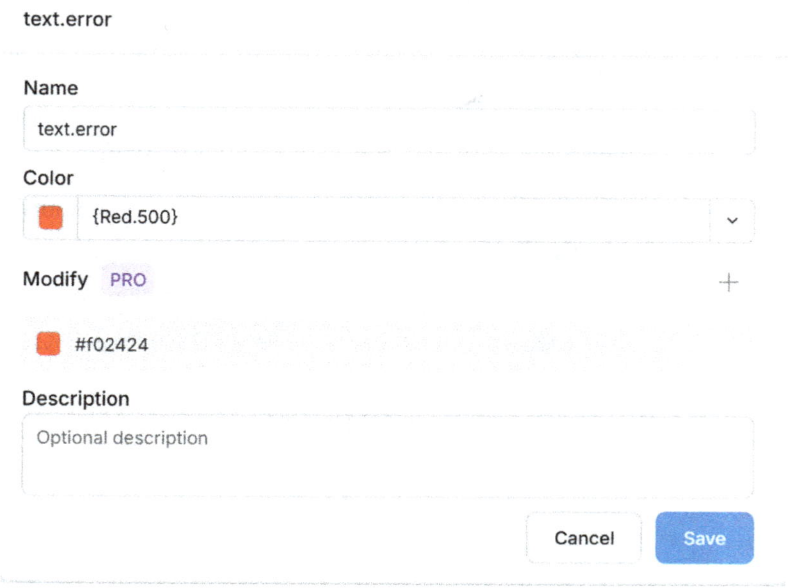

Figure 6.15 – Showcase of selected reference token

Your sets should now look like the following figure:

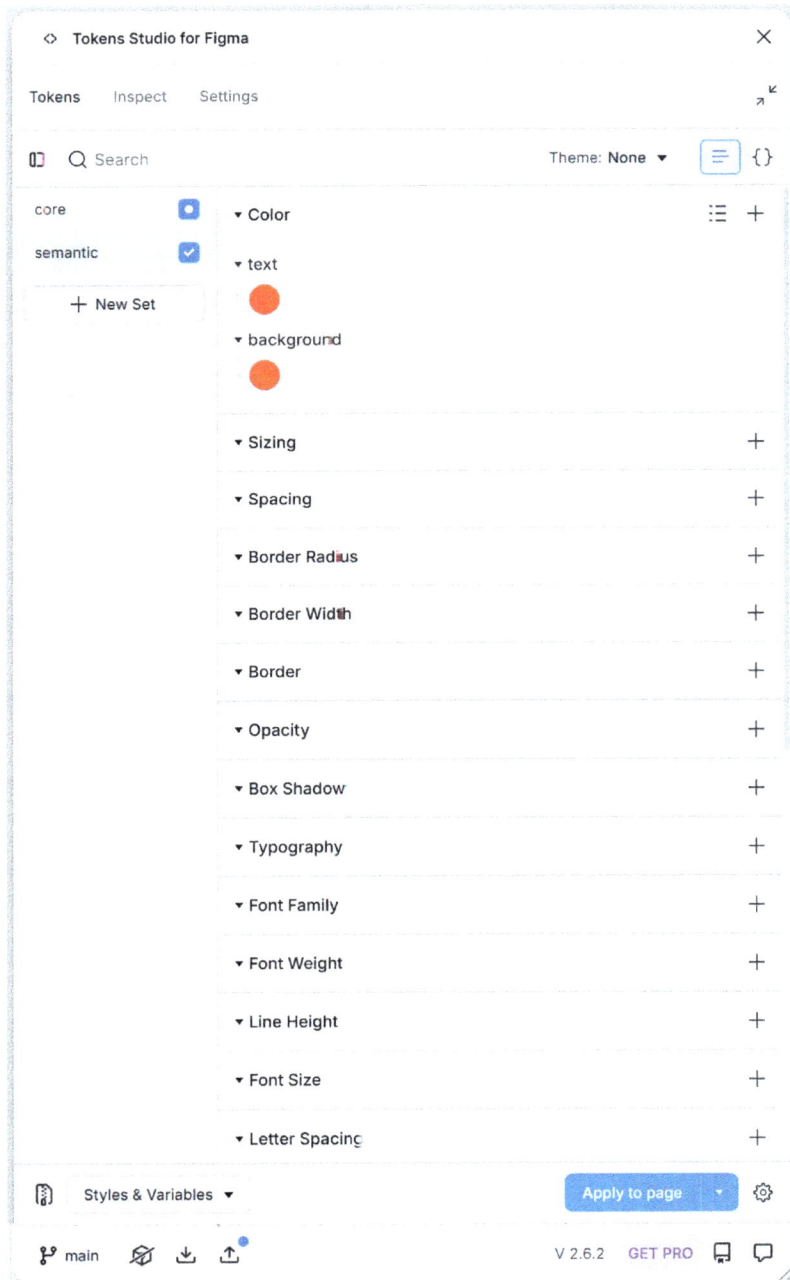

Figure 6.16 – Token Studio list of tokens

Why should you use alias tokens? The power becomes clear when you need to make changes. If you update the reference token (Red/500), the change automatically propagates to every alias token connected to it. This means you can update a single core token and have the change reflected across your entire design system instantly.

Applying design tokens to your design

Now that we've created our semantic tokens, let's put them to use. Here's how to apply these tokens to your Figma designs. The process is the same for any token type, though each type can only be applied to appropriate properties—you can't apply a color token to font-size or a pixel-based token to a color property.

For beginners, Token Studio offers a more familiar approach: you can export your tokens as native Figma variables or styles. This means you can apply them using Figma's standard interface instead of learning about the plugin-based method. To do this, look for the export options in Token Studio's settings, which will create native Figma elements that you can use just like any other variables or styles in your workflow.

However, if you prefer to work directly with Token Studio or want to see the tokens in action immediately, here's the plugin-based application process:

1. Create a simple element in Figma to apply the background/discount token to. A basic rectangle will work perfectly.

2. With your element selected in the Figma design file, simply click on the token in Token Studio, and it will be applied. Color tokens are applied to the most common property by default:

   - **Fill** (default option)
   - **Border**

3. If you want to use this token for a border instead of a fill, right-click on the token in Token Studio (or two-finger click on a touchpad). This will display all available application options beyond the default.

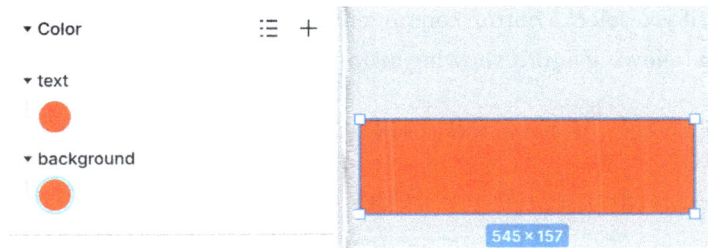

Figure 6.17 – Applying a design token

When you apply a token, you'll notice a blue border around the element, as shown in the preceding figure. This visual indicator helps you identify which elements have tokens applied to them.

Using the Inspect tab

The **Inspect** tab is a powerful feature for quality control. Here, you can see all design tokens applied to any selected element. You can select an individual element, a group, or an entire component to view all applied tokens at once.

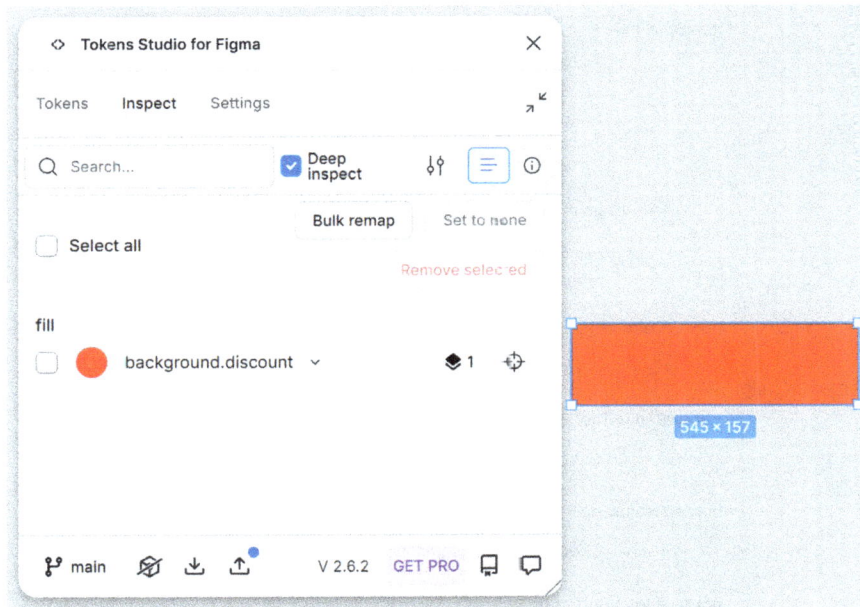

Figure 6.18 – The Inspect panel in Token Studio

For example, if you select a button component from our Dotidot design system, you'll see something like the following figure, showing all tokens applied to various properties of the button.

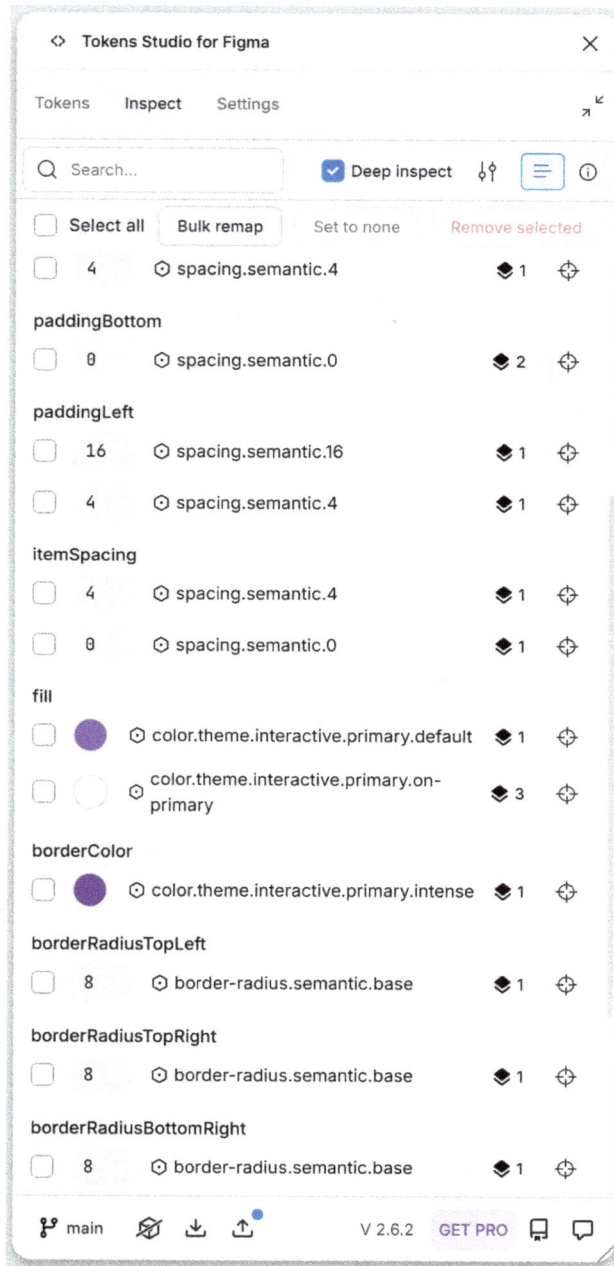

Figure 6.19 – The Inspect panel in Token Studio on the button element

This tab is invaluable for checking components before publishing to ensure everything is applied correctly. It helps you catch inconsistencies or missing token applications that might otherwise go unnoticed.

Implementing Figma variables

After exploring Token Studio, let's look at Figma's native approach to design tokens: Figma variables. As I mentioned earlier, this approach might be preferable if you're building a smaller design system that will primarily live within Figma. It's worth noting that variables now support better dev mode integration than when initially launched, and will most likely keep improving, making them increasingly valuable for design-to-development workflows. Let me guide you through the process of setting up and using Figma variables.

First steps with variables

Unlike Token Studio, Figma variables are built directly into Figma, so you don't need to use any plugins to get started. Here's how to begin:

1. Open your Figma file where you want to implement variables.
2. In the right sidebar, you should see a tab for **Variables**. Click on it to open the **Variables** panel.

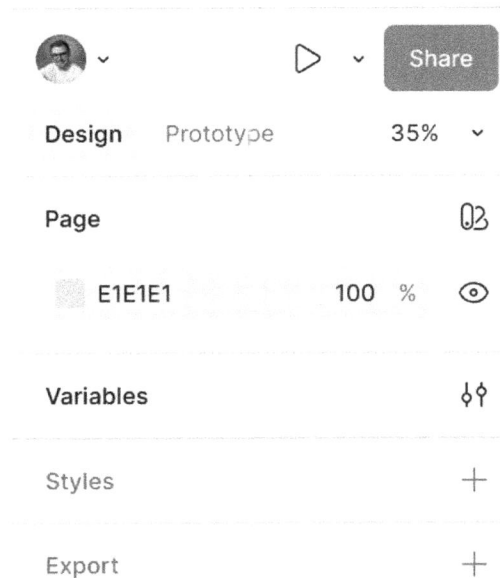

Figure 6.20 – Right sidebar in Figma

3. If this is your first time using variables in this file, you'll see an empty state with a prompt to create your first variable collection.

Variables in Figma are organized into collections, which are similar to the "sets" we created in Token Studio. These collections help you categorize your variables logically.

If you want to visualize your variables in a different way or need help managing them, check out the **Variable Inspector** plugin by *Mr. Biscuits* (`https://www.figma.com/community/plugin/1457362132545070106`), which provides an alternative interface for working with Figma variables.

Creating your first variable and collection

Let's create our first collection following the same structure we used in Token Studio. Unfortunately, Figma's workflow is slightly different—you can't start with empty collections, so you need to create your first variable first and then work with the collection:

1. Click on + **Create variable** and select **Color** as the type.
2. Name it `Red/500` and add your desired hex value.
3. You'll notice Figma automatically creates a collection called **Collection 1** in the top-left corner of the **Variables** panel. Click on the three dots next to it and select **Rename** to change it to `Core`.

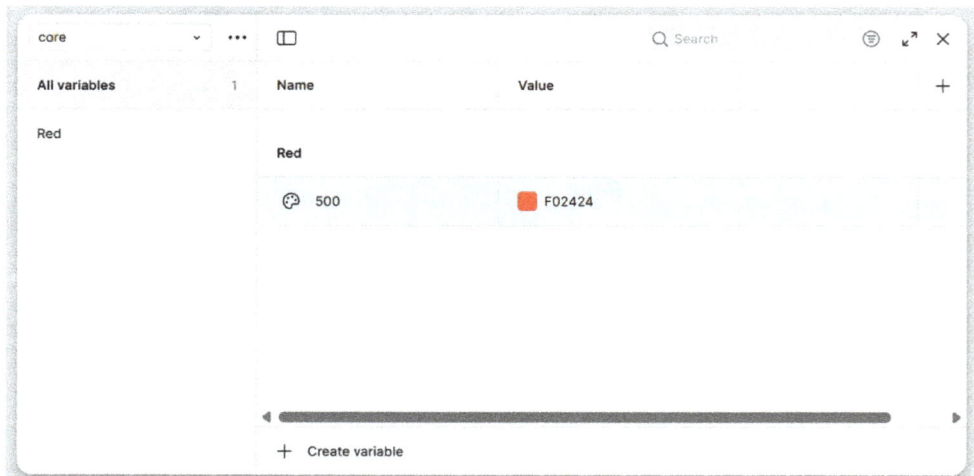

Figure 6.21 – Figma variables collection

You should now see a structure similar to what we created in Token Studio, as shown in the preceding figure. This core collection will hold all your primitive values, such as colors, spacing, and typography variables.

If you want to practice working with variables before implementing them in your own project, check out Figma's official variables playground in the community: `https://www.figma.com/community/file/1234936397107899445`.

Creating semantic variables

Now that we have our core variables, let's create semantic variables that reference them. In Figma, we'll need to create a new collection for these:

1. Click on the three dots next to your **Core** collection name and select **Create collection**.

2. Figma will automatically create a new collection with a default name such as **Collection**. Click on the three dots next to this new collection and select **Rename** to change it to `Semantic`.

3. With your **Semantic** collection selected, click on **+ Create variable**.

4. Choose the appropriate type (**Color**, in this case).

5. Create two variables with semantic names that clearly describe their usage:

   • `text/error`: For error messages in your design
   • `background/discount`: For discount badges in your design

6. Instead of entering a direct value, click on the color selector and then **Libraries**. Here you should see our already created core variables, such as **Red/500**. Select this variable to create an alias connection. Now, your new `text/error` variable is connected to the `Red/500` core variable.

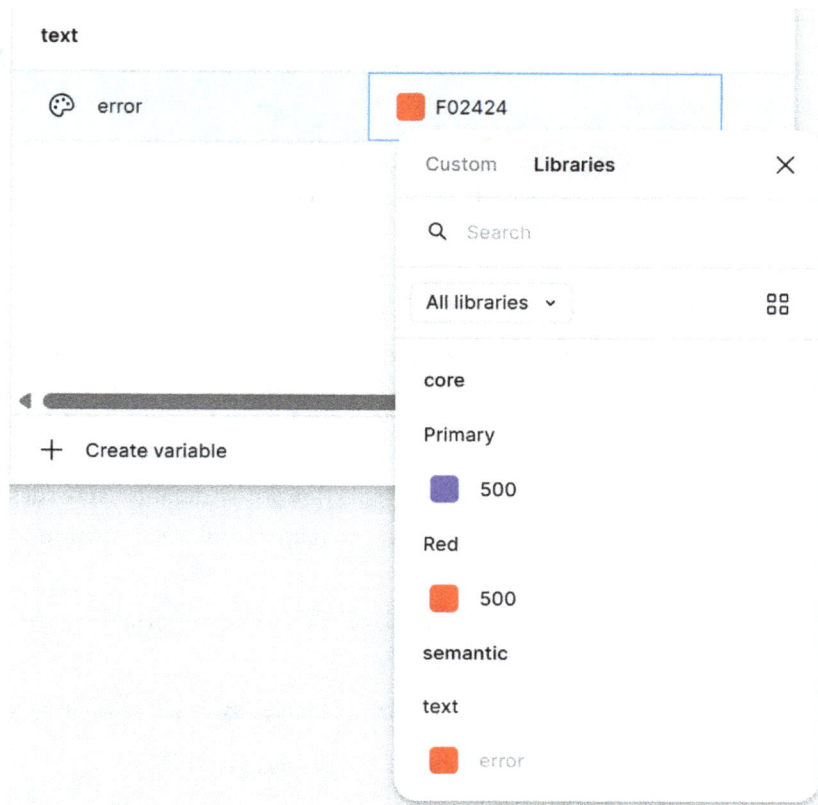

Figure 6.22 – Selecting an alias connection in Figma variables

The power of this approach is similar to what we saw in Token Studio—changes to core variables will automatically propagate to all semantic variables that reference them.

Why should you use alias variables? The power becomes clear when you need to make changes. If you update the reference variable (Red/500), the change automatically propagates to every alias variable connected to it. This means you can update a single core variable and have the change reflected across your entire design system instantly.

Variable constraints and scoping

One powerful feature unique to Figma variables is the ability to set constraints on how variables can be used. This helps maintain design system integrity by preventing misuse of tokens.

When creating or editing a variable, you can set scoping constraints that determine where the variable can be applied:

- For color variables:

    - **Fill**: Can be used as background colors, shape fills

    - **Frame**: Can be used for frame backgrounds

    - **Shape**: Can be used for shape elements

    - **Text**: Can be used for text color

    - **Stroke**: Can be used for borders and outlines

    - **Effects**: Can be used for drop shadows and other effects

- For number variables:

    - **Corner radius**: For border radius values

    - **Width and height**: For element dimensions

    - **Gap (Auto layout)**: For spacing between elements in auto layout

    - **Text content**: For general text-related values

    - **Stroke**: For stroke width

    - **Layer opacity**: For transparency values

    - **Effects**: For effect-related values

- Typography-specific constraints:

    - **Font weight**: For font weight values

    - **Font size**: For font size values

    - **Line height**: For line height values

    - **Letter spacing**: For letter spacing values

    - **Paragraph spacing**: For spacing between paragraphs

    - **Paragraph indent**: For paragraph indentation

Why use constraints?

Constraints prevent common mistakes, such as accidentally using a font-size variable for spacing or applying a border color to text. This is especially valuable in larger teams where multiple designers work with the same variable system.

For example, you might create a number variable called typography/heading/large and constrain it to **Text content** only. This ensures it can only be used for font sizes and related typography properties, preventing someone from accidentally using it for spacing or dimensions.

This scoping feature is one advantage that Figma variables have over Token Studio, where such constraints aren't available. It adds an extra layer of protection for your design system's consistency.

Organizing collections for modes

When planning your variable structure, consider how you'll use modes. Different types of variables often need different mode structures, which means you might want to organize them into separate collections:

- **Colors collection**: You might create light/dark modes to handle theming:
    - **Light mode**: text/primary = dark gray
    - **Dark mode**: text/primary = light gray
- **Spacing collection**: You might create mobile/desktop modes for responsive design:
    - **Mobile mode**: spacing/large = 16px
    - **Desktop mode**: spacing/large = 24px

By separating colors and spacing into different collections, each can have its own relevant modes without forcing unnecessary complexity. You don't want to create light/dark modes for spacing values that don't change between themes, just as you don't need mobile/desktop modes for colors that stay the same across screen sizes.

This approach keeps your variable system clean and logical, with each collection focused on its specific use case and mode requirements.

Applying variables to designs

Applying variables to your designs in Figma is straightforward:

1. Select an element in your design.
2. In the property panel on the right, look for the property you want to apply a variable to (such as **Fill**).
3. Click on the color selector and switch to **Libraries**.
4. Here, you can see all of your variables and styles. The dropdown isn't the most UX-friendly, so be careful with your selection—it's easy to misclick.

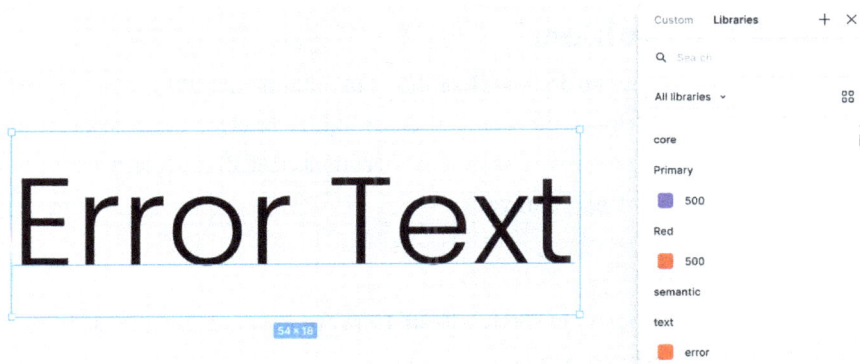

Figure 6.23 – Styles and variables selection panel in Figma

5. Select the appropriate variable from the list.

Your element will now use the variable value, and you'll see the variable name in the input where you usually see the hex code of the color.

Variables versus styles

You might wonder how variables relate to Figma's existing styles (color styles, text styles, etc.). While they serve similar purposes, variables offer more flexibility:

- Variables can be referenced by other variables, creating a hierarchy
- Variables support different modes for theming
- Variables can be used for more properties than styles can
- Variables can store more types of data (such as numbers and Booleans)

That said, styles are still useful for certain cases, particularly for text styles that combine multiple properties.

Version controlling design tokens with GitHub or GitLab

A significant advantage of using Token Studio with GitHub is that GitHub is built for developer needs, with excellent versioning capabilities built right in. This "simple" feature becomes invaluable when working with larger design systems. While you can use Figma's native versioning features, as I mentioned in *Chapter 1*, it's not ideal for managing token changes specifically.

What's the problem?

As design systems grow, so does the likelihood of making mistakes. When working with hundreds of tokens across multiple collections, the possibility of error increases significantly. Having an easy solution to revert to previous versions becomes crucial, especially when changes could affect products across an entire organization.

How to fix it

You can leverage the power of GitHub itself. Here are the main benefits of using GitHub for version controlling your design tokens:

- **Comprehensive history tracking**: Every commit (push from Token Studio to GitHub) creates a record in the history, allowing you to see exactly what changed and when.

Figure 6.24 – Commits history in GitHub

- **Visual change comparisons:** You can see all changes in one simple view for quick reference, with additions highlighted in green and deletions in red.

- **Contributor tracking:** GitHub automatically tracks who made which changes, providing greater visibility when multiple people work on the same design system.

If you need to check a previous version, you can access it with just a few clicks from the history. You can also download the file and import it back into Token Studio for better testing before deciding whether to roll back to that version. This workflow gives you a safety net that encourages experimentation while minimizing risk.

Maintaining token documentation for cross-team consistency

Documentation isn't the most fun part of our job, but it's necessary for success. Let me share a few tips on how you can effectively manage documentation to ensure consistency for collaboration between designers and developers.

What's the problem?

When you're designing something and spending dozens of hours in a complex web of design tokens, it's easy to think of certain decisions as "obvious." But remember that many people will encounter your design system for the first time and face a large, potentially intimidating structure. Proper documentation isn't only for developers—it's crucial for your fellow designers as well.

Without clear documentation, your carefully crafted token system may go unused or be applied inconsistently. New team members might struggle to understand the rationale behind certain tokens, leading to the creation of duplicate tokens or inconsistent application across projects.

How to fix it

You have multiple ways to improve your documentation and information transfer. Here are some tips to consider. Remember, even small steps will make a big impact, so start with something manageable.

Show them visually

Design tokens may live in Token Studio or Figma variables, but designers and developers work in the canvas in Figma. Make your tokens visible:

- For colors, create frames where each color is displayed
- For dimensions, show them visually so everyone can see the sequence
- For typography, display text examples using each typography token

EXAMPLE	FONT FAMILY	FONT WEIGHT	LINE HEIGHT	FONT SIZE	LETTER SPACING
Display 4XL	Poppins	Semi-Bold	120%	32	0
Display 3XL	Poppins	Semi-Bold	120%	22	0
Display 2XL	Poppins	Semi-Bold	120%	18	0
Display XL	Poppins	Semi-Bold	120%	16	0
Display LG	Poppins	Semi-Bold	120%	14	0
Display MD	Poppins	Semi-Bold	120%	12	0
Display SM	Poppins	Semi-Bold	120%	10	0
DISPLAY XS	Poppins	Semi-Bold	120%	10	2px

Figure 6.25 – Typography documentation in Figma

Visual representation creates an immediate understanding that text descriptions alone can't achieve.

Proper categorization

This might seem obvious, but proper categorization is key. Don't leave all your design tokens on one page or frame. Display them across multiple pages with clear names that will help your team find them quickly. Consider organizing by the following:

- Token type (colors, spacing, and typography)
- Usage domain (global or component-specific)
- Product area (if you have multiple products)

Use consistent vocabulary

I've mentioned this multiple times, but it bears repeating: use the same vocabulary across design and development. This will save you countless hours and prevent many mistakes. When designers say "spacing/medium" and developers say "gap-md," confusion inevitably follows.

Proper naming

Consistent naming is crucial for semantic tokens and documentation. Every token's purpose should be obvious from its name. Choose naming conventions that clearly indicate the following:

- What the token is (color, spacing, etc.)
- Where it should be used (background, text, etc.)

- Any variants or states (default, hover, etc.)

Token descriptions

For large design token sets, names alone aren't enough—you'll need additional descriptions. Both Token Studio and Figma variables support descriptions, making it easier to document the purpose and usage of each token.

In Token Studio, you can write descriptions directly into the design token itself. In Figma variables, you can add descriptions by right-clicking on a variable and selecting **Edit variable**—you'll find a description field where you can document the token's purpose and usage guidelines.

Connected descriptions in design

Token Studio has an amazing feature that allows you to connect token descriptions directly to text elements in Figma. When you update the description, it automatically updates everywhere. Here's how to set it up:

1. Create an empty text element on your canvas.
2. Make sure your design token has a description. If not, edit the token and add one.

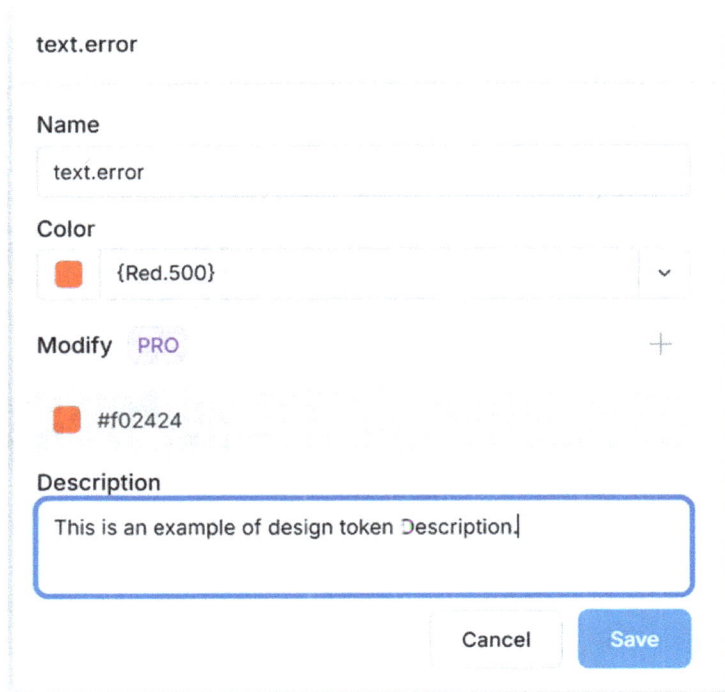

Figure 6.26 – Design token detail in Token Studio

3. Right-click on the design token you want to describe.

4. Select **Documentation Tokens**.

5. Choose **Description**.

That's it—your text is now automatically synchronized. When you change the description in the token, it updates in Figma as well. This also works for token names and values.

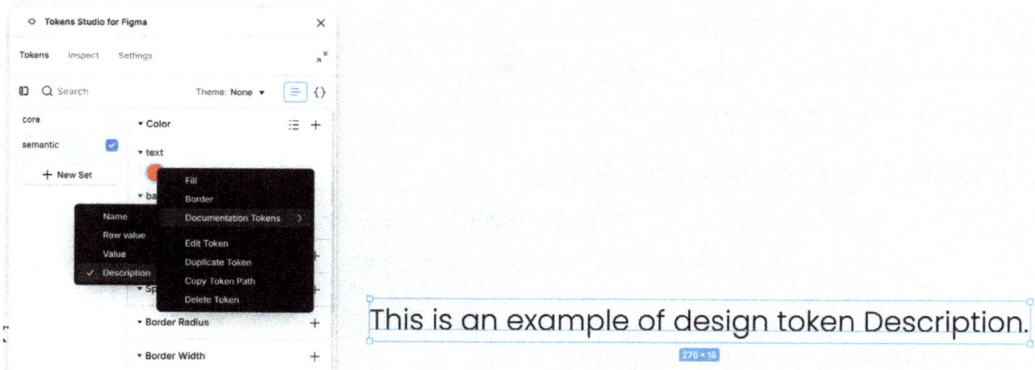

Figure 6.27 – Applying token documentation on a text element in Figma

What's particularly powerful is that this syncing works with your GitHub repository, too. Developers can add or modify descriptions in GitHub, and with your next pull (synchronization from GitHub), those changes will appear in your Figma file. This creates a true two-way documentation system that keeps everyone aligned.

7

Building Accessible Design Systems

Accessibility has become a critical topic for designers in recent years. A few years ago, I didn't give it much thought—it seemed like a complex, distant subject with limited resources available. However, when the **European Accessibility Act (EAA)** was approved, the landscape changed dramatically. This legislation, which came into force in June 2025, requires companies across the EU to make their digital products and services accessible to people with disabilities. The EAA applies to companies with 10 or more employees and annual revenue above €2 million (micro-enterprises with fewer than 10 employees and under €2 million annual turnover are exempt). Importantly, this also affects non-EU companies that sell products or provide services to European consumers through e-commerce, digital platforms, or online services. The consequences for non-compliance include significant fines and potential exclusion from the European market, making accessibility not just a moral imperative but a business necessity. Accessibility suddenly became a much broader conversation among designers, which is a positive shift. During this time, I discovered how much I didn't know and how my perspective on the topic had been misguided.

In this chapter, I want to share these insights with you—both from the perspective of a designer and a C-level manager—to help you build more accessible products. I'm still learning in this field every day, and I believe all of us as designers are continually learning because accessibility isn't just about design—it's about communicating accessibility principles across companies and to management.

In this chapter, we'll explore the following:

- Understanding the importance of accessibility in design
- Creating components with proper color contrast ratios
- Designing for keyboard accessibility and navigation
- Ensuring screen reader compatibility in your design system
- Documenting accessibility features in Figma
- Integrating WCAG standards into your design process
- Testing and validating accessibility across platforms

Let's start with the first topic.

Understanding the importance of accessibility in design

As I mentioned, I made the mistake of not taking accessibility seriously because it seemed distant from my everyday experience. I don't have anyone in my close circle with a disability, so I didn't think much about it—and this was the first problem. Accessibility isn't only about permanent disabilities, which is what I initially associated with the topic. It also encompasses temporary conditions (such as a broken arm) and situational limitations (bright sunlight, working with gloves, using a phone with one hand while carrying coffee or groceries, or my personal favorite— sitting on a bumpy public transit ride). Even watching videos in a noisy environment or without headphones shows how captions benefit everyone, not just people with hearing impairments.

What's the problem?

Many managers view accessibility as a marginal topic that exists primarily because of regulations. In start-up environments especially, you need to make tough decisions every day to pare products down to their **Minimum Viable Product** (**MVP**), and accessibility often takes a back seat. However, this approach is problematic because accessibility isn't binary—it's a scale. It's not simply a matter of "we have it" or "we don't." Rather, it's about how comprehensively we address it, and you can build on your approach incrementally.

How to fix it

I want to describe the two worlds I inhabit: the design world and the C-level management world. In both environments, you need to use different arguments to advocate for accessibility. Perhaps you work in an organization where accessibility has been a priority from day one—if so, you're fortunate and might be able to skip this chapter. However, from my experience, this is rare, especially in smaller or mid-sized companies. In many workplaces, the primary motivation has traditionally been fear of legal penalties, but this is gradually changing. I'm seeing a shift toward a genuine understanding of why accessibility matters and how it makes our products better for everyone. This evolution in thinking is crucial for meaningful progress.

Management perspective

I'll start with this one because it's straightforward. According to a Forrester study, approximately 1 billion people worldwide have some form of disability (`https://www.forrester.com/blogs/the-billion-customer-digital-accessibility-opportunity/`). That's an enormous market that most managers overlook because they make the same mistake I did—they think only about the small group of people with the most visible disabilities and don't understand the range of individuals included in this demographic. The Forrester study references $1.2 trillion in annual disposable income. I wish I could tell you that other arguments are equally compelling, but numbers speak volumes here. Accessibility isn't a niche concern—it's about including a vast user base that you may be inadvertently ignoring.

Designer perspective

As designers, we can do a lot in our day-to-day work without investing significantly more time. Sometimes, all you need is a little knowledge about the topic to make a substantial difference that you might not even realize. I encourage you to invest time in learning—watch videos, read articles, listen to podcasts, or simply think about accessibility regularly. Remember, it's a scale, and some changes can be implemented quickly. For example, ensuring your colors have good contrast won't take much time, while implementing full descriptions for screen readers might require more effort. You can choose where to start and begin with small changes that can make a meaningful difference.

Creating components with proper color contrast ratios

Design systems are powerful tools for promoting accessibility adoption across your company. Let's start with one of the most straightforward "quick fixes"—color contrast. This issue has an enormous impact even beyond traditional accessibility conversations. I'd venture to say that proper contrast is generally addressed in most products because insufficient contrast significantly impacts conversion rates. Nevertheless, let's explore this topic more deeply.

What's the problem?

Poor color contrast creates barriers for many users, not just those with diagnosed visual impairments. When text blends too closely with its background, it becomes difficult or impossible to read, leading to user frustration and potential abandonment of your product. When I was starting in design, many designers chose colors based purely on aesthetic preferences without considering their functional impact on readability. Thankfully, the situation is much better now, with greater awareness around contrast requirements and their importance.

This issue extends beyond obvious cases such as light gray text on white backgrounds. Even seemingly clear color combinations can fail to meet accessibility standards when measured objectively. Additionally, what appears legible on your high-end monitor might be nearly invisible on other devices or in different lighting conditions. When I was actively designing websites and apps, I always kept reference devices next to me. For desktop designs, I had the cheapest Full HD monitor plugged in alongside my main display. For mobile apps, I kept a budget Android phone and an iPhone SE nearby to always check the "reality" of my designs—not just how they looked on my high-end device, where everything appears amazing because the device cost a few thousand dollars. This simple practice helped me catch contrast issues that would have otherwise slipped through, especially with subtle color combinations that might be perfectly visible on a premium device but barely distinguishable on average consumer devices.

Consider everyday scenarios that affect everyone: working in bright office lighting or outdoors can wash out screens, while battery saver mode makes displays dimmer to conserve power. These common situations mean that good contrast benefits all users, not just those with visual impairments.

How to fix it

Adequate contrast between text (or icons) and background is vital so that users with low vision or color vision deficiencies can read content easily. The WCAG guidelines recommend a contrast ratio of at least **4.5:1 for regular body text** and **3:1 for large text** (typically 18px+ or bold 14px+), as these thresholds significantly improve readability.

Figma Color Contrast Checker

In the past, we had to rely on plugins to check contrast ratios. I mentioned Stark in *Chapter 2*, but fortunately, one of the releases in 2025 introduced this feature natively within Figma's color palette.

Every element with color can be automatically checked against its background element. For example, text is checked against its parent frame. Without a frame, it will be checked against the canvas color.

Here's how to use this feature:

1. Click on the **Check color contrast** option on the right side of the color picker.
2. This tab will display a different color picker where you'll immediately see the contrast ratio and can adjust various settings.
3. The main settings you can modify are based on context (large text, normal text, graphics) and your target compliance level (AA or AAA). For **EAA** compliance, you need to meet at least the AA standard.
4. Based on these settings, you'll see whether your color choice follows WCAG guidelines.

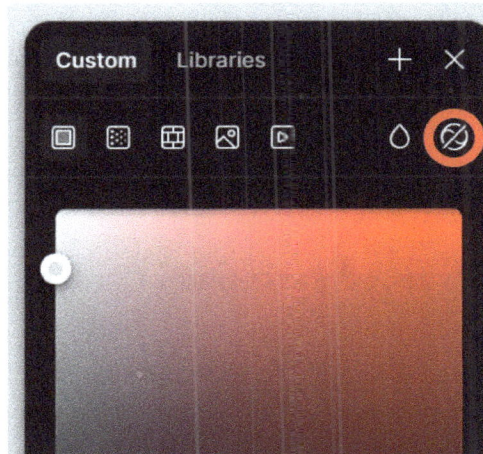

Figure 7.1 – Figma Contrast Checker

I recommend building a small testing environment (with typical screens where you'll use these tokens) alongside your design system. This allows you to quickly see many "real" cases where tokens will be used together. While Figma's native contrast checker is perfect when you're creating design tokens and working on individual components, if you want to audit a whole project or design system, use **Stark**. The Stark plugin can do much more than just contrast checking and offers bulk auditing capabilities that can scan entire design files, checking multiple accessibility issues across all your components at once.

Multiple design token sets/modes

One of the great use cases for Tokens Studio is that you can build multiple Token Sets. Figma variables also support multiple modes, but you're limited to 4 (Professional and Organization pricing plans) or 40 (Enterprise plan). Given this limitation, I haven't encountered anyone using modes for this purpose, so I'll focus on Token Sets.

You can create different Token Sets that help you manage contrast ratios. For example, your baseline goal might be to meet AA standards, but you can easily build a new token set aimed at AAA compliance and give users the option to switch to it in their app settings. I found this approach in one of my favorite games, Star Wars Battlefront II. You can easily change the design Token Set to be more inclusive.

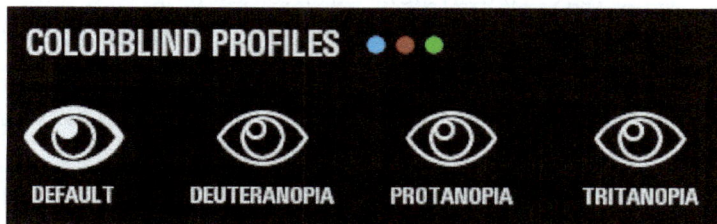

Figure 7.2 – Star Wars Battlefront II settings

If you want to learn more about using Token Studio, check out *Chapter 6*, where we covered this topic in detail.

Looking ahead—Advanced Perceptual Contrast Algorithm (APCA)

If you're reading this after mid-2025, you might want to explore **APCA** as well. The **Advanced Perceptual Contrast Algorithm** is a new method for calculating contrast that's expected to be part of WCAG 3.0. Unlike WCAG 2.1's simple ratio system, APCA takes into account font size and font weight, and provides perceptually accurate contrast measurements across all color ranges.

Right now, WCAG 2.1 AA remains the standard that regulations such as the EEA reference, so stick with those guidelines for compliance. However, APCA offers more accurate readability predictions and can help you make better color choices, especially for mid-range colors where WCAG 2.1 sometimes falls short. You can experiment with APCA at https://apcacontrast.com/ to see how it compares to traditional contrast checking and get a sense of what the future of accessible color contrast might look like.

Designing for keyboard accessibility and navigation

Our designs are mainly built around mouse/trackpad interaction or touch on phones, but not everyone can operate these input methods. If you've had a broken arm in the past, you know exactly what I mean. If not, try using your favorite website without a mouse and you'll quickly see how hard or easy it can be (depending on the team's approach to accessibility). Even common situations, such as a laptop trackpad not working or using a computer at a small standing desk setup where reaching for a mouse is inconvenient, show how keyboard navigation benefits everyone, not just people with motor impairments.

What's the problem?

Not everyone can operate a mouse or a touch interface. What's interesting is that this limitation can be very easily simulated by you, allowing you to see firsthand how your product performs. A good rule of thumb is: *if an action can be done with a mouse, it **must** be doable with a keyboard as well*, and any interactive element should receive a visible focus indicator when navigated via keyboard. There can be significant problems with tab ordering that we'll explain.

How to fix it

I want to focus on three main areas that you can improve:

- Focus states
- Movement order
- Proper file handoff

Focus states

First, the easiest things to check are clear focus states for buttons, links, form fields, and so on. These should use an outline or highlight that meets contrast guidelines, making them easy to spot. You can test this on any website by pressing the *Tab* key and observing how elements respond.

The good news is that most browsers have focus states built in, but sometimes you'll want to customize them. If you do, be extra careful. The default color is light blue, which isn't always the best option. Consider using a different color with better contrast—for example, a thick yellow outline can work much better (you can see this approach in action in the UK Government Design System: `https://design-system.service.gov.uk/get-started/focus-states/`).

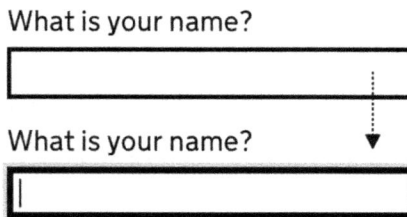

What is your name?

What is your name?

Figure 7.3 – Custom focus state from UK Government Design System

Always check the contrast of your custom focus states if you need to change the default ones.

Movement order

Try visiting your favorite website and pressing the *Tab* key repeatedly. You should move through the page from left to right and top to bottom on English-language websites, and you should be able to reach all needed elements. This tab order is crucial because it directly affects usability, and it's entirely within your control.

A common problem I've observed on many websites involves cookie consent banners that are placed at the bottom of the code (and thus the tab order). This forces users who navigate by keyboard to tab through the entire page before they can interact with this essential element, which is incredibly frustrating. Try testing for this issue on various websites—it's more common than you might think.

Tab order can become particularly challenging when you add certain popups (modals) or complex vertical hierarchies to your site. Always test the production code before releasing it. But how do you incorporate tab order into your design process? Let's explore that now.

Proper file handoff

If we focus on how to improve Figma files and avoid leaving tab order to chance or the development team's discretion, I want to tell you about an amazing plugin supported by Microsoft: A11y - Focus Order (`https://www.figma.com/community/plugin/731310036968334777/a11y-focus-order`). This plugin helps you add annotations to your designs that show developers your intended tab order for building the final product.

I created a simple demonstration app using Figma's First Draft AI feature (don't focus on the design quality). This plugin helps you build automatic documentation for developers in seconds. Here's how it works:

1. Open the plugin and select the frame you want to document (annotate).
2. Select elements in the frame and click **Add**.
3. Choose the appropriate component type based on guidelines (W3C for web, iOS, or Android) and add any necessary additional information, such as descriptions.
4. The plugin quickly creates new layers with numbered references indicating your intended tab order, along with descriptions next to the design.

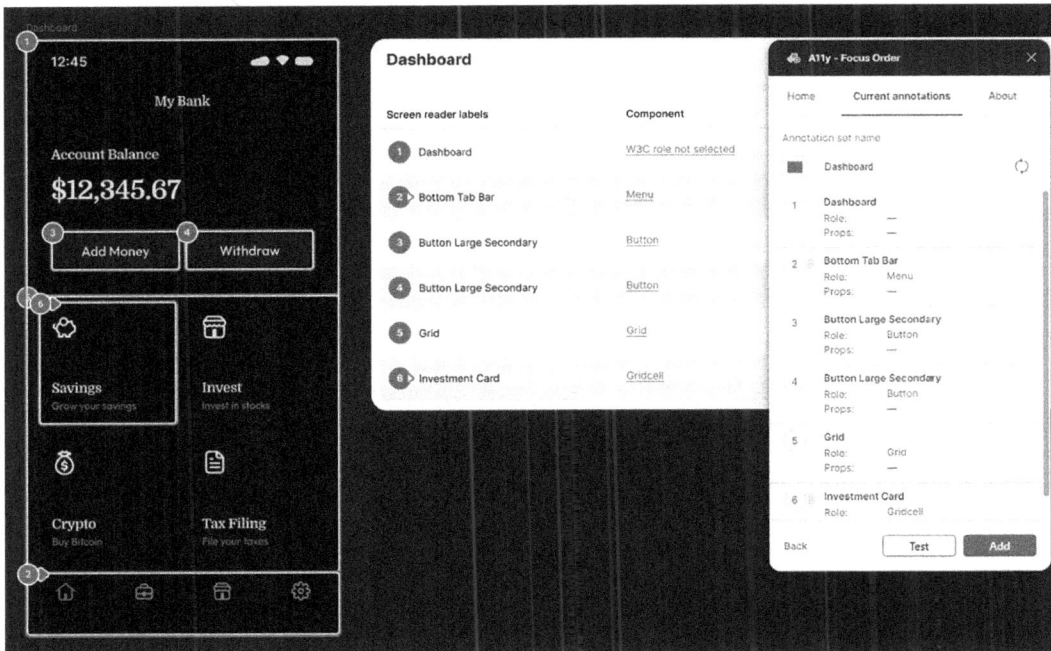

Figure 7.4 – Focus order handoff via A11y plugin

This process is super fast, and you can easily change the order by simply dragging items up and down—the documentation updates automatically. For complex layouts, such as sites with navigation at the bottom of the screen (as in my example), spend an afternoon experimenting with the plugin to make developers' jobs much easier.

You can also include additional information about keyboard navigation, such as using arrow keys for carousels or keyboard shortcuts. For example, you might note that the *Esc* key should close modals and the *Enter* key should select items in drop-down menus.

Additional plugin for comprehensive accessibility annotations

One of my beta readers also recommended the Include Accessibility Annotations plugin (`https://www.figma.com/community/plugin/1208180794570801545/include-accessibility-annotations`), which offers a more comprehensive approach to accessibility documentation. Built by the accessibility and design teams at eBay, Include provides step-by-step guidance for both web and native annotations.

The plugin includes features such as landmarks, focus grouping, headings, reading order, touch targets, alternative text detection, contrast checking, and even color deficiency simulation. While the A11y - Focus Order plugin excels at tab order documentation, Include covers a broader range of accessibility considerations, making it valuable for teams that want to document accessibility requirements comprehensively across their entire design system.

Ensuring screen reader compatibility in your design system

Screen readers are essential tools for users with visual impairments. Before I dive into this topic, I want to share a small disclaimer: I didn't design specifically for screen readers in my daily work. What I'll share comes from conversations with other designers and my own research. I'd love to tell you that I'm an expert in this area, but in reality, I'm still learning—and I want to be transparent with you from the start.

What's the problem?

Screen readers do exactly what their name suggests—they read content on the screen. But it's not that simple, because they can only work with what you (or mainly developers) provide to them. Without proper structure, meaningful alt text, and semantic markup, screen readers face significant challenges.

You can experience this firsthand by trying a screen reader on any website—the results can be eye-opening. On Windows, use the shortcut *Control + Windows + Enter*, and on macOS, use *Command + F5* to activate the built-in screen readers. Try navigating your own website or a well-built one such as a major news outlet. You'll quickly understand how different the experience can be when content isn't properly structured for accessibility.

How to fix it

Let's focus on practical steps you can include in your design system to help your developers build better experiences for screen reader users. Remember that this work requires active involvement from your development team as well—there are aspects of screen reader compatibility that are beyond what designers can fully address on their own.

Alternative text

First, let's clarify what alt text (alternative text) is: it's the brief description attached to an image or icon that screen readers will read aloud to users who can't see the visual element. Let's check a short list of what to do:

- **Create standardized alt text guidelines**: Build your design system documentation with simple rules such as "describe meaning or function." For example, all close icons should have alt text that begins with "Close [context]" (e.g., "Close settings panel"). Don't start with phrases such as "Icon description" or "Image description" because screen readers will already announce the element type ("image") before reading your alt text, creating redundancy.

- **Include alt text fields in components**: Add dedicated alt text input fields to your component properties in Figma. This serves as a constant reminder for designers to fill them out. How often do you actually add alt text to your designs for developers? Having this built into your components makes it a natural part of the workflow rather than an afterthought.

- **Document icon meanings**: Create a comprehensive library of your icons with their intended meanings in your design system documentation. Developers can reference this when implementing alt text, ensuring consistency across your product.

Semantic structure

Screen readers need "rails" to follow as they navigate content. Your job is to create a clear path through proper semantic structure. While much of this falls to developers during implementation, designers can and should establish guidelines before development begins.

- **Create clear heading hierarchies**: Design your text sections with a logical heading structure using Heading 1 (H1) through Heading 6 (H6). This isn't just about visual differences in size—it provides essential navigation landmarks for screen reader users. A common mistake I've seen is designers using a style named "Heading 1" repeatedly throughout a website simply because it looks appealing. This practice confuses screen readers and harms both accessibility and **SEO** (**Search Engine Optimization**, which affects how well your site ranks in search results).

> There should typically be only one H1 per page, followed by H2s as section headers, and so on.

- **Group related content blocks**: In your designs, visually group related components together and document these relationships. While the final implementation happens in code, your designs can guide developers toward proper grouping. For example, when building forms, keep labels, input fields, and error messages visually connected and indicate in your documentation that they should be grouped semantically in the code.

- **Design with accessibility in mind**: Let's continue with the forms example, where I frequently see a common problem: the use of placeholder text instead of proper labels. This approach fails not just from an accessibility standpoint but from general UX principles as well. Every input field needs a persistent, visible label—placeholders disappear when users start typing, leaving them without context if they get distracted.

- **Use multiple requirement indicators**: For required form fields, use multiple indicators that help all users understand what's mandatory. Relying solely on color (such as red asterisks) isn't sufficient—include text markers such as "(required)" or an asterisk with a legend explaining its meaning. Avoid indicating required fields through only bold text or color differences, as these cues aren't accessible to all users.

- **Prioritize clear text:** While visual elements such as icons and images enhance the experience for sighted users, screen reader users rely entirely on text and alt text. Sometimes we don't invest enough time in writing clear, descriptive text because there's an amazing icon or image that "tells the whole story." This approach excludes users who can't see those visual elements. Make sure your content stands on its own without visual support.

Accessible Rich Internet Applications (ARIA)

ARIA (officially WAI-ARIA) is a W3C specification that adds extra semantics to HTML so assistive technologies—screen readers, braille displays, voice control, switch devices—can understand and interact with complex web UI components.

This is primarily the development team's responsibility and concerns the underlying code structure. I won't go into great depth here, as I mentioned at the beginning of this section that I'm not an expert on this topic. However, it's important to know that these standards exist so you can initiate conversations with your development team about implementing them.

Some basic ARIA concepts that designers should be familiar with include the following:

- **ARIA landmarks:** These define regions of the page (navigation, main content, search, etc.) that help screen reader users navigate more efficiently
- **ARIA states and properties:** These communicate the current state of interactive elements (expanded/collapsed, checked/unchecked, etc.) to assistive technologies
- **ARIA live regions:** These announce dynamic content changes (such as error messages or notifications) to screen reader users without requiring them to navigate to that content

In your design system documentation, you can include recommendations for when and how developers should implement these ARIA attributes based on your components. While you don't need to specify the exact code, you can note which components should have particular ARIA roles or states.

Testing with real screen readers

The most effective way to ensure your designs work well with screen readers is to test them. Encourage both designers and developers to do the following:

- **Learn basic screen reader commands:** Familiarize yourself with the basic navigation commands of at least one screen reader. You can test your website using the built-in screen readers: on Windows, use the shortcut *Control + Windows + Enter*, and on macOS, use *Command + F5*.

- **Test components individually**: Before integrating components into larger designs, test them individually with a screen reader to identify and fix issues early. You can test them in tools such as Storybook before they're distributed to all developers, making it easier to isolate and address accessibility issues at the component level.

By incorporating these practices into your design system, you'll create a foundation for more accessible products that work well with screen readers. Remember that this is an ongoing learning process—even experienced accessibility specialists continue to discover new ways to improve screen reader compatibility.

Documenting accessibility features in Figma

Documentation is a topic we've discussed in many previous chapters, and it's equally relevant here. I'll admit that I've been one of those managers who have sometimes pushed documentation aside as non-critical when facing tight deadlines. In small, stable teams where people rarely leave, this approach might work to some extent. But for larger teams—and especially for accessibility—this simply isn't effective. Accessibility remains a relatively new concept for many designers and developers, and it encompasses numerous considerations that aren't immediately obvious. These details need to be explicitly documented and shared.

What's the problem?

Many design systems thoroughly document components from visual and functional perspectives (how they look and behave in their basic state) but neglect accessibility considerations. This creates a significant gap in understanding how components should be implemented to support all users.

I believe we should include as much documentation as possible directly within Figma, since that's where designers and developers are already working. While there are excellent external documentation tools, such as Czech Supernova (try them out and tell them you heard about them from me), for small to mid-sized projects, Figma itself can be a perfectly adequate documentation hub.

How to fix it

Let's explore several methods you can implement in your process. As always, choose what best suits your team's specific needs—even small changes can make a meaningful difference.

Component documentation

Here are the key strategies for documenting accessibility within your component system:

1. **Leverage component descriptions in Figma:** This often-overlooked feature provides a dedicated space to communicate important information. Use it to explain accessibility considerations specific to each component. For example, for a drop-down menu, you might note **Ensure keyboard navigation with arrow keys and tab focusing. Must be operable with screen readers announcing current selection.**

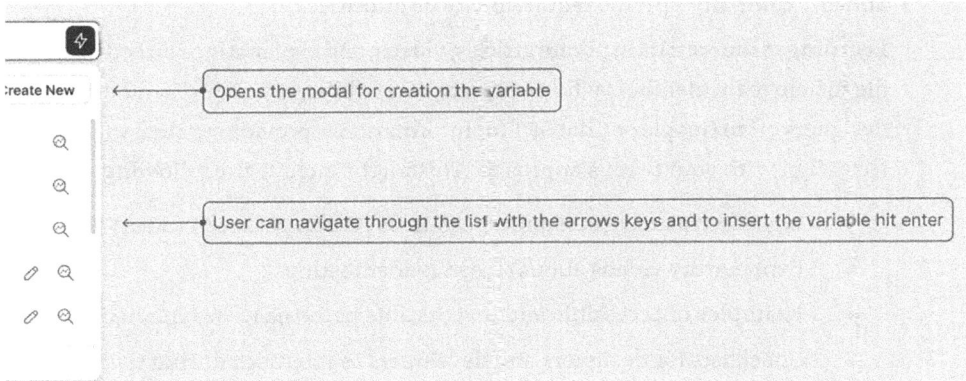

Figure 7.5 – Part of our Dotidot component documentation

2. **Add accessibility sections to component documentation:** When you create documentation templates for components, include a dedicated accessibility section by default. When this section exists but remains empty, it creates a visible reminder that something is incomplete—pushing you and your team to fill it in. If you think, "We'll add this section in the future when we have time," let's be honest—you probably won't. Building it into your documentation structure from the beginning creates accountability.

3. **Document all states, including focus states:** Ensure your component documentation includes every possible state, paying particular attention to focus states for interactive elements. Too often, focus states are treated as an afterthought, but they're essential for keyboard navigation. Document not just how they look, but also the expected behavior (tab order, keyboard shortcuts, etc.).

Dedicated accessibility documentation

Create a dedicated space in your design system for accessibility-specific documentation. By allocating this space upfront, you establish an expectation that it will be filled with valuable information. Here's what to include:

- **Accessibility guidelines**: Develop a comprehensive guide explaining the fundamental principles of accessibility, why it matters for your products, and your team's approach to implementing it. Include specific standards you're following (WCAG 2.1 AA, for example) and any company-specific requirements or priorities.

- **Learning resources**: Incorporate articles, videos, and explanations directly into your Figma file to help team members who are new to accessibility. Don't just send developers or new designers off to Google or ChatGPT for information—provide curated, validated resources that align with your team's approach. This might include the following:

    - Links to trusted accessibility resources (WebAIM, A11Y Project)
    - Explanatory videos about screen reader testing
    - Examples of accessible and inaccessible patterns with explanations
    - Checklists for designers and developers to reference during their work

- **Testing procedures**: Document how your team should test for accessibility, including which tools to use, what to look for, and how to report issues. This creates consistency in your approach to identifying and resolving accessibility problems.

- **Team responsibilities**: Clarify who is responsible for different aspects of accessibility implementation. Is color contrast the designer's responsibility? Who ensures that proper ARIA attributes are implemented? By documenting these expectations, you prevent important considerations from falling through the cracks.

By thoroughly documenting accessibility features directly in Figma, you make it much easier for your team to create consistently accessible products. You also reduce the learning curve for new team members and create a valuable reference that evolves alongside your design system. Remember that good documentation isn't static—update it regularly as you learn more about accessibility best practices and as your components evolve.

Accessibility acceptance criteria in user stories and tickets

One area that many teams overlook is including accessibility requirements directly in their development workflows through user stories and tickets. This bridges the gap between your beautifully documented Figma files and the actual development work.

How to include accessibility in user stories

When writing user stories or creating development tickets, include specific accessibility acceptance criteria alongside your functional requirements. This ensures accessibility isn't treated as an optional add-on but as a core requirement for the feature to be considered complete.

Here are some practical examples of how to structure accessibility acceptance criteria:

For a button component:

- The button must be keyboard accessible (*Tab* to focus, *Enter/Space* to activate)
- The focus state must be visible with a 3:1 contrast ratio against the background
- The button text must have a 4.5:1 contrast ratio in all states
- The screen reader must announce the button's purpose and current state
- The button must include appropriate ARIA attributes if it toggles content

For a form:

- All form fields must have persistent, visible labels
- Required fields must be indicated with both visual and text indicators
- Error messages must be announced to screen readers when they appear
- Form must be completeable using only keyboard navigation
- Field validation must not rely solely on color

For a modal dialog:

- The focus must be trapped within the modal when open
- The *Esc* key must close the modal
- The focus must return to the trigger element when the modal closes
- The modal must be announced to screen readers when it opens
- Background content must be hidden from screen readers while the modal is active

Integration with your workflow

Work with your product managers and developers to establish these accessibility criteria as standard practice. When you hand off designs, reference the specific accessibility requirements in the development tickets. This creates accountability and ensures that accessibility considerations don't get lost in translation from design to development.

You can even create a template or checklist of common accessibility criteria that can be quickly adapted for different types of components or features. This standardizes the process and makes it easier for your team to consistently include accessibility requirements in their planning and development work.

Integrating WCAG standards into your design process

Web Content Accessibility Guidelines (WCAG) are the foundation of accessible design. Unfortunately, they're often viewed as a long and complex checklist of requirements you need to satisfy to make your product "accessible." I want to show you that this checklist approach isn't the best solution and demonstrate how to work with these standards to improve accessibility without creating additional overhead in your workflow.

What's the problem?

WCAG has become the industry standard for measuring accessibility compliance across three main levels (A, AA, AAA). You might remember these from our discussion about color contrast earlier in this chapter. These guidelines should help us design better, more inclusive products, but they can often feel very technical and, let's be honest, quite boring to read through.

The design industry is slowly improving its approach to accessibility, but I'll admit that even I've made this mistake in the past: we'd design something and then check it against WCAG guidelines afterward, trying to "fix" the biggest issues. This retrofit approach isn't ideal or sustainable. It creates more work, often compromises the original design vision, and frequently results in accessibility solutions that feel tacked on rather than thoughtfully integrated.

How to fix it

The key is to integrate WCAG principles into your design process from the beginning, rather than treating them as an afterthought. Here's how to make this integration seamless and effective:

- Start with understanding
- Design tokens are your best friend
- Build WCAG into your components
- Use AI assistants strategically
- Train yourself and your team
- Remember the scale

Start with understanding

Before implementing any workflows, invest time in reading through the design-focused guides available at https://www.w3.org/WAI/tips/designing/ or https://www.wcag.com/designers/. These resources will help shift your perspective on accessibility from a compliance checkbox to a design consideration.

Many of these guidelines will seem like common knowledge—which is actually encouraging! It means you're already thinking about some accessibility principles. However, reading through them systematically helps you internalize the reasoning behind each guideline and recognize opportunities to implement them more consistently.

Design tokens are your best friend

Remember our discussion about design tokens and Figma variables in *Chapter 6*? If this topic is new to you, please review that chapter before continuing here. Design tokens offer one of the most effective ways to bake WCAG compliance into your design system from the ground up.

When you implement WCAG standards directly into your tokens, you solve potential accessibility issues at their source, eliminating the need to revisit and fix them later. Focus on meeting at least AA standards for background-to-foreground color contrast (text on backgrounds). Fortunately, you can now quickly check this directly in Figma using the built-in Figma Contrast Checker we discussed earlier.

Beyond colors, consider typography when creating composite tokens. Proper text spacing and line height are essential for readability. Remember that even you might find yourself in situational limitations where good typography becomes crucial for your product to be used normally – for example, as I mentioned, bumpy public transport.

When building typography tokens, focus on these key accessibility considerations:

- **Font size and scaling**: Establish minimum font sizes (typically 16px for body text) and use relative units that scale properly when users zoom up to 200%. Test your typography tokens at different zoom levels to ensure text remains readable.

- **Line height ratios**: Set line height between 1.4 and 1.6 times the font size for body text. Tighter line heights can make text difficult to read, especially for people with dyslexia or visual processing difficulties.

- **Font selection**: Choose fonts that remain clear at small sizes and avoid overly decorative typefaces for body text. Sans-serif fonts often work better for digital interfaces, though well-designed serif fonts can also be accessible.

- **Text spacing**: Include adequate spacing between paragraphs and sections. Dense text blocks are harder to navigate, especially for screen reader users who rely on clear content structure.

If you're using design tokens to standardize animations, create stricter guidelines for speed and complex motion. While complex animations might look "cool," they can be challenging to make inclusive unless you're focusing specifically on accessibility considerations. Consider providing reduced-motion alternatives for users who prefer less visual movement or adding an option to disable all animations with a single click. Microsoft uses this approach on its websites, so go check them out for reference.

Build WCAG into your components

Components are your building blocks, and in my experience, it's much harder to retroactively rebuild them to meet accessibility standards. Trust me, I've made this mistake multiple times, and honestly, I sometimes still do it because I'm not designing as actively as I used to. It's much easier to build components correctly from day one.

For complex components, you probably already sit down before creating them to properly plan all variants, states, and how they'll be built. Now it's time to add one additional planning step: identifying applicable WCAG success criteria.

Before you start designing, create a list of the WCAG criteria you want to meet for each component, and let these guide both your design and development process. This proactive approach ensures accessibility considerations influence your design decisions rather than constraining them afterward.

Make sure to agree with your team on your target compliance level. There's a significant difference between A, AA, and AAA standards. I'd recommend focusing on AA compliance as your baseline, with AAA for critical components, especially considering the EAA requirements.

Use AI assistants strategically

AI tools such as ChatGPT or Claude can be invaluable helpers for understanding accessibility requirements. Since accessibility is a new topic for many designers and can involve lengthy, technical documentation, don't hesitate to ask questions and share screenshots for analysis.

Here's a helpful prompt you can use with AI assistants to check WCAG compliance for your components:

"I'm designing a [component type] for a web application. Can you help me identify the relevant WCAG 2.1 AA success criteria I should consider? Here are the component details: [describe functionality, user interactions, visual elements]. Please provide specific guidance on how to ensure this component meets accessibility standards, including any potential issues I should watch for and testing recommendations."

Follow up by sharing screenshots or Figma links to get more specific feedback on your designs.

Train yourself and your team

Knowledge is power, so share it actively within your team. When you discover useful resources or learn from mistakes, document and share these insights. Accessibility is complex, and you don't need to tackle it alone.

Conduct regular accessibility reviews of your design system components. These audits serve a dual purpose: they improve your design system's accessibility while building your team's knowledge and confidence in addressing accessibility challenges.

Remember the scale

Always keep in mind that accessibility isn't a yes-or-no question. It's a scale. You don't need to achieve perfect accessibility overnight. Start with foundational improvements such as color contrast and keyboard navigation, then gradually expand your focus to more complex considerations such as screen reader compatibility and advanced ARIA implementations.

Every improvement you make benefits your users, even if you haven't achieved full AAA compliance across every component. Progress is more valuable than perfection, especially when that progress is sustainable and builds momentum for further improvements.

Testing and validating accessibility across platforms

You can test your accessibility in two main places: in Figma before development and in code after development. Both places are important, but honestly, the main testing happens in the code. An amazingly prepared Figma file with all the states, documentation, alt text, and accessibility considerations means nothing without proper implementation. However, you can still significantly help your developers by preparing your files properly from the start.

What's the problem?

I've seen multiple times that designers don't want to take responsibility for the production code, but as I've said repeatedly throughout this book, the final output isn't a Figma file but production code. You, as a designer, need to take responsibility for the final product and help your developers achieve the best possible implementation.

Many teams treat accessibility testing as an afterthought, checking for issues only after everything is built. This approach creates more work and often results in compromises that could have been avoided with earlier testing. Additionally, designers often feel intimidated by testing in code, thinking it's outside their expertise, but there are many accessibility tests that designers can and should perform.

How to fix it

As I mentioned, there are two main environments where you can test your accessibility solutions. Let's explore both of them and the specific techniques you can use in each.

Testing in Figma

In Figma, you can establish processes to hand off your designs in better shape than before, helping developers build more accessible products from the start.

Contrast checking

As I've mentioned multiple times throughout this chapter, check the contrast of your colors ideally at the design token level before you share designs with developers. You can use Figma's native color contrast checking tool or plugins such as Stark to perform bulk contrast checks across your entire design system.

Make this part of your design review process. Don't wait until the end of a project to discover contrast issues that require you to rebuild components or reconsider your color palette.

Color blindness simulation

This was honestly my first introduction to accessibility testing years back when I tried a Figma plugin that showed me how people with different visual impairments see my designs. I tried it more than 5 years ago, and I still recommend it today: Color Blind by Sam Mason de Caires (`https://www.figma.com/community/plugin/733343906244951586/color-blind`).

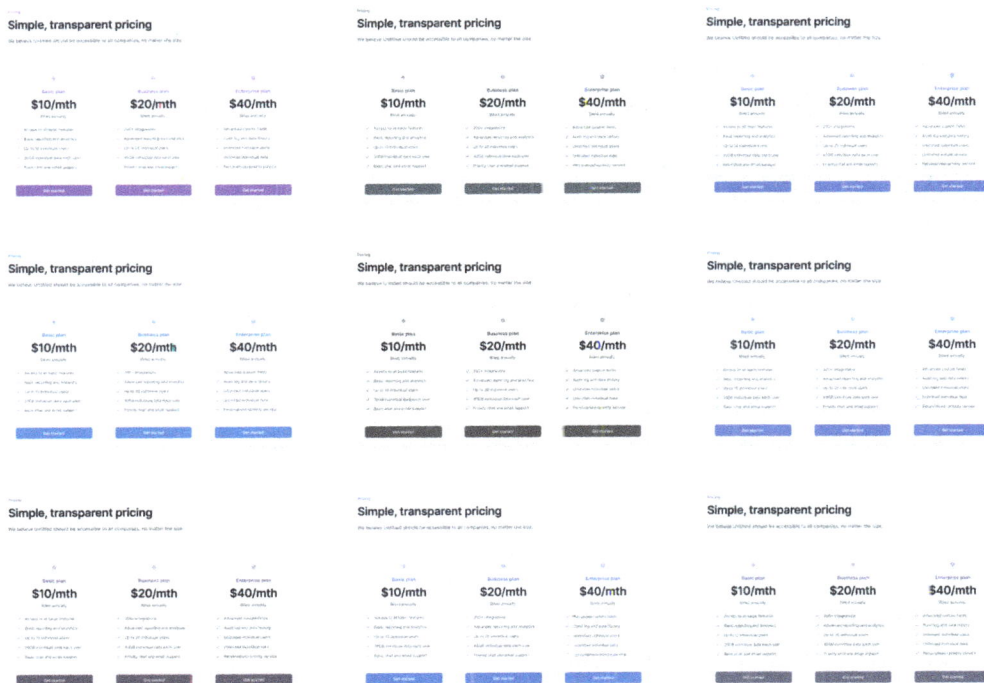

Figure 7.6 – Color blind plugin test

Running your designs through color blindness simulation helps you identify when you're relying too heavily on color alone to convey information. This is particularly important for status indicators, error states, and interactive elements.

Map edge cases

Try to build your designs and components with edge cases in mind. For example, test how your design looks when someone zooms to 200% (making text 200% bigger). One of my weird habits is that when I'm on the metro, I never use my phone and instead watch how others work and play on their devices. Very often, you can see older people with settings that make their text much larger, and you'll quickly spot the problems.

For example, in many popular messaging apps, names start to truncate with "..." when text is enlarged. I once saw a lady with a whole list of WhatsApp contacts showing only first names (very common first names in the Czech Republic) without surnames. She needed to check every chat before finding the right person. Think about these scenarios, and sometimes just observe the world around you. You're designers, after all.

Set component guidelines

Components are the building blocks of your design, and it's much easier when they're built correctly with accessibility in mind from the start. Set up clear guidelines for your team. Many of these I've already mentioned throughout this chapter, but here's a consolidated checklist:

- Remember all states (especially focus states for interactive elements)
- Check the usage of correct design tokens before handoff
- Images need to have appropriate alternative text (descriptive alt text for informative images, empty `alt=""` for purely decorative images)
- Add accessibility sections to component documentation
- Include keyboard navigation instructions where relevant
- Document expected ARIA attributes for complex components
- Specify tab order for complex layouts

Testing in code

Even as a designer, you can test many accessibility aspects in the production code, though some tests will require developer involvement.

Cross-browser and cross-platform testing

This shouldn't be tied only to accessibility, but please check your product on something other than MacBooks and Safari. I once worked with a team that was building keyboard shortcuts into their product. They had a company policy that everyone used only MacBooks. Maybe you know where I'm going with this. When I found out they didn't have shortcuts working on Windows, their reaction was "Oh, we didn't think about that." By the way, based on Google Analytics, 70% of their users were on Windows.

Test your accessibility features across different browsers, operating systems, and devices. What works perfectly on Chrome might have issues in Firefox or Safari. What works on desktop might break on mobile.

Keyboard testing

You can launch your product and try hitting *Tab* to move forward or *Shift* + *Tab* to move backward through interactive elements. You can test the tab order very quickly and give immediate feedback to your developers about any issues you discover.

Pay attention to the following:

- Can you reach all interactive elements using only the keyboard?
- Is the tab order logical and does it follow the visual flow of the page?
- Are focus indicators clearly visible on all interactive elements?
- Can you activate buttons, links, and form elements using *Enter* or the *Spacebar*?
- Can you close modals and dropdowns using the *Esc* key?

Screen reader testing

Very similar to keyboard testing, just open your product and activate the built-in screen readers: *Ctrl* + *Windows* + *Enter* on Windows, or *Command* + *F5* on macOS.

Listen to how your content is announced and whether the information makes sense without visual context. This gives you immediate insight into the screen reader experience and helps you identify areas where additional labels or descriptions might be needed.

Automatic testing (designer-friendly)

You can test your product using automated tools that don't require development knowledge. For example, add the amazing extension "Accessibility Insights for Web" to Chrome (https:// chromewebstore.google.com/detail/accessibility-insights-fo/pbjjkligggfmakdaogkfomd dhfmpjeni). This extension will scan your page and give you quick wins to focus on, highlighting issues with clear explanations of what's wrong and how to fix it.

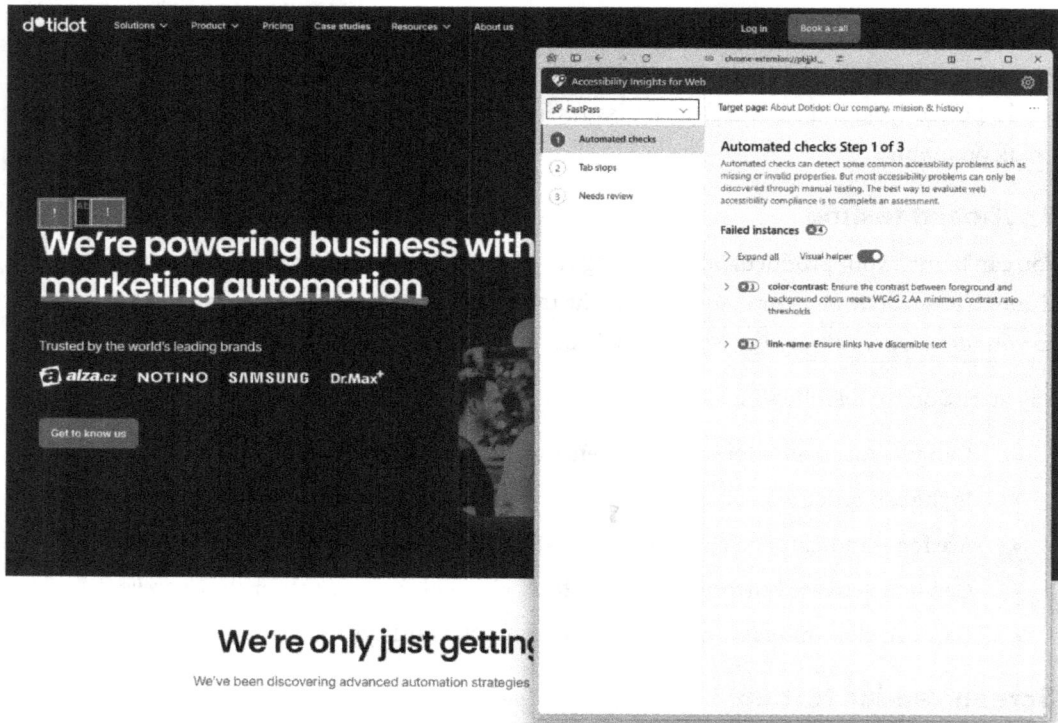

Figure 7.7 – Quick showcase of Dotidot About Us page that needs some improvements

Automatic testing (developer-required)

Your development team almost certainly (okay, maybe 99% certain) has automated tests covering different user flows and states in your product. Work with them to add automated accessibility tests that cover the main accessibility pain points. This ensures that before every release, the system checks whether everything meets your accessibility standards.

The most popular tool for this is axe-core (`https://github.com/dequelabs/axe-core`), an open source accessibility testing library created by Deque Systems. axe-core can be integrated directly into automated testing pipelines, allowing developers to catch accessibility issues as part of their regular development workflow. It's the same technology that powers tools such as Google Lighthouse and many browser extensions, so it's battle-tested and widely trusted.

What makes axe-core particularly valuable is that developers can set it up to automatically check every code change for accessibility problems before the website goes live. Think of it like a spell-checker, but for accessibility. If the code has accessibility issues, the system can prevent the update from being published until those problems are fixed. This means accessibility becomes a must-have requirement, not something that gets skipped when deadlines are tight.

Deque (`https://www.deque.com/`) offers enterprise tools built on top of axe-core that provide additional features such as reporting dashboards and advanced integrations, but the core testing engine is free and open source, making it accessible to teams of all sizes.

User testing with actual users

This is, of course, the best approach. Invite users from your target demographic who can test your product and provide direct feedback about their experience. In reality, you need substantial resources to conduct proper accessibility user testing, so this option is typically available only for larger teams. But asking your leadership about this never hurt anyone, right?

When you do have the opportunity for user testing with people who have disabilities, remember that they're the experts about their own experience. Listen to their feedback without being defensive, and be prepared to learn things about your product that automated testing could never reveal.

Creating a testing routine

Don't treat accessibility testing as a one-time checklist. Instead, build it into your regular workflow:

1. **Design phase**: Use contrast checkers and color blindness simulators during design
2. **Pre-handoff**: Run through your component guidelines checklist
3. **Post-development**: Perform keyboard and screen reader testing on new features
4. **Regular audits**: Schedule periodic accessibility reviews of your entire product

By incorporating testing into multiple stages of your process, you catch issues early, when they're easier and less expensive to fix, while also building accessibility awareness across your entire team.

Unlock this book's exclusive benefits now

Scan this QR code or go to packtpub.com/ unlock, then search this book by name.

Note: Keep your purchase invoice ready before you start.

8

Precision Handoff Techniques

The handoff phase is often the most challenging aspect of collaboration between design and development teams. I've discussed this throughout multiple chapters because I truly believe it from experience. You can design the best product on the planet, but if it won't be developed properly, it will stay only in Figma for your next Dribbble post.

Throughout this book, we've touched on various aspects of the handoff process that are essential for successful collaboration between designers and developers:

- In *Chapter 1*, we discussed how screen annotations and proper documentation are crucial for every Figma handoff, and we explored the communication gaps that often exist between design and development teams
- *Chapter 2* showed us how plugins can streamline the handoff process, particularly tools such as *Variables to CSS* that help bridge the gap between Figma designs and production code
- In *Chapter 4*, we dove deep into structuring design files for developer accessibility and explored proper file handoff techniques, including accessibility documentation using specialized plugins
- *Chapter 6* demonstrated how design tokens serve as a bridge between design and code, making handoffs more systematic and reliable
- In *Chapter 7*, we covered how to document accessibility features properly during the handoff process

This chapter won't repeat these points, but I'll add new techniques that should help you prepare better designs for your developers to build upon.

When I started my career, handoffs were painful. We'd export static images, write lengthy emails explaining interactions, and hope developers would interpret everything correctly. My favorite memory was sharing PSD files that were several gigabytes and named something like `project-final-version-2016-final-V2.psd`. The result? Endless back-and-forth conversations, frustrated developers, and final products that looked "similar enough" for us to finally say "*OK*."

Thankfully, those days are behind us. Modern tools such as Figma have revolutionized the handoff process, but you still need to know how to use them effectively. In this chapter, we'll explore advanced techniques that will help you achieve flawless design handoffs and reduce development errors.

The following are the sections we will cover:

- Setting precise export options for accurate delivery
- SVG icon optimization for clean export
- Preparing Figma variables for specific platforms
- Ensuring high-fidelity implementation
- Interactive prototype handoffs
- Animation handoffs
- Quality assurance process

Setting precise export options for accurate delivery

Figma can be used by developers, and it should be used by developers. In many teams, developers navigating through Figma files is a daily routine, but are they just "looking" or actively using Figma's features? One of the most important features is **asset export**, which can make or break the development process.

What's the problem?

Long gone are the days when you shared a drive folder filled with assets. Everyone can export assets from Figma now, but you, as a designer, need to prepare them correctly to make the process easier and ensure that developers use them the right way. Here are some common mistakes with assets:

- Large export files that slow down applications
- Wrong naming conventions that confuse developers

- Complex layers without clear indicators of what frame or group to export
- Poorly prepared export settings for multiple devices and platforms

These issues lead to frustrated developers, slow-loading applications, and ultimately, poor user experiences. When developers can't easily find or use the assets they need, they either skip optimizations or create their own versions, leading to inconsistencies.

How to fix it

Let's address each of these problems with practical solutions you can implement immediately.

Large export files

Large image files slow down applications and frustrate users. Before exporting, consider whether each asset really needs maximum quality. For background images or decorative elements, you can often reduce quality significantly without visible impact.

Figma recently added new export settings, and if you're exporting images as JPG, check the quality settings under the additional options (three dots icon).

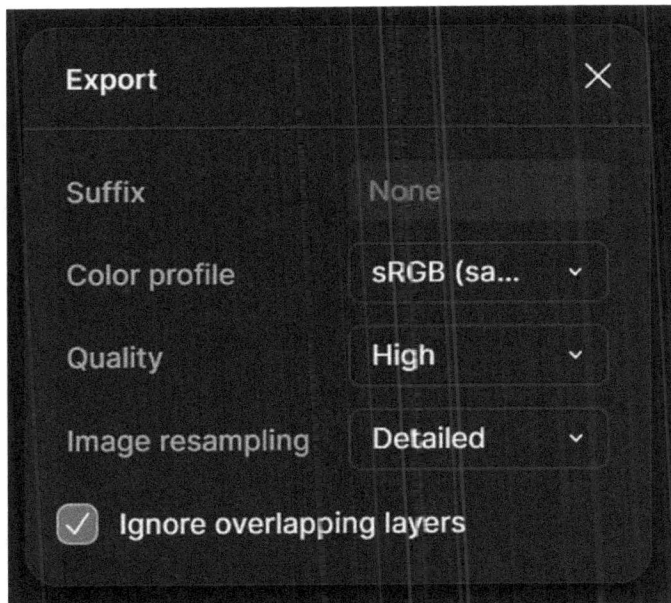

Figure 8.1 – Figma default JPG settings (Quality is set on High)

Background images don't need high quality, and you'll be fine with **Quality** set to **Low**. I tested this with an image at 1920x1080 resolution: at **High** quality it was 1.54 MB, while at **Low** quality it was 0.64 MB—that's a 58.4% saving in file size. On first glance, you can't tell the difference.

> If you prefer alternative tools for image optimization, consider using ImageOptim (Mac) or TinyPNG (web-based) to compress your exported images without quality loss.

Modern file formats

Figma exports the "typical" file types, such as PNG, JPG, and SVG, but modern websites can use WebP or AVIF formats for even better compression. For WebP or AVIF conversion, you can use online converters or Figma plugins. Unfortunately, most useful plugins aren't free, but you can try InnoExport, which offers 20 free exports to test it out.

Choose the right format for your content:

- **SVG**: Best for simple graphics, icons, and illustrations that need to scale perfectly
- **PNG**: Ideal for graphics with transparency or sharp edges (logos and UI elements)
- **JPG**: Perfect for photographs and complex images with many colors
- **WebP**: Modern replacement for PNG/JPG with better compression; works for both graphics and photos
- **AVIF**: Newest format with the best compression; excellent for photos and complex graphics

In my tests, the same image converted to WebP was 0.20 MB (87% data savings), and AVIF was 0.094 MB (93.9% data savings)—incredible compression with no visible quality loss. If you don't want to use paid plugins, try online converters such as Google's Squoosh (https://squoosh.app/).

Wrong naming conventions

Yes, naming layers is back again! If you want developers to easily export assets from Figma, they need to know what to export. Unified naming is the key to success. For consistency with your broader design system, consider following the same naming patterns you use for design tokens (covered in *Chapter 6*) when naming your assets. Let me share two specific cases where proper naming makes a huge difference.

Exporting icons

If you want developers to export icons efficiently, place them all on one dedicated page with a clear prefix (for example, `icon-` or `ico-`). This allows them to re-export the entire icon set at once, even if you change just one icon. They'll know they have everything up to date without you having to explain which specific icons changed.

Here are some examples:

- `icon-arrow-left`
- `icon-arrow-right`
- `icon-close`
- `icon-menu`

Exporting images

You should always use clear names in layers for images that need to be exported. More importantly, always use a wrapper frame and set up export settings on that frame. This way, developers can easily identify and export the correct assets without guessing.

Complex layers without clear export guidelines

This issue connects directly to the wrong naming conventions. Sometimes, you create very complex images built with multiple elements, such as a testimonial section with multiple user photos arranged in a layout.

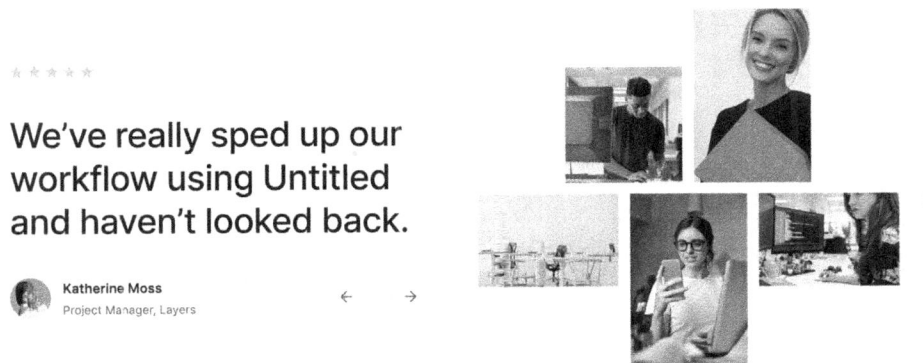

Figure 8.2 – Showcase from Untitled UI with complex image structure

Every element can be exported individually, or you can export everything at once. You should always give this decision to developers, because you don't know exactly how they'll implement the design. The best approach is to follow these steps:

1. Create one main frame containing all the assets.
2. Create logical content blocks within that frame for modular export options.
3. Use clear naming for both the main frame and individual components.

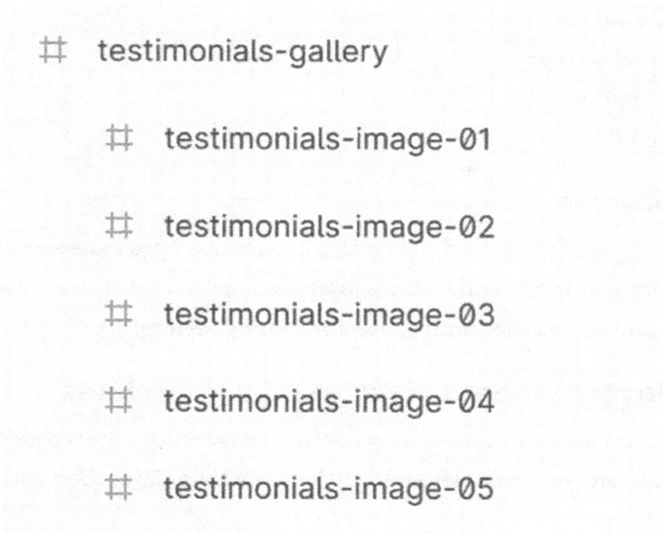

     #   testimonials-gallery

         #   testimonials-image-01

         #   testimonials-image-02

         #   testimonials-image-03

         #   testimonials-image-04

         #   testimonials-image-05

Figure 8.3 – Figma proper layers naming

This gives developers flexibility to export the entire composition or just the pieces they need for their specific implementation approach.

Poorly prepared export settings for multiple devices

Before exporting anything, clarify with your development team what formats and resolutions they need. Web projects typically need 1x and 2x versions, while mobile apps might require 1x, 2x, and 3x variants. Some teams prefer SVG files for icons, while others need PNG exports at specific sizes.

You can prepare export settings for each asset so developers will see every option in Dev mode. This creates a one-click export solution—they don't need to set up everything themselves, which reduces errors and saves time.

Export   +

1x	⌄	SVG	⌄	•••	—
2x	⌄	PNG	⌄	•••	—
1.5x	⌄	PNG	⌄	•••	—
1x	⌄	PNG	⌄	•••	—

Export icon-social-facebook

Figure 8.4 – Figma export settings for icons

Here are some common export configurations:

- **Web icons**: SVG format (scalable) or PNG at 24px, 32px, or 48px
- **Web images**: JPG/PNG at 1x and 2x for retina displays
- **Mobile icons**: PNG at 1x, 2x, and 3x resolutions
- **Mobile images**: Multiple resolutions based on device requirements

Test your exports

Please test your exports! As I showed you with file size optimization, you can make huge improvements to user experience with simple testing. Try different export settings and find the best balance between file size and quality for your specific assets.

Don't assume your first export settings are optimal. Spend time experimenting with different formats, quality levels, and compression settings. Your users will benefit from faster loading times, and your developers will appreciate assets that are properly optimized from the start.

SVG icon optimization for clean export

SVG icons are among the most frequently exported assets in any design project, yet they're often the source of significant developer frustration. Many designers don't realize how their design choices directly affect the exported SVG code quality, leading to bloated files, browser compatibility issues, and unnecessary cleanup work for developers. Understanding how to design icons properly can dramatically improve your handoff process and reduce implementation time.

What's the problem?

When designers create icons without considering the final SVG output, they often use design techniques that create unnecessarily complex code. A simple-looking icon might export as hundreds of lines of SVG code filled with masks, filters, and complex path data that browsers struggle to render consistently.

Another common issue is using design approaches that work perfectly in Figma but translate poorly to the SVG format. Features such as multiple strokes, complex gradients, or layered effects might look great in your design tool but create compatibility nightmares across different browsers, especially older versions of Edge.

Additionally, many designers treat icon creation as purely visual work, not considering that icons need to be scalable, performant, and maintainable in code. This disconnect often leads to icons that look perfect at design time but cause technical problems during implementation.

How to fix it

Creating clean, developer-friendly SVG icons requires understanding both design principles and technical constraints. The goal is to design icons that export as clean, simple SVG code that performs well across all browsers and devices.

Design with simple paths and shapes

Build your icons using basic geometric shapes and simple paths rather than complex effects or detailed illustrations. This fundamental approach ensures your icons export as clean, efficient SVG code.

Here are some best practices:

- Use rectangles, circles, and polygons as building blocks
- Create complex shapes by combining simple ones
- Avoid intricate details that don't scale well
- Keep designs geometric and systematic

Here are the things to avoid:

- Complex illustrations with many small details
- Hand-drawn or sketch-like elements
- Overly decorative elements that don't serve the icon's purpose

Flatten and combine paths instead of grouping

One of the most important technical considerations is how you structure your icon's elements. Instead of simply grouping multiple shapes, use Figma's path operations to create unified, clean shapes:

- **Recommended path operations:**
    - **Union:** Combine overlapping shapes into single paths
    - **Subtract:** Cut shapes out of each other cleanly
    - **Intersect:** Create shapes from overlapping areas
    - **Exclude:** Remove overlapping areas while keeping the rest
- **Why this matters:**
    - Creates single, clean paths instead of multiple layered elements
    - Dramatically reduces the complexity of exported SVG code
    - Improves rendering performance across all browsers
    - Makes icons easier for developers to modify programmatically

Avoid masks, gradients, and complex effects

These features create significantly more complex SVG code and can cause compatibility issues across different browsers and devices.

Here are some effects to avoid:

- Drop shadows and inner shadows
- Blur effects and other filters
- Complex gradients (especially radial gradients)
- Masks and clipping paths
- Multiple overlapping strokes

Here are some alternative approaches:

- Use solid colors instead of gradients
- Create depth through clever use of geometry rather than shadows
- If you must use gradients, discuss implementation complexity with developers first
- Design variations for different states, rather than relying on effects

Test your SVG export quality

Before finalizing any icon, export it as SVG and examine the code quality. This quick check can reveal potential issues and help you refine your design approach.

Here's how to do a quick quality test:

1. Export your icon as SVG from Figma.

2. Open the SVG file in a text editor.

3. Check the file size and code complexity.

Here are some red flags to look for:

- Files larger than a few KB for simple icons

- Hundreds of lines of code for seemingly simple designs

- Presence of `<mask>`, `<filter>`, or `<clipPath>` elements

- Extremely long or complex `<path>` data

- Multiple `<defs>` sections with gradients or patterns

Here are the good SVG characteristics:

- Clean, readable code structure

- Minimal `<path>` elements with simple coordinates

- No complex effects or filters

- File sizes typically under 2 KB for most icons

Preparing Figma variables for specific platforms

Figma variables are powerful tools for maintaining design consistency, but they become even more valuable when properly prepared for different development platforms. Each platform—web, iOS, Android, or desktop applications, TVs, and watches—has its own conventions, limitations, and requirements that should be reflected in how you structure and name your variables.

What's the problem?

Many designers create variables that work perfectly in Figma but don't translate well to development environments. Generic variable names such as `Color 1` or `Spacing Large` might make sense in a design context, but they create confusion when developers try to implement them across different platforms.

Different platforms also have varying technical constraints. What works as a web CSS variable might not be suitable for iOS development, and Android has its own naming conventions that differ from both. Without considering these platform-specific needs, your variables can become a source of confusion rather than clarity.

Additionally, many teams don't think about how variables will be consumed by developers until the handoff phase, missing opportunities to create a more streamlined development process.

How to fix it

The key is to structure your variables with the end platform in mind, creating a system that works seamlessly from design to production code.

Understand platform conventions

Before creating variables, research the naming conventions and organizational patterns used by your target platforms:

- **Web development:**

    - CSS custom properties use *kebab-case*: `--color-primary-500`

- **iOS development:**

    - Uses *camelCase*: `colorPrimary500`

- **Android development:**

    - Uses *snake_case*: `color_primary_500`

Set up the variables for each platform

Figma Variables has an amazing **code syntax** feature that not many people are using. You don't need to set up platform-specific variables, because that would create multiple variables without any reason and build a super complex system for almost nothing. What you do instead is prepare platform-specific naming via **Code syntax** for each variable.

This means you'll have only one variable, but it will be named differently for web, iOS, or Android, so each developer will see the specific naming convention they expect. Here's how you can set this up—it's super easy:

1. Open the **Variables** tab in your Figma file.
2. Select a specific variable you want to configure.
3. Click on the **Edit Variable** icon (pencil icon).

4. Hit the + button next to **Code syntax**.

5. Select your platform (for example, **Web**).

6. Enter the desired syntax into the input field.

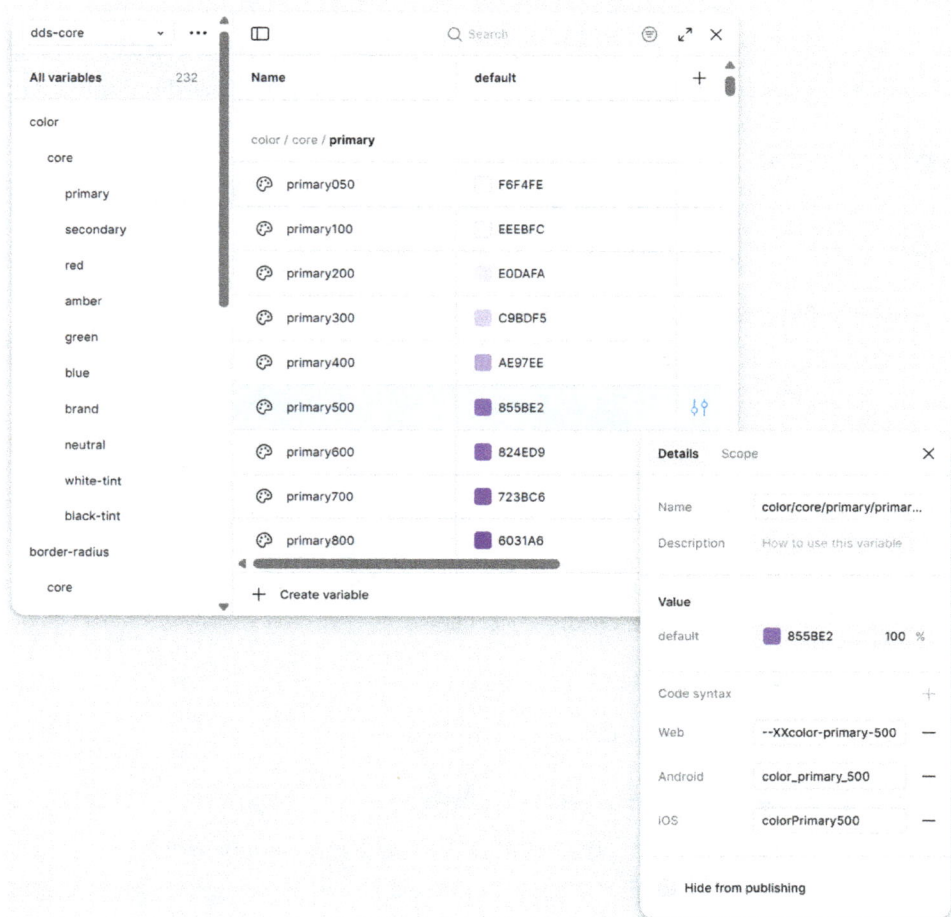

Figure 8.5 – Figma variables Code syntax modal

For example, if your variable is called **Primary Blue** in Figma, you can set it to appear as the following:

- `--color-primary-500` for web developers
- `colorPrimary500` for iOS developers
- `color_primary_500` for Android developers

Once you've set this up, you can easily check how it will appear to developers by switching to Dev mode. The same variable will show the appropriate naming convention based on the platform context, as shown in the following figures:

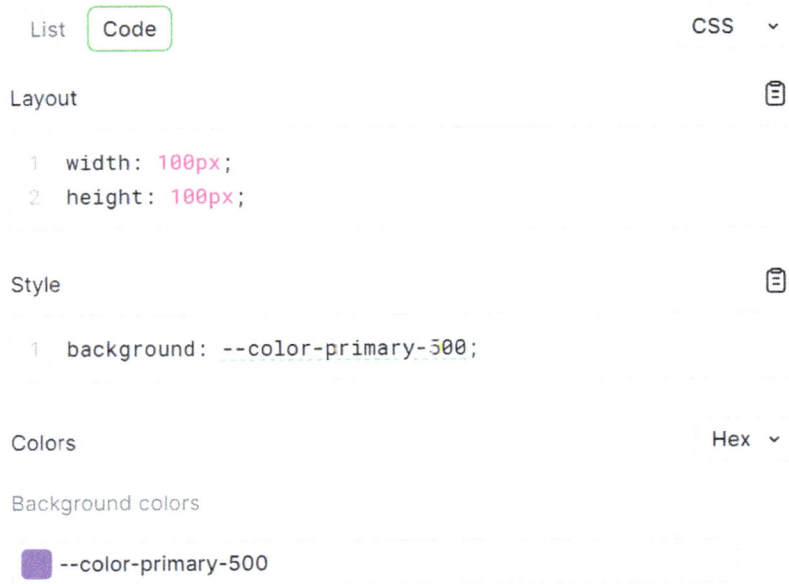

List | Code   CSS ⌄

Layout   ▤

```
1  width: 100px;
2  height: 100px;
```

Style   ▤

```
1  background: --color-primary-500;
```

Colors   Hex ⌄

Background colors

■ --color-primary-500

Figure 8.6 – Variable naming format in Dev mode for CSS

List | Code   SwiftUI ⌄

Rectangle   ▤

```
1  Rectangle()
2      .foregroundColor(.clear)
3      .frame(width: 100, height: 100)
4      .background(colorPrimary500)
```

Colors   Hex ⌄

Background colors

■ colorPrimary500

Figure 8.7 – Variable naming format in Dev mode for iOS (SwiftUI)

List   Code   Compose   ⌄

Modifier

```
1  Modifier
2      .width(100.dp)
3      .height(100.dp)
4      .background(color = color_primary_500)
```

Colors   Hex ⌄

Background colors

color_primary_500

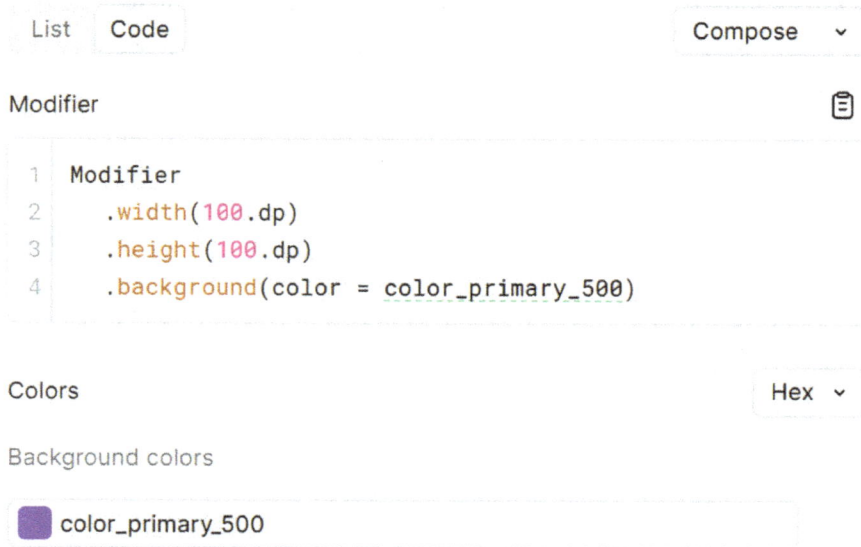

Figure 8.8 – Variable naming format in Dev mode for Android

If you have many variables already prepared, don't do this manually. Check out this short and funny Figma tutorial video on how to do it via JavaScript in seconds: https://www.youtube.com/watch?v=t2bMxHk7D5k.

Ensuring high-fidelity implementation

Good design isn't about pixel-perfect implementation—it's about solving the right problems. But at the same time, when the product is developed differently than you designed, you don't know whether it will solve the problem you originally designed for. Sometimes, the reason something is developed differently lies in the handoff process itself. I've found that the best implementations come from treating the handoff as the beginning of a collaborative process, not the end of the design phase.

What's the problem?

Even with perfect documentation and assets, implementations can drift from the original design due to technical constraints, time pressure, or simple misunderstandings. Small deviations compound over time, eventually creating products that feel inconsistent and unpolished compared to the original vision.

Many teams lack a systematic approach to verifying implementation accuracy. Designers might not see the implemented version until it's nearly complete, making significant corrections expensive and time-consuming. Or you'll hear the dreaded *"Create a ticket and we'll come back when we have time"*—which, let's be honest, is never.

How to fix it

High-fidelity implementation requires proactive involvement throughout the development cycle. Here's how to maintain design quality from handoff through launch:

1. Open communication channels with developers.
2. Establish review checkpoints.
3. Use shared testing environments.
4. Build quality assurance into the process.
5. Document approved deviations.
6. Create implementation guidelines.

Open communication channels with developers

Make sure developers know they can and should reach out to you when they have questions or doubts about implementation details. Creating an environment where developers feel comfortable asking for clarification upfront prevents costly fixes later and ensures better implementation quality.

Here's how to encourage open communication:

- Make yourself available for quick questions during development sprints
- Set clear expectations about response times for different types of questions
- Use collaborative tools (Slack, Teams, etc.) for quick clarifications
- Schedule regular check-ins during complex feature development
- Celebrate when developers ask questions rather than making assumptions

> **Remember**
>
> It's always better to spend 5 minutes clarifying something than 5 hours fixing it after implementation

Establish review checkpoints

Set up clear review checkpoints with your development team and product manager. Account for this time in your project timeline and treat it as part of the project (same as QA for development), not a nice-to-have phase if you have time.

Remember, you as a designer should be the final review stage for the design and behavior of components or larger blocks (search functionality, for example). If you find inconsistencies, ask developers *why* they implemented it differently. I was mentoring one team where designers were doing these reviews by generating dozens of Jira tickets with changes, but they didn't understand why developers implemented things differently. Is it a misunderstanding or a technical limitation? That's a huge difference in how you approach the "problem."

Use shared testing environments

Get access to staging environments where you can interact with implemented designs regularly. This hands-on experience helps you catch usability issues that aren't apparent in static designs and ensures that interactions feel smooth and natural.

Test implementations on multiple devices and browsers to verify consistency across platforms. What looks perfect on your development machine might have issues on older devices or different operating systems. I've mentioned this before, but check the product on multiple platforms—not only on your expensive MacBook Pro.

> **Tip from beta reader**
>
> Consider using Figma's branching feature to create separate testing branches instead of testing everything in one shared file. This is particularly valuable for design system changes, as it helps separate your design updates from other teams' changes that could potentially interfere. Ad-hoc branches give you better control and help trouble-shoot potential design issues more effectively by isolating different types of changes.

Build quality assurance into the process

Make design review an official part of the development workflow. Just as code gets reviewed before merging, implemented designs should be verified for accuracy before being marked complete.

Create simple checklists that developers can use to self-assess their work before requesting design review. This approach catches obvious issues early and makes the review process more efficient for everyone.

Here is an example checklist:

- Does the spacing match the design specifications?
- Are the correct fonts and font weights applied?
- Do interactive states (hover, focus, and active) work as intended?
- Is the component responsive across different screen sizes?
- Does the color contrast meet accessibility requirements?

Document approved deviations

When technical constraints require changes from the original design, document these decisions clearly. This documentation prevents the same discussions from happening repeatedly and helps maintain consistency when similar situations arise in the future.

Remember, not all designers are working on the same features, and if you encounter a challenge, it's very likely another team member will face it too. Share these findings with your design team and document them where your team can access them. For example, if it's a limitation in a certain component, include this information in Figma or even in the component's description.

Create implementation guidelines

Beyond individual component reviews, establish broader guidelines for how designs should be interpreted. This includes guidance on the following:

- **Spacing consistency**: How should developers handle spacing when content length varies?
- **Responsive behavior**: How should components adapt across different screen sizes?
- **Animation and transitions**: What timing and easing should be used for interactions?
- **Error states**: How should components behave when something goes wrong?

These guidelines reduce guesswork and help developers make design-aligned decisions when you haven't explicitly designed for edge cases.

Interactive prototype handoffs

Interactive prototypes can be incredibly powerful for communicating complex user flows and interactions that static designs simply can't convey. However, not all prototypes are created equal when it comes to handoffs. The key is creating prototypes that enhance understanding rather than confuse developers about what needs to be built.

What's the problem?

Many designers create prototypes that are either too basic to be useful or so complex that developers can't extract actionable information from them. I've seen prototypes that take longer to create than the actual development would take, and others so simplified that they miss crucial interaction details.

Another common issue is the disconnect between what's possible in a Figma prototype and what's feasible in production code. Figma allows for interactions that might be technically challenging or impossible to implement, leading to frustration when developers can't replicate the exact prototype behavior.

Additionally, many teams use prototypes for stakeholder presentations but forget to optimize them for developer handoffs. A prototype that impresses clients might not contain the technical details developers need to build the actual product.

How to fix it

The goal is to create prototypes that serve as clear communication tools between design and development, not just impressive demos. There's a simple decision workflow that I use and teach my team to follow. Based on this approach, we can invest the minimum time needed in prototypes.

Isn't a video enough?

Sometimes, you need something more interactive than static design, but do you really need to prototype it? Isn't a short Loom video with verbal explanation and some showcases from other parts of your product enough? Maybe something is already developed in production, but you don't have the interaction built in Figma yet.

In many cases, a video is sufficient, and it's the least time-consuming decision you can make. You can save hours by replacing complex interactive prototypes with just a short recording.

Use someone else's interaction/check technical feasibility

Ask your development team how they're planning to build this flow. If they'll use a third-party library, maybe there's a Figma file for it that you can use and adapt the interaction from. No need to reinvent the wheel.

For example, this was a common case when our development team planned to use a specific component (in our case, it was a date picker). We found a free Figma file from the community, redesigned it with our design tokens in mind, and it was done. Easy and fast.

Focus on user flows

For handoff purposes, prioritize demonstrating user flows over visual polish. Developers need to understand how users move through the interface, what triggers state changes, and how different screens connect to each other.

Your prototype should clearly show the following:

- **Entry points**: How do users access this flow?
- **Decision points**: What choices do users make along the way?
- **Success states**: What happens when everything goes right?
- **Error handling**: How does the system respond to problems?
- **Exit points**: How do users leave this flow?

Create multiple prototype versions

If you have the time and resources, consider creating different prototype versions for different audiences:

- **Stakeholder version**: Polished, impressive, and shows the big picture
- **Developer version**: Detailed, technical, and shows edge cases and states
- **User testing version**: Functional, realistic, and allows for genuine feedback

This approach ensures that each audience gets the information they need without overwhelming anyone with irrelevant details.

Besides this decision workflow, there are two additional points that are important to consider when creating prototypes for developer handoffs.

Talk with your developers

Yes, here it is again. Talk with them before you design something, and talk with them regularly, because many teams have different workflows and needs.

Before building your prototype, talk with your development team about what information would be most helpful. Some developers prefer detailed micro-interactions, while others need high-level flow understanding. Knowing their preferences helps you focus your prototype efforts where they'll have the most impact.

Ask specific questions such as the following:

- Do you prefer to see detailed transitions or just understand the flow?
- What interaction patterns are you familiar with implementing?
- Are there any technical limitations I should consider?
- How do you typically handle complex state changes?

Use realistic content and data

Prototype with real or realistic content whenever possible. You can check *Chapter 2* about plugins (specifically *data.to.design* and *Content Reel*) that help you load realistic content and data. Lorem ipsum and placeholder data can hide important layout and interaction issues. If your prototype shows a user dashboard, use actual user names, realistic data volumes, and varied content lengths.

This approach helps developers understand edge cases such as the following:

- How does the interface handle very long user names?
- What happens when lists are empty or have hundreds of items?
- How should the design adapt to different data types?

For international projects, consider the localization aspect when prototyping with realistic content. Different languages can dramatically affect layout and spacing. Use plugins such as CopyDoc, Localiser, or Transifex Figma Plugin to test your designs with actual translated content. This helps identify potential issues with text expansion (German text can be 30% longer than English) or text contraction (Chinese text might be much shorter) before development begins.

For more detailed guidance on accessibility testing and considerations, refer to *Chapter 7*, which covers comprehensive approaches to ensuring your designs work for all users.

Animation handoffs

Animation handoffs can be one of the trickiest aspects of the design-to-development process. While static designs and even interactive prototypes are relatively straightforward to communicate, animations involve timing, easing, sequencing, and technical performance considerations that can easily get lost in translation. The goal is to provide developers with clear, actionable specifications that result in smooth, polished animations that enhance the user experience rather than detract from it.

What's the problem?

Many designers create beautiful animations in Figma or Adobe After Effects that look perfect in the design environment but are difficult or impossible to implement in production code. The disconnect often happens because Figma's animation capabilities don't always align with what's technically feasible or performant in real applications.

Another common issue is incomplete animation specifications. Designers might show the end states of an animation but forget to document crucial details such as timing, easing curves, or what triggers the animation. This leaves developers guessing about implementation details, often resulting in animations that feel different from the original design intent.

Performance is also a major concern that's often overlooked during the design phase. An animation that runs smoothly in Figma might cause performance issues on lower-end devices or older browsers, but these constraints aren't always considered during the handoff process.

How to fix it

Successful animation handoffs require clear communication about both the visual aspects and the technical specifications that make animations feel polished and perform well.

Try to prepare the final form of the animation

You, as a designer, have many tools at your disposal to deliver not just an animation "showcase" but the final "product" that can be used by developers. First, ask them whether they're planning to use some of the amazing libraries that are available online, such as GSAP (`https://gsap.com/`) or AnimeJS (`https://animejs.com/`). If you know they want to use something like this, it's your guideline to prepare something that will be easy to implement, because you'll be working within the guardrails of the library.

A second option is to use my favorite LottieFiles (`https://lottiefiles.com/`) with their amazing Figma plugin. In a few clicks, you can have production-ready animations without any guessing and complex information transfer to developers—just deliver them the final output of the animation, and you're good to go.

> Rive (`https://rive.app/`) is another excellent alternative to LottieFiles, offering more advanced animation capabilities and real-time interactive features that can be particularly useful for complex prototypes.

> **Performance warning (from engineer beta reader)**
>
> While these animation libraries are powerful, consider the trade-offs. Adding 100+ KB of library weight just for simple transitions can hurt performance. For basic animations, CSS animations or utility-based systems such as Tailwind's animation classes often provide better performance with minimal complexity. Reserve heavy animation libraries for truly complex animations that justify the overhead. Sometimes, less is more.

If this isn't an option, try to think about the following points.

Animation patterns and styles

Even in animations, you should follow strict guidelines. You can have animations as part of your design tokens in Tokens Studio or simply as part of your design system. My point is, if you need to invest time into custom animation, try to limit their variety and create repeatable "components" from them.

It sounds obvious, but Figma doesn't have an easy way to make animation settings (duration and motion curve) into components to repeat again and again. This could cause complex implementation, because every animation will be slightly different, even when it doesn't make any sense. Try to build your own animation library to use repeatedly.

Document animation specifications

For every animation you design, provide developers with comprehensive specifications that include the following:

- Distinguishing essential animations from aesthetic animations
- Timing and duration

- Easing and motion curves
- Trigger conditions
- Performance considerations

Distinguish essential animations from aesthetic animations

In my mind, there are two types of animations: essential animations that communicate key interaction concepts, such as system status, and aesthetic animations that are there to entertain or please users with nice transitions and visual flourishes. (I originally called these *UX animations*, but my beta reader pointed out this could be confusing terminology.)

Essential animations are more important, and the implementation should be as close as possible to the design. For nice-to-have animations, developers can implement them more easily and make them slightly different if technical capabilities make your original design harder to achieve.

Here are some examples:

- **Essential animation**: In a long form with an error, the browser scrolls to the first input with an error that changes color to red and does a little bouncy size change to grab your attention
- **Nice-to-have**: A delightful animation of a flying unicorn when you mark your task as done in Asana

Timing and duration

Be specific about timing requirements to ensure animations feel consistent and intentional:

- How long should the animation take from start to finish?
- Are there different phases with different timing?
- Should the animation speed adapt based on content or device capabilities? For example, should loading animations always finish, even if the actual loading is faster?

Easing and motion curves

Define the motion characteristics that create the right emotional response and feel:

- What type of easing should be used (linear, ease-in, ease-out, or ease-in-out)?
- Are there custom cubic Bezier curves that create the desired feel?

Be aware that easing terminology varies across platforms. While the concepts are universal, the naming differs:

Concept	CSS/Web	iOS	Android	Material Design
Linear	`linear`	`.linear`	`LinearInterpolator`	N/A (rarely used)
Ease-in	`ease-in`	`.easeIn`	`AccelerateInterpolator`	Acceleration `cubic-bezier(0.4, 0.0, 1, 1)`
Ease-out	`ease-out`	`.easeOut`	`DecelerateInterpolator`	Deceleration `cubic-bezier(0.0, 0.0, 0.2, 1)`
Ease-in-out	`ease-in-out`	`.easeInOut`	`AccelerateDecelerateInterpolator`	Standard `cubic-bezier(0.4, 0.0, 0.2, 1)`
(Emphasis)	-	-	-	Sharp `cubic-bezier(0.4, 0.0, 0.6, 1)`

Table 8.1 - Specific platform terminology

Trigger conditions

Clearly specify when and how animations should be activated to prevent implementation confusion:

- What user action or system event starts the animation?
- Are there conditions where the animation should be skipped or modified?
- How should the animation behave if triggered multiple times quickly (for example, rapidly clicking a button)?
- Should the animation work bidirectionally? (For example, when scrolling down, elements animate in, but when scrolling back up, they should reverse and animate out.)

Performance considerations

Address technical constraints early to ensure animations work smoothly across all devices and platforms:

- Which properties are being animated (position, opacity, transform, etc.)?
- Are there performance-friendly alternatives to achieve the same visual effect?
- Should the animation be disabled on lower-end devices?

When animating movement, always prefer CSS `transform` properties over `position` properties (`left`, `top`, `right`, and `bottom`). Transform animations use hardware acceleration and don't trigger layout recalculations, resulting in smooth 60 fps animations. Position-based animations force the browser to recalculate the layout, which can cause stuttering and poor performance, especially on mobile devices. The visual result may look identical, but the performance difference is dramatic.

Showcase the animation

When you want to show the animation, you have two main options:

- **Build it**: In Figma using Smart Animate or in tools such as Adobe After Effects
- **Loom it**: (Yes, that's certainly a word!) Try to show the animation using examples from other sources. For example, you can find interesting animations on CodePen (`https://codepen.io/`), where, alongside your Loom video, developers have the code ready. For additional inspiration, check out Landing Love (`https://www.landing.love/`) for curated web animations, and Dribbble's micro-interaction collection (`https://dribbble.com/tags/micro-interaction`). If you want small changes, you can try modifying the code yourself, or explain the changes in the video.

Talk about technical implementation approaches

Work with your development team to understand which animation techniques work best for your specific platform and performance requirements. For example, for web development, you can use the following:

- CSS transitions
- CSS animations
- JavaScript animations

Create fallback options

Always design with graceful degradation in mind. What happens if the animation can't be implemented as designed due to technical constraints or performance requirements? Having fallback options ready prevents your carefully designed user experience from being completely abandoned when implementation challenges arise.

Fallback options might include the following:

- Simpler animations that achieve the same functional goal
- Static state changes that maintain usability
- Alternative feedback mechanisms that don't rely on motion

Quality assurance process

Quality assurance in design handoffs isn't just about catching bugs—it's about ensuring that the implemented design maintains the intended user experience, visual consistency, and functional behavior across different devices and platforms. A good QA process for design implementation bridges the gap between what was designed and what was built, catching discrepancies before they reach users.

What's the problem?

Many teams treat design QA as an afterthought, only checking whether the implementation "looks close enough" to the original design. This approach misses subtle but important details that affect user experience: inconsistent spacing, wrong fonts, poor color contrast, or incorrect design tokens.

Another common issue is the lack of structured design review processes. Designers might check implementations randomly or only when developers specifically ask for feedback, leading to inconsistent quality standards across different features or projects.

Additionally, many QA processes focus primarily on functional testing (does the button work?) while overlooking design fidelity (does the button look and feel right?). This can result in products that function correctly but feel unpolished or inconsistent with the brand and design system.

How to fix it

Implementing a systematic approach to design QA ensures that the quality of implementation matches the quality of your design work.

Establish design review checkpoints

Create specific moments in your development workflow where design review is mandatory, not optional. These checkpoints should be built into your project timeline and treated as essential as code reviews or functional testing.

Here are some recommended checkpoints:

- **Component completion**: Before any new component is marked as "done"
- **Feature milestone**: When a complete user flow is implemented
- **Pre-staging**: Before the code moves to the staging environment
- **Pre-production**: Final design sign-off before release

Create design QA checklists

Develop comprehensive checklists that cover both visual and functional aspects of design implementation. These checklists help ensure consistency across different reviewers and prevent important details from being overlooked.

Here are some example points that I would look for. Remember that you need to adjust them for your specific project. If you're building a mobile app, the checklist will be different from if you're building a web app.

> For more comprehensive QA guidance, especially for design system components, check out the *Design System Checklist* (https://www.designsystemchecklist. com/) and Nathan Curtis's article on *Component Visual Test Cases* (https://medium. com/eightshapes-llc/component-visual-test-cases-e501e2d21def). These resources provide in-depth checklists that are particularly helpful for QA teams working with design system components

> **Note from engineer beta reader**
>
> Many of these checklist items should ideally be automated through testing frameworks such as Playwright rather than checked manually by humans. Automation ensures consistency, saves time, and catches issues more reliably than manual reviews.

Here is a visual fidelity checklist:

- Are fonts, sizes, and weights correct?
- Is spacing consistent with design specifications?
- Do colors match the design system exactly?
- Are images properly sized and optimized?
- Do icons and graphics display correctly?

And here is an interaction design checklist:

- Do interactive states work as intended (hover, focus, active, disabled, etc.)?
- Are loading states implemented correctly?
- Do animations match timing and easing specifications?
- Are error states properly designed and functional?
- Does keyboard navigation work smoothly?

Here is a responsive design checklist:

- Does the layout work across different screen sizes?
- Are touch targets appropriately sized for mobile?
- Do components adapt gracefully to content changes?
- Are breakpoints implemented as designed?

Involve designers in sprint reviews and retrospectives

Make design review a standard part of your sprint review or demo process. This ensures that design quality is evaluated alongside functional requirements and prevents design issues from accumulating over time.

During sprint reviews, designers should specifically check the following:

- How well the implementation matches the intended user experience
- Whether any technical constraints led to design compromises
- Whether the implementation reveals any gaps in the original design specifications
- How the new implementation affects overall product consistency

Test across real devices and conditions

Don't rely solely on desktop browsers or device simulators for design QA. Test on actual devices, in different lighting conditions, and with various user settings to ensure your design works in real-world scenarios.

Back in the days when I was designing a lot, I always kept 2–3 phones next to my computer (low-end and high-end Android, plus an iPhone SE—the tiny one) to check the designs and pre-production apps before they received the green light from me.

Here are some real-world testing considerations:

- Different screen sizes and resolutions
- Various browser versions and operating systems
- Different user accessibility settings
- Slow network connections
- Different input methods (mouse, touch, or keyboard)

For more detailed guidance on accessibility testing and considerations, refer to *Chapter 7*, which covers comprehensive approaches to ensuring your designs work for all users.

Unlock this book's exclusive benefits now	
Scan this QR code or go to packtpub.com/unlock, then search this book by name.	
Note: Keep your purchase invoice ready before you start.	

9

Elevating Stakeholder Engagement

Working with stakeholders can be one of the most rewarding parts of the design process, but it can also be incredibly frustrating. I know this because I've been on both sides of the discussion many times, both as a designer and as a C-level manager. The funny thing is that in both cases, I was telling myself, "Why don't they get it? It's so simple!" But the reality is, it's not simple at all.

Stakeholder management is challenging because you're dealing with people. These are people who, in many cases, have years of experience in their field behind them. This can be incredibly beneficial, but they're also carrying patterns and prejudices from their past experiences. Understanding this human element is crucial to successful stakeholder engagement.

Over the years, I've seen teams struggle with unclear feedback, endless revision cycles, and stakeholders who seem to change their minds constantly. However, I've also witnessed the magic that happens when stakeholder engagement is done right. When stakeholders feel heard, understood, and truly involved in the design process, they become your biggest advocates rather than obstacles.

The key insight I want to share is this: stakeholder engagement isn't about managing people or controlling their input. It's about creating systems and processes that channel their expertise, concerns, and vision into actionable design decisions. The best stakeholder relationships I've built weren't based on perfect presentations or flawless prototypes. They were built on transparency, clear communication, and making stakeholders feel like true partners in the design process. The key is ensuring stakeholders feel genuinely involved in creating solutions, not just evaluating them.

In this chapter, we'll explore five essential areas that will transform how you work with stakeholders:

- Running collaborative reviews with stakeholders
- Using interactive prototypes to gather live feedback
- Implementing agile design changes based on stakeholder input
- Presenting design rationale for stakeholder alignment
- Managing complex feedback loops for stronger stakeholder relationships

Let's dive into the first area.

Running collaborative reviews with stakeholders

In many companies that I've worked with, the traditional design review process was fundamentally broken. You know the drill: spend hours preparing a presentation, walk through designs, get bombarded with conflicting feedback, then spend days trying to make sense of scattered comments across email, Slack, and Figma. If you don't know this routine, consider yourself lucky and thank your stakeholders for it, because this scenario is more common than you might think.

What's the problem?

Most design reviews fail because they lack structure and clear objectives. Stakeholders arrive unprepared, discussions go in circles, and decisions get postponed. Without proper facilitation, reviews become showcase events where designers present work and stakeholders provide scattered, often conflicting feedback. This approach wastes everyone's time and rarely leads to actionable outcomes.

Another common issue is the "design by committee" trap, where stakeholders try to redesign everything during the review. This happens when stakeholders don't understand the design rationale or haven't been involved enough in the process leading up to the review.

How to fix it

The solution really depends on your internal workflows, but here are some key strategies I've found effective across different organizations.

Establish a clear project narrative

Before you can have productive design reviews, everyone needs to be on the same starting line. Every project should have a clear narrative that answers the fundamental questions: Why are we doing this? What problem are we solving? Who are we solving it for? What does success look like?

This isn't just about having a project brief sitting in a shared folder somewhere. It's about actively ensuring every stakeholder understands and agrees on the project's core purpose. I've seen too many review sessions derail because stakeholders had different assumptions about the project goals or user needs.

Create a simple one-page project narrative that includes the following:

- **The problem:** What specific user or business challenge are we addressing?
- **The opportunity:** Why is solving this problem important right now?
- **Success metrics:** How will we know if our solution works?
- **Constraints:** What limitations do we need to work within?

Share this narrative before your first review session and reference it throughout the project. When feedback discussions go off track, you can always return to this foundation: "Let's check whether this suggestion aligns with our core objective of [insert problem statement]."

Review preparation

Stakeholders are busy people, and don't assume they're at the same level of understanding about design processes or project phases as you are. They're probably not, and you need to guide them. You can make small changes to your review process to be more effective.

Make a proper calendar event

Many times, even now at Dotidot, I receive calendar events with just a title and zero description. This sets everyone up for failure. Here's what should be included:

- **Context setting:** Briefly remind stakeholders of the project goals, target users, and any constraints you're working within. Even if they were part of earlier conversations, this refresher ensures everyone starts from the same foundation. These details are crucial. If you need any preparation or expect clear outcomes from the meeting, put it in the calendar invite.

- **Review objectives:** Clearly state what you want to achieve in this session. Are you validating the overall direction, gathering feedback on specific interactions, or making final decisions before development? Different objectives require different types of feedback.

- **Specific questions**: Instead of asking *"What do you think?"* provide targeted questions such as the following:

    - Does this solution address the main user pain point we identified?
    - Are there any business constraints we haven't considered?
    - How does this align with our technical capabilities?
    - Do you agree with the proposed direction?

Use video for complex topics

For more complex topics, or when you're introducing new concepts, consider recording a short Loom video instead of just sending text. A 2-3 minute video where you walk through the key points or show the Figma prototype can be much more effective than a written explanation, especially when stakeholders need to understand context or see specific interactions.

Figma tutorial

Include some basic guidance with your invite. Not every stakeholder is a Figma pro, so I send a short pre-recorded video (I have one that I send repeatedly) covering the basics: how to navigate, that Figma has multiple pages you can switch between (a common mistake is when stakeholders only check the first page), how to comment, etc..

Send a reminder

One or two days before a crucial meeting, send a reminder with the information from the event description. Set up this email or Slack message when you're creating the event and schedule it to send later, so you don't need to think about it.

Review session structure

Start every review with a five-minute agenda overview. This might seem obvious, but it sets expectations and keeps the conversation focused.

Ask everyone whether they completed their preparation from the event description. If not, don't be afraid to postpone the meeting with an honest explanation:

"To be productive, we need to have the same starting point. That starting point is the preparation outlined in the event description. If you didn't have time to review it, that's completely understandable. I know more important things come up. But in this case, it doesn't make sense for us to proceed. It would be a waste of time for those who did prepare. What date works best to reschedule?"

I always remember the faces of stakeholders who come to every meeting unprepared when this is said for the first time by the meeting organizers I'm mentoring. Priceless. You can be sure that next time they'll either be prepared or they'll decline the meeting.

If everyone is ready, the meeting can start. Here's my agenda template, but remember to adapt it to your situation:

- **Design walk-through (15-20 minutes)**: Present the work systematically, explaining your thinking as you go. Don't just show the final designs; walk through your decision-making process.

- **Targeted feedback (20-30 minutes)**: Work through your prepared questions systematically. Use techniques such as dot voting for prioritization when you have multiple options to evaluate.

- **Action items and next steps (5-10 minutes)**: Clearly document decisions made, action items assigned, and the timeline for next steps.

Managing the conversation

For larger stakeholder groups, appoint a dedicated facilitator. In my experience with larger groups or senior stakeholders, it's beneficial to have a different facilitator than the presenting designer. While it's often the same person, this isn't ideal because the facilitator's role often involves saying "stop," and it's difficult to switch between a neutral role (facilitator) and an opinionated role (designer).

If you don't have the option to have two separate people in the meeting (facilitator and designer), try setting up a safe word. At Dotidot, we use "strawberry." Anyone can use it, and when they do, the discussion stops and we return to the original topic. It doesn't matter if a product manager says it in the middle of the CEO talking. That's the rule, and everyone respects it. This approach works better in smaller, more open companies than in large corporations, in my opinion, but it's an interesting strategy worth considering for the right team culture.

The facilitator keeps the conversation on track and ensures everyone has a chance to contribute. When working with senior stakeholders, this role becomes even more critical because power dynamics can prevent honest feedback.

As a designer, use the "yes, and" approach when stakeholders suggest changes. Instead of immediately explaining why something won't work, acknowledge their concern and build on it. Take the following example:

"Yes, I understand the concern about the checkout flow being too long, and let me show you how we addressed that with the progress indicator and by reducing form fields."

Scripts for unclear feedback

When stakeholders give vague feedback such as "make it pop more" or "it doesn't feel right," use the "help me understand" script to turn subjective opinions into actionable design direction:

"Help me understand what [repeat their words] means for our users trying to [complete specific task]. Are you thinking about [offer 2-3 specific options such as visual hierarchy, color contrast, call-to-action prominence, etc.]?"

Take the following example:

- **Stakeholder**: *"This page needs more energy"*

    - **Response**: *"Help me understand what 'more energy' means for users trying to find our pricing information. Are you thinking about brighter colors, larger typography, or more prominent call-to-action buttons?"*

- **Stakeholder**: *"The design feels off"*

    - **Response**: *"Help me understand what feels off for users trying to complete their purchase. Are you thinking about the layout structure, visual hierarchy, or the flow between steps?"*

This approach validates their concern while gathering specific, actionable information you can actually design with.

Documenting decisions

Every meeting needs to have all decisions documented in one place and shared with everyone. You can make this step super easy with automated notetaking tools such as Loom, Fathom, Otter. ai, or Zoom's built-in transcription that can automatically join meetings when you connect your calendar.

Even if the meeting is offline, I usually start a Google Meet with myself and add a Loom recording bot. The meeting will automatically create a recording with a clear transcript that you can input into ChatGPT or Claude to extract action steps, decisions, tasks, deadlines, and so on from the meeting in seconds. This allows you to focus solely on the presentation rather than note-taking.

Follow-up actions

Send a review summary within 24 hours that includes the following:

- Key decisions made
- Action items with owners and deadlines
- Updated timeline if changes affect the schedule
- Link to the updated Figma file with any changes made during the session

This follow-up email or Slack message serves as a record and ensures everyone remembers what was agreed upon.

Using interactive prototypes to gather live feedback

Interactive prototypes are powerful tools for stakeholder engagement because they make abstract design concepts tangible. Instead of asking stakeholders to imagine how something will work, you can show them. This dramatically improves the quality of feedback you receive and helps stakeholders understand the user experience in a way static designs cannot achieve.

We talked more about prototypes in *Chapter 4*, but I want to share only a few new points about them tied to stakeholder engagement.

What's the problem?

Static presentations force stakeholders to mentally simulate interactions, often leading to wrong assumptions about user behavior and technical complexity. This imagination gap creates multiple collaboration challenges:

- **Lack of historical references**: When I put a bunch of static designs in front of you, I'm pretty sure you would see interactions in your head, just based on your past experience and the reality that you're a designer who thinks about design every day when you encounter it around you. But stakeholders usually aren't these people, and something that is super clear for you may be completely new to them.
- **Imagination gap**: Stakeholders see a static checkout flow and think "looks good," but they don't understand how confusing the actual clicking experience might be until it's built and too late to change.
- **Interface intimidation**: Figma's interface overwhelms non-designers. They're afraid to click around and explore, so they provide surface-level feedback instead of engaging deeply with the design.

- **Ownership absence**: When stakeholders can't interact with designs, they don't develop emotional investment in the solutions. They see themselves as critics rather than collaborators.

- **Decision-making in a vacuum**: Executives approve designs based on static screens or screenshots in boardrooms, never experiencing the actual user journey that leads to those moments.

How to fix it

The solution is making interactive prototypes central to your stakeholder collaboration, not just something you create for user testing.

Scale prototype complexity to stakeholder needs

Different stakeholders need different levels of prototype fidelity and complexity:

- **Executive stakeholders**: Remember, these people are juggling a lot of projects, and they don't need the high level of granularity that you need or know. Don't bury them in details, or they will feel lost and overwhelmed. Use simple, high-level flow prototypes showing key user journeys and business outcomes. Focus on the big picture rather than interaction details:

    - 3-5 key screens maximum
    - Clear business value demonstration
    - Simple click-through without complex interactions
    - Include brief explanatory annotations

- **Product stakeholders**: Mid-fidelity prototypes with realistic content and interactions. Show edge cases, error states, and feature integration:

    - Complete user flows with realistic data
    - Error states and edge case handling
    - Integration points with existing features
    - Conditional logic and dynamic content

- **Technical stakeholders**: High-fidelity prototypes with complex interactions, micro-animations, and responsive behavior:

  - Detailed interaction specifications
  - Component behavior documentation
  - Performance considerations and constraints
  - Accessibility features and considerations

Start early and progress from low to high fidelity

One of my beta readers pointed out something crucial that I almost missed: the importance of starting feedback sessions early and often, iterating from low-fidelity prototypes to high-fidelity ones. This progression is critical for getting the right kind of feedback at the right time.

I probably missed this because at Dotidot, as a small start-up, this isn't as much of a problem. Our stakeholders are fairly knowledgeable about the design process and can focus on functionality even when looking at polished designs. But in larger organizations where stakeholders aren't as familiar with design thinking, this progression becomes absolutely crucial.

When you show high-fidelity prototypes right away, stakeholders tend to focus on colors, spacing, and specific numbers instead of fundamental issues such as information architecture and user flow. This can derail productive conversations about core functionality.

Here's the progressive approach:

- **Round 1 – Low-fidelity wireframes**: Get feedback on structure, layout, and basic user flow without visual distractions. Stakeholders focus on "does this make sense?" rather than "I don't like this shade of blue."
- **Round 2 – Mid-fidelity with real content**: Once the structure is validated, add realistic content and basic styling. This helps stakeholders understand how the design works with actual data.
- **Round 3 – High-fidelity polish**: Only after the flow and content strategy are solid should you introduce final visual design, micro-interactions, and detailed styling.

This approach prevents the common scenario where stakeholders approve a beautiful high-fidelity design, only to realize later that the underlying user flow doesn't work for their business needs.

Integrate real user feedback with stakeholder sessions

One of the most powerful stakeholder engagement techniques is bringing real user voices into the design process through prototype testing.

User testing integration

The most effective approach is to make user feedback a central part of your stakeholder conversations, not something that happens separately:

- Use tools such as Maze (there are other tools, but I have very good experience with Maze) to test your Figma prototypes with actual users
- Collect quantitative data (task completion rates and time on task) and qualitative feedback
- Create user testing summary reports for stakeholder review
- Record everything, because for stakeholders, users are often a distant entity, but when they see a video of the user testing, it's much more impactful than just a Google Docs report
- Schedule stakeholder sessions to review user testing results together

Stakeholder-user comparison sessions

Another powerful technique is having stakeholders experience the design exactly as your test users did, then comparing the results:

- Have stakeholders complete the same tasks you tested with users
- Compare stakeholder assumptions with actual user behavior
- Identify gaps between stakeholder expectations and user reality
- Use data to guide design iteration priorities

Create stakeholder testing scenarios

Turn stakeholder reviews into structured usability sessions that build empathy for user challenges.

Task-based testing

Take the following examples:

- "Try to find information about our pricing plans"
- "Complete a purchase for the premium subscription"
- "Update your account notification preferences"
- "Find help documentation for a billing question"

Observe them

The real insights come from watching how stakeholders actually interact with your design, not just listening to what they say about it:

- Watch where stakeholders hesitate or get confused
- Note what they click first versus what you intended
- Ask questions about their expectations versus reality
- Document their mental model versus your design assumptions
- Compare their behavior with real user testing data

Implementing agile design changes based on stakeholder input

One of the biggest challenges in stakeholder engagement is managing change requests efficiently. Stakeholders will have new ideas, shifting priorities, and evolving requirements. The goal isn't to prevent changes but to implement them in a way that maintains project momentum and design quality.

What's the problem?

Once we were in a meeting and there was one C-level manager saying, "I don't understand why these small changes take so long." The changes were small in her eyes. To be honest, they would have looked small to me too if I didn't have the details.

Agile development methodologies have transformed how software is built, but they've created an expectation that everything can be done *now*, or at least by the end of the day. This often isn't the case, and this misalignment of expectations creates distrust between stakeholders and design/development teams.

How to fix it

In my experience, disappointments come from wrongly set expectations, so the solution to this problem is to create a clear and transparent environment where stakeholders can see for themselves what's going on and why.

Clear feedback windows

I mentioned this in *Chapter 1*, but when you're expecting feedback from multiple people, you need to add strict deadlines. The importance of your project can be different for each stakeholder, and they will prioritize accordingly. For example, for one person, it will have priority number 1, so when you ask for feedback, they'll provide it by the end of the day. But there's a second stakeholder who sees this project as priority number 3, and you'll need to wait a week for their feedback. If the first person doesn't know this, they'll be frustrated that their feedback is taking so long to implement, but in the meantime, you're waiting for complete feedback to be able to start working.

Change request prioritization

Show all stakeholders and decide together where every piece of feedback falls. Based on that, they will understand, or at least agree on, what the priority order is.

Critical

- **Business impact**: Directly affects revenue, prevents core task completion, or creates legal/ compliance issues.
- **Ask yourself**: Does this prevent users from completing their main goal? Would this block a product launch?
- **Examples**: "Login button doesn't work on mobile," "Payment processing fails," "Site violates accessibility standards."

Important

- **Business impact**: Significantly improves conversion rates, reduces support burden, or enhances user retention.
- **Ask yourself**: Would fixing this measurably improve our key metrics? Do multiple users struggle with this?
- **Examples**: "Checkout flow is confusing (affects conversion)," "Search results aren't relevant," "Mobile navigation is hard to use."

Enhancement

- **Business impact**: Increases user satisfaction or brand perception but doesn't affect core metrics.
- **Ask yourself**: Is this nice-to-have? Would users notice if we didn't fix it immediately?
- **Examples**: "Button could be more visually appealing," "Animation could be smoother," "Better micro-copy."

Experimental

- **Business impact**: An unproven concept that needs validation before investment
- **Ask yourself**: Are we guessing this would help? Do we need data before deciding?
- **Examples**: "Maybe we should add social login," "Consider adding a chatbot," "What if we tried a different layout?"

Tiered feedback integration

You need to teach stakeholders and the whole company that not all feedback is equal, and based on the "tier," they can expect different timelines for results:

- **Immediate changes (same day)**: Business-critical changes that can't wait and need to be done ASAP. These should only be small tweaks. An example is: "Copy changes on the website about discounts ending today."
- **Sprint changes (1-2 weeks)**: User flow modifications, new feature integration.
- **Roadmap changes (future sprints)**: Structural changes requiring research and planning.

Communicating change impact

Always explain the implications of requested changes. Stakeholders might not realize that what seems like a small visual adjustment could require significant development work or impact other parts of the system.

The trade-off conversation script

Use this framework to make trade-offs concrete and help stakeholders make informed decisions rather than assuming everything can be done simultaneously:

"I understand this looks like a small change. If we prioritize this, it means [X hours of work], which would delay [Y feature] or push back our timeline by [Z time]. Which would you prefer we focus on first?"

Here are some examples:

- "I understand moving the search bar looks simple. If we prioritize this, it means eight hours of development work, which would delay the user dashboard feature by two days. Which would you prefer we focus on first?"
- "I see why you'd want that animation added. If we prioritize this, it means 12 hours of design and development time, which would push back our testing phase by a week. Which is more important for our launch deadline?"

This approach transforms "can we just add this small thing?" conversations into strategic priority discussions.

Use visual aids to show change impact. Create simple before/after comparisons or use Figma's version comparison feature to highlight what's different.

Provide time estimates for implementing changes. This helps stakeholders make informed decisions about whether the change is worth the investment.

Branches or versioning

We talked about branches and versions in *Chapter 1*, but I want to repeat it again. I was part of many projects where we started running in circles, and stakeholders were providing feedback on things we had in our design earlier. Some designers just deleted the previous versions or redesigned them, and when this happened, they needed to redesign them again. Do your versions in Figma. Save them before every feedback session so you can come back quickly if needed.

Design Sprint

I could write a whole book about this point. In fact, Jake Knapp did write it, and I have it right behind me on my bookshelf. But if you feel pushed to perform super fast, try suggesting a Design Sprint. It will be very time-consuming for all stakeholders, but in calendar days, it's the fastest way you can deliver results. If you're more interested in the whole Design Sprint topic, check out his book (`https://www.thesprintbook.com/`).

Set AI boundaries and expectations

This is quite a new topic in my opinion, but in recent months, I've been part of sessions where AI was brought up in a way that suggested everything can be quickly vibe-coded in an hour because that's what people saw on LinkedIn. The discussion in that meeting wasn't handled properly, and the meeting ended with designers and developers feeling that managers know nothing, and management thinking we only have slow people on the team who don't want to learn new things.

Think about this and have a more deeply open conversation about it. The LinkedIn hype train is real, and you need to set clear expectations about the capabilities of these tools and what they're built for. Show them live examples where AI is limited and explain where you're using it every day to be faster and more productive.

Presenting the design rationale for stakeholder alignment

One of the biggest challenges in stakeholder collaboration is getting everyone aligned on not just what the design looks like but why specific decisions were made. Stakeholders who understand the reasoning behind design choices become advocates rather than critics, leading to smoother approvals and better long-term collaboration.

Remember, you live and breathe design, but they don't, and that's okay. It isn't their job to be enthusiastic about it and get everything on the first try. That's your job. This is, in my opinion, one of the main differences between junior and senior designers: how you can align the whole team behind your decisions.

What's the problem?

Many designers present solutions without adequately explaining the thinking process that led to those solutions. This creates several collaboration challenges that can derail even the best design work:

- **Solution without story**: Stakeholders see the final design but don't understand the user research, business constraints, and strategic thinking that informed the solution.
- **Personal preference debates**: Without a clear rationale, stakeholder feedback defaults to personal preferences rather than evidence-based evaluation.
- **Decision reversal**: Stakeholders who don't understand why decisions were made are more likely to request changes that undermine the design strategy.
- **Lack of design advocacy**: When stakeholders don't understand design value, they can't defend design decisions in meetings where designers aren't present. This is a big problem for your whole design team. I was part of meetings in one multinational company where they looked at designers as the "painters" who create nice mockups. You don't want to be in this role, but don't blame the stakeholders if you don't know how to explain your job and added value. It's your mistake.

How to fix it

Don't assume that stakeholders know what you know. Be ready to have different stories about the project based on your target groups. For example, I can talk about decisions at Dotidot in formats of 2 minutes, 5 minutes, 30 minutes, or hours. I have ready in my head the main points that I want to include in these stories based on the available time and target group.

Imagine it with something super easy to grasp. Think for a minute how you would explain why you chose the destination of your last vacation if you had 2 minutes, 5 minutes, 30 minutes, or hours. You'll see how the arguments and key points will be slightly different, based on the priority for your decision. You need to have the same thing ready for your current projects and decisions.

Different stakeholders need different levels of detail

Different stakeholders need different levels of detail about your design thinking.

Executive summary level (2 minutes)

- Business problem being solved
- Key user need being addressed
- Success metrics and expected outcomes
- High-level solution approach

Strategic overview level (5 minutes)

- User research insights driving design decisions
- Competitive analysis and market positioning
- Technical constraints and opportunities
- Brand alignment and consistency considerations

Detailed rationale level (30 minutes)

- Design principle application and trade-offs
- User testing results and iteration history
- Component and interaction decision reasoning
- Accessibility and performance considerations

The interesting thing is that every one of these stories has the same structure for me, and that's this:

- **The challenge:** What problem are we trying to solve?
- **Our approach:** How did we decide to tackle this challenge?

- **The solution**: What did we create and why?
- **The impact (if you already have some data)**: How does this solution address the original challenge?

Use data-driven storytelling

Most stakeholders love data. Data is something they can rely on, and if the project goes sideways, they can always point to the data and say, "But this is what the data told us." Try to find this data and add it to your stories.

User research integration

- Quote specific user feedback that influenced design decisions
- Show user journey pain points that your design addresses
- Reference user personas and scenarios driving design choices

Business impact connection

- Link design decisions to business goals and KPIs
- Show competitive advantages created by design choices
- Quantify expected improvements in user behavior

Technical feasibility evidence

- Document engineering input that shaped design decisions (another team's input gives your opinion more value. If more teams think the same, it needs to be good, right?).
- Explain performance considerations affecting interface choices.
- Show how design decisions support development efficiency.
- Include accessibility compliance and inclusive design rationale.

Hard data

- Use analytics tools such as Google Analytics 4 to show current user behavior patterns that inform design decisions
- Include session recordings from tools such as Microsoft Clarity or Hotjar to demonstrate actual user struggles and behavior patterns
- Reference conversion funnel data that shows where users drop off in current flows
- Show page performance metrics that justify design choices (load times, bounce rates, etc.)
- Include A/B testing results from previous design changes to demonstrate impact

Document decisions for future reference

One of my beta readers suggested adding this concept, and I'm grateful for it because it's such a practical addition. **Design Decision Records (DDRs)** are lightweight documents that capture important design decisions and their reasoning. Think of them as a permanent record of your design rationale that stakeholders can reference months later.

The concept comes from software development (where they're called architecture decision records), but it works brilliantly for design teams facing the same challenges we discuss in this chapter.

Here's a basic DDR structure:

- **Context**: What situation led to this decision?
- **Decision**: What exactly was decided?
- **Status**: Proposed, accepted, or rejected?
- **Consequences**: Positive and negative outcomes expected

The following is an example DDR.

Title: Allow Guest Checkout Without Account Creation

Status: Accepted

Context: Cart abandonment rate was 68%, with user research showing that 43% of users abandoned when forced to create an account. Competitors such as Amazon and Target offer guest checkout.

Decision: Implement a guest checkout option with optional account creation at the end of purchase process.

Consequences:

- **Positive**: Reduced friction, faster checkout, likely improved conversion rates
- **Negative**: Fewer registered users initially, harder to track customer lifetime value

How do DDRs solve common stakeholder problems?

- **Prevent decision reversal**: When stakeholders question decisions months later, you have documented reasoning
- **Enable design advocacy**: Stakeholders can reference DDRs to defend decisions when you're not in meetings

- **Stop relitigation**: "We already decided this, here's the documented reasoning…"
- **Help onboarding**: New stakeholders understand the design evolution and current state

You can create DDRs in Notion, Confluence, or even simple Google Docs. The key is making them easily searchable and accessible to all stakeholders.

Different stories for different teams, but at their core, they are the same

Every team and every stakeholder speaks a little bit of a different language. This is a crucial point because what will work for a development team won't work for product, sales, or marketing.

The same design decision can be explained differently to different stakeholders based on what they care about most. You need to adjust this based on your situation, but these are some general points that these teams care about.

For product managers

- Feature adoption and user engagement implications
- Roadmap integration and development prioritization
- Competitive positioning and market differentiation
- User satisfaction and retention impact

For development teams

- Implementation complexity and timeline estimates
- Performance considerations and technical trade-offs
- Reusability and maintainability benefits
- Integration requirements with existing systems

For marketing teams

- Brand consistency and visual identity alignment
- Campaign integration opportunities and constraints
- Message clarity and conversion optimization

For executive stakeholders

- Business value and revenue impact potential
- Risk mitigation and competitive advantages

- Resource requirements and ROI expectations
- Strategic alignment with company objectives

If you're talking about design systems, use Figma's built-in analytics (if you're on Organization/Enterprise plans) to show stakeholders how design decisions ripple through your organization:

- Component usage tracking showing adoption patterns
- Detach rate analysis indicating component effectiveness
- File activity metrics revealing stakeholder engagement patterns
- Design consistency improvements over time

Managing complex feedback loops for stronger stakeholder relationships

When working with multiple stakeholders across different departments and seniority levels, feedback can quickly become overwhelming and contradictory. The challenge isn't just collecting feedback but synthesizing it into actionable design decisions while maintaining strong relationships with all stakeholders involved.

What's the problem?

Complex stakeholder groups often provide conflicting feedback because they have different priorities, perspectives, and levels of context about the design decisions. Without proper management, these feedback loops can become circular, with stakeholders contradicting each other and designers caught in the middle.

Additionally, stakeholder fatigue is real. If the feedback process is too cumbersome or if stakeholders feel their input isn't being heard, they'll either disengage entirely or become increasingly critical and difficult to work with.

How to fix it

The solution involves creating clear feedback structures and managing expectations effectively.

Establishing feedback hierarchies

Not all stakeholder feedback carries equal weight, and it's important to establish this clearly from the beginning. In bigger teams where there are a lot of stakeholders at once, this is usually not clear. Don't just agree on it verbally. Have it as part of your project brief so you can always come back to it and reference it.

Identify decision-makers for different types of choices. For example, the product manager might have the final say on feature prioritization, while the tech lead decides on implementation feasibility, and the design lead determines consistency with the design system. At first glance, this sounds obvious, but don't assume that everyone has the same point of view as you.

I once witnessed a big disagreement about who should have the final say on feature prioritization: a new product manager or a senior tech lead who had been at the company from the start. The tech lead thought he knew much more than the product manager because he'd been there for a long time, and he was correct about having more knowledge. But there's a big difference between providing feedback and having the final say. It's a completely different responsibility level.

Sequential versus parallel feedback collection

Based on the preceding point, decide how you will gather feedback. I started doing this deliberately, and it had a big impact on the smoothness of the process:

- **Sequential**: Gather feedback from stakeholders in priority order, with each round building on previous input. This usually takes a little bit longer, but you have fewer rounds overall.
- **Parallel**: Collect feedback simultaneously and synthesize conflicts through facilitated discussion. You get some feedback fast, but there will be more rounds of feedback because some points from stakeholders will contradict each other.
- **Hybrid**: Use parallel collection for initial input, then sequential refinement for conflict resolution.

Consolidating and synthesizing feedback

Use structured feedback collection methods. Instead of collecting random comments, provide stakeholders with specific frameworks for giving feedback. For example, ask them to categorize their input as "must fix," "should consider," or "nice to have."

I also mentioned this before in *Chapter 1*, but be sure to create a simple guide on how to comment in Figma: how to tag people, how to use emojis, and so on. It will help you a lot.

If your company doesn't use Loom, try to encourage stakeholders to adopt it, because often video feedback is much better than written messages. You'll save time on long meetings where you still need to do recording to understand everything, or spend half the time writing notes.

Maintaining stakeholder relationships

If you want to be in this role, some part of your job as a designer will be invested in managing relationships. That's the reality.

Acknowledge all feedback, even when you can't implement it. Explain your reasoning for not implementing certain suggestions and show how you considered their perspective in your decision-making.

Provide regular updates on how feedback is being incorporated. This keeps stakeholders engaged and demonstrates that their input is valued and considered.

Create opportunities for stakeholders to see each other's perspectives. Sometimes the best way to resolve conflicting feedback is to facilitate a conversation between stakeholders rather than trying to mediate separately.

Relationship repair process

My last point is about repair. Not everything will go smoothly, and that's okay. Sometimes we need to cool down and take another breath. In the end, it's just a job.

I try to follow these short guidelines in face-to-face meetings (if possible) or online calls:

1. **Acknowledge the problem**: Recognize relationship damage and its impact on design work.
2. **Understand root causes**: Investigate underlying issues beyond surface-level conflicts.
3. **Facilitate direct communication**: Help stakeholders discuss issues with appropriate mediation (be neutral, that's your job in this meeting).
4. **Rebuild trust gradually**: Create small wins and positive interaction opportunities.

Managing complex feedback doesn't mean avoiding stakeholder disagreements. Instead, it's about turning different viewpoints into better design solutions that work for both users and the business. When stakeholders see their feedback valued and thoughtfully integrated, they stop being critics and become true collaborators.

Building strong stakeholder relationships through these five advanced techniques transforms design work from a solitary activity into a collaborative partnership. When stakeholders understand design rationale, participate in interactive exploration, and see their feedback integrated systematically, they become advocates for good design throughout your organization.

The key is consistent application of these techniques over time. Start with the approaches that address your biggest stakeholder challenges, then gradually implement more sophisticated collaboration methods as relationships strengthen and trust builds.

Remember, every stakeholder interaction is an opportunity to demonstrate design value and build the foundation for even better collaboration on future projects. The investment you make in stakeholder relationships today pays dividends in smoother approvals, better design outcomes, and more strategic influence for design in your organization.

Unlock this book's exclusive benefits now Scan this QR code or go to packtpub.com/unlock, then search this book by name. *Note: Keep your purchase invoice ready before you start.*	

10

Unlock Your Book's Exclusive Benefits

Your copy of this book comes with the following exclusive benefits:

⌂ Next-gen Packt Reader

✦ AI assistant (beta)

📄 DRM-free PDF/ePub downloads

Use the following guide to unlock them if you haven't already. The process takes just a few minutes and needs to be done only once.

How to unlock these benefits in three easy steps

Step 1

Have your purchase invoice for this book ready, as you'll need it in *Step 3*. If you received a physical invoice, scan it on your phone and have it ready as either a PDF, JPG, or PNG.

For more help on finding your invoice, visit https://www.packtpub.com/unlock-benefits/help.

Note: Did you buy this book directly from Packt? You don't need an invoice. After completing Step 2, you can jump straight to your exclusive content.

Note: Bought this book directly from Packt? You don't need an invoice. After completing *Step 2*, you can jump straight to your exclusive content.

Step 2

Scan this QR code or go to `packtpub.com/unlock`.

On the page that opens (which will look similar to Figure 10.1 if you're on desktop), search for this book by name. Make sure you select the correct edition.

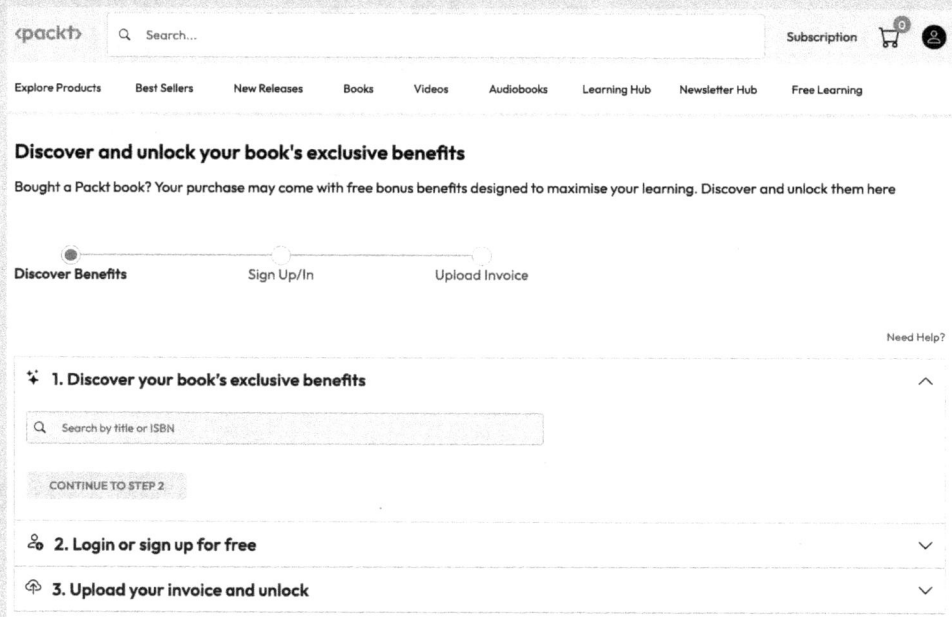

Figure 10.1: Packt unlock landing page on desktop

Step 3

Once you've selected your book, sign in to your Packt account or create a new one for free. Once you're logged in, upload your invoice. It can be in PDF, PNG, or JPG format and must be no larger than 10 MB. Follow the rest of the instructions on the screen to complete the process.

Need help?

If you get stuck and need help, visit `https://www.packtpub.com/unlock-benefits/help` for a detailed FAQ on how to find your invoices and more. The following QR code will take you to the help page directly:

Note: If you are still facing issues, reach out to `customercare@packt.com`.

‹packt›

packtpub.com

Subscribe to our online digital library for full access to over 7,000 books and videos, as well as industry leading tools to help you plan your personal development and advance your career. For more information, please visit our website.

Why subscribe?

- Spend less time learning and more time coding with practical eBooks and Videos from over 4,000 industry professionals
- Improve your learning with Skill Plans built especially for you
- Get a free eBook or video every month
- Fully searchable for easy access to vital information
- Copy and paste, print, and bookmark content

At www.packt.com, you can also read a collection of free technical articles, sign up for a range of free newsletters, and receive exclusive discounts and offers on Packt books and eBooks.

Other Books You May Enjoy

If you enjoyed this book, you may be interested in these other books by Packt:

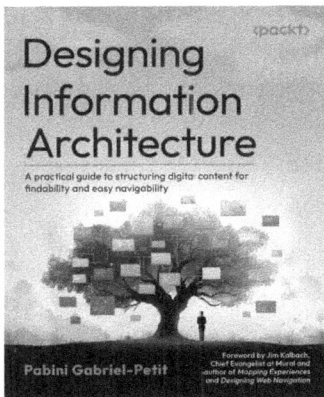

Designing Information Architecture

Pabini Gabriel-Petit

ISBN: 978-1-83882-719-9

- Information-seeking models, strategies, tactics, and behaviors
- Principles for designing IAs that support human cognitive and visual capabilities
- Wayfinding principles for placemaking, orientation, navigation, labeling, and search
- Useful structural patterns and information-organization schemes
- UX research methods and analytics for information architecture
- Content analysis, modeling, and mapping methods
- Categorizing content and creating controlled vocabularies
- Designing and mapping information architectures
- Leveraging artificial intelligence (AI) to deliver optimal search results

Inclusive Design for Accessibility

Dale Cruse, Denis Boudreau

ISBN: 978-1-83588-822-3

- Master the core principles of inclusive design to create products that serve all
- Conduct diverse user research to gain insights into accessible experiences
- Implement accessibility best practices in your web and mobile deployments
- Create fully accessible content in text, audio, and video formats
- Explore the accessibility challenges and opportunities with AI, VR, and AR
- Navigate the legal and ethical implications of accessibility to protect users and your brand
- Establish accessibility-focused workflows and practices in your teams

Packt is searching for authors like you

If you're interested in becoming an author for Packt, please visit authors.packtpub.com and apply today. We have worked with thousands of developers and tech professionals, just like you, to help them share their insight with the global tech community. You can make a general application, apply for a specific hot topic that we are recruiting an author for, or submit your own idea.

Share your thoughts

Now you've finished *Design Beyond Limits with Figma*, we'd love to hear your thoughts! Scan the QR code below to go straight to the Amazon review page for this book and share your feedback or leave a review on the site that you purchased it from.

https://packt.link/r/1836207719

Your review is important to us and the tech community and will help us make sure we're delivering excellent quality content.

Index

W

www.ingramcontent.com/pod-product-compliance
Lightning Source LLC
Chambersburg PA
CBHW061807210326
41599CB00034B/6905